THE TRUTH ABOUT
GRACE

THE TRUTH ABOUT
GRACE

VINSON SYNAN, *Editor*

FOREWORD BY WILLIAM M. WILSON

PRESIDENT, ORAL ROBERTS UNIVERSITY

CHARISMA
HOUSE

Most CHARISMA HOUSE BOOK GROUP products are available at special quantity discounts for bulk purchase for sales promotions, premiums, fund-raising, and educational needs. For details, write Charisma House Book Group, 600 Rinehart Road, Lake Mary, Florida 32746, or telephone (407) 333-0600.

THE TRUTH ABOUT GRACE by Vinson Synan, PhD, Editor
Published by Charisma House
Charisma Media/Charisma House Book Group
600 Rinehart Road
Lake Mary, Florida 32746
www.charismahouse.com

Scripture quotations marked ESV are from the Holy Bible, English Standard Version. Copyright © 2001 by Crossway Bibles, a division of Good News Publishers. Used by permission.

Scripture quotations marked ISV are from International Standard Version. Copyright © 1995-2014 by ISV Foundation. All rights reserved internationally. Used by permission of Davidson Press, LLC.

Scripture quotations marked KJV are from the King James Version of the Bible.

Scripture quotations marked MEV are from the Modern English Version. Copyright © 2014 by Military Bible Association. Used by permission. All rights reserved.

Scripture quotations marked NASB are from the New American Standard Bible, copyright © 1960, 1962, 1963, 1968, 1971, 1972, 1973, 1975, 1977, 1995 by The Lockman Foundation. Used by permission. (www.Lockman.org)

Cover design by Lisa Rae McClure
Design Director: Justin Evans

Visit the Empowered21 website at https://empowered21.com/.

Library of Congress Cataloging-in-Publication Data:
An application to register this book for cataloging has been submitted to the Library of Congress.
International Standard Book Number: 978-1-62999-504-5
E-book ISBN: 978-1-62999-505-2

18 19 20 21 22 — 987654321
Printed in the United States of America

CONTENTS

Foreword *by William M. Wilson*...................................xi

Preface xiii

Introduction:
From Graceless Law to Lawless Grace
by Vinson Synan 1

Chapter 1:
Jack Hayford, the Security of the Believer,
and the Need for Pentecostal Pastor-Theologians
by S. David Moore...7

Chapter 2:
Are All Our Sins—Past, Present, and Future—
Already Forgiven in Jesus?
by Michael L. Brown 21

Chapter 3:
The Hyper-Grace Gospel
by Trevor Grizzle...31

Chapter 4:
John Wesley's Fuller Understanding of Grace
by Henry H. Knight III 48

Chapter 5:
The Grace Revolution and Person-Centered Therapy:
A Comparative Analysis From a Pastoral Care Perspective
by Thomson K. Mathew..58

Chapter 6:
Reformed Theology and Grace in Newfrontiers Churches
by William K. Kay...71

Chapter 7:
A Spirit of Unity and Grace:
Learning from the Assemblies of God Ireland
by Miriam (Mimi) A. Kelly 82

Chapter 8:
Grace, Sanctification, and Italian Pentecostalism
by Paolo Mauriello..94

Chapter 9:
Manifestations of Grace: A Latin American Witness
by Miguel Álvarez 107

Chapter 10:
Still and Still Moving: Grace in the Anglican Tradition
by Andy Lord..123

Chapter 11:
Law and Grace as Partners:
An Examination of Reformed Theology
by Mark Jumper..141

Chapter 12:
Evidence of Grace in the Old Testament
by Mark E. Roberts..153

Chapter 13:
Grace and Works—A Johannine Perspective
by John Christopher Thomas 166

Chapter 14:
Grace and Spirit Baptism
by Scott T. Kelso...184

Chapter 15:
Glossolalia and Groaning:
A Manifestation of God's Grace
by Mark R. Hall................................199

Chapter 16:
Going Beyond the Debate on Grace:
Learning From a South Asian Tradition
by Brainerd Prince................................210

Chapter 17:
Beware of Counterfeit Grace
by Joseph Prince................................225

Notes 241

FOREWORD

IN THE FALL of 1517, Martin Luther, monk, professor, and church reformer, nailed his 95 Theses to the entrance door of Castle Church in Wittenberg, Germany. Five hundred years later, we celebrate Luther's years of research and study, and his commitment to understand Scripture. His expository revelations of God's grace changed the history of the world!

Luther challenged the culture of his day and the popular belief that the goodness of God could be earned or purchased. Moving forward to the twenty-first century, the topic of God's grace is still being debated. As global ministry leaders have identified, accurate scriptural interpretation of grace remains a significant challenge to the church due to erroneous perceptions pertaining to the application of grace to the sins of mankind.

Empowered21, a global relational network, serves the more than six hundred million Spirit-empowered believers around the world by addressing crucial issues facing the movement and connecting generations for intergenerational blessing and impartation. The Empowered21 Global Council, a group of distinguished leaders from international denominations and ministry organizations, commissioned select accomplished scholars from around the world to address the current controversies and trends confronting today's church.

The Truth About Grace endeavors to study grace from a historical and theological perspective, looking into all aspects of the current grace movements and trends. This book is the sixth to appear under the sponsorship of the Empowered21 movement (E21). Charisma House has published all of the volumes under the leadership of Stephen Strang. The previous books include *Spirit-Empowered Christianity in the 21st Century*, edited by Vinson Synan, and the four-volume *Global Renewal Christianity: Spirit-Empowered Movements Past, Present, and Future* (covering Asia, Latin America, Africa, and North America and Europe), edited by Vinson Synan and Amos Yong.

Vinson Synan, editor of *The Truth About Grace*, is a premier and respected scholar and historian of the Pentecostal and Charismatic movements. Synan served as dean of the Regent University School of Divinity for twelve years and as interim dean of Oral Roberts University (ORU) for one year. He is currently a Scholar in Residence at ORU. Synan assembled an elite group of international scholars in London in 2016 to consider and review the topic of grace as it is currently understood from varied cultural perspectives. The men and women featured in this volume researched the subject extensively to offer a better understanding of the grace message being presented at this time in salvation history. Their prayer is that this book will be an inspired and valuable resource for those who want to know more about contemporary views on grace.

One can never diminish the beauty and significance of God's grace. One of the most beloved hymns is John Newton's classic "Amazing Grace." Indeed, this epic British hymn has become an anthem of declaration for the church. God's grace is continually and ever amazing!

—WILLIAM M. WILSON
PRESIDENT, ORAL ROBERTS UNIVERSITY
GLOBAL CO-CHAIR, EMPOWERED21

PREFACE

S OME BELIEVE THE great crisis of the twenty-first century church is its understanding of grace. Has costly grace been cheapened? What is the responsibility of the believer in order to walk in God's grace? Is the grace of God truly greater than all our sin? Can there be forgiveness without repentance? Are there conditions to receiving grace?

With conflicting teachings on God's grace, it is essential to look deep into Scripture to examine how the miraculous gift works in our daily Christian walk. Culture has created a compromise in the global church and is directing many to make choices of convenience rather than following Jesus in devout consecration.

The Truth About Grace is the latest in a series of books commissioned by Empowered21, a relational network for Spirit-empowered denominations, organizations, and ministries. Under the direction of global co-chairs William M. Wilson and George O. Wood, Empowered21 seeks to shape the future of the global Spirit-empowered movement throughout the world by focusing on crucial issues facing the body of Christ and connecting generations for intergenerational blessing and impartation.

Empowered21 is built on three pillars: leaders, scholars, and next generation voices. Beginning in 2012, a select group of international Pentecostal and Charismatic scholars representing different academic disciplines was commissioned to gain perspectives on the shape, potential, and global impact of issues within these movements.

During the first E21 Europe Congress, held in London in 2016, scholars gathered to discuss the implications of the grace movement that has been growing in global influence. "Grace in the Spirit-Empowered Movement" was the selected topic in response to requests from Pentecostal and Charismatic leaders around the world for scholars to research the controversial so-called "hyper-grace movement" that had become quite popular with several prominent ministries. *The Truth About Grace* is the result of that meeting.

The scholars presenting on the topic of grace came from the United States, the United Kingdom, Italy, Ireland, Jamaica, South Africa, and Singapore. The writers approached the topic from many ecclesiastical perspectives including the Anglican tradition (Andy Lord), the Methodist tradition (Henry H. Knight III), the Reformed tradition (Mark Jumper), and the Pentecostal tradition (S. David Moore). Several chapters deal with grace from biblical and theological perspectives, including those by John Christopher Thomas, Mark E. Roberts, Thomson K. Mathew, and Mark R. Hall. Other chapters deal with grace as seen in different nations such as those written by Miguel Álvarez (Latin America), Paolo Mauriello (Italy), William K. Kay (the United Kingdom), and Miriam (Mimi) A. Kelly (Ireland).

Some of the chapters address the excesses of "hyper-grace" teachings from a biblical and pastoral perspective. These include chapters by Brainerd Prince (no relation to Joseph Prince), who contributed "Going Beyond the Debate on Grace: Learning From a South Asian Tradition," and another by Trevor Grizzle, who wrote "The Hyper-Grace Gospel." In addition, Joseph Prince contributed a chapter titled "Beware of Counterfeit Grace," which is a major defense of Prince's teachings on grace and an answer to critics who claim he teaches a hyper-grace message. Meanwhile, Michael L. Brown, perhaps the most prominent critic of the hyper-grace message, has contributed a rebuttal of some of the movement's teachings.

Other chapters are more general and present a balanced view of grace from various perspectives. My opening chapter explores the scope of the problems created by an overemphasis on grace, which could sometimes produce tragic results. This chapter calls for a balanced approach between the extremes of "graceless law" and "lawless grace." With grace being a notable topic of interest, it is believed that *The Truth About Grace* will be well received as a useful reference tool for pastors, church leaders, and academic scholars for years to come.

—VINSON SYNAN, EDITOR

FROM GRACELESS LAW TO LAWLESS GRACE

Vinson Synan

"I HAVE RECENTLY DISCOVERED the wonderful freedom of grace, and I have changed my views on holiness as the church has taught it," a fellow minister told me a few years ago. "I have grown to see the dangers of Phariseeism and legalism that has plagued us for so long."[1]

He then exulted, "Now that I am free from the demands of the law, I am free to serve the Lord, not because I have to, but because I want to."

Although this sounded interesting to me at the time, I felt a twinge of concern for this friend who had long been a stalwart champion of holy living. Years before, I had known this young man to be a devout ministerial student with extraordinary gifts. His subsequent pastorates were successful, and he was marked for future leadership in his denomination.

A few months after hearing him exult about "discovering grace," I heard the shocking news that he had left the ministry in disgrace after being caught in a sexual affair with a woman in the community. The resulting divorce wrecked his family and forced him to resign his pastorate. For him, the discovery of grace had become a license to sin, which led to the ruin of his ministry.

Over the years, I have seen the same pattern repeated several times and usually with the same tragic results. For some persons, the discovery of grace becomes a convenient way to cover sin and attempt to avoid the guilt that inevitably follows. When someone tells me he has suddenly "discovered grace," I often shudder. This "grace-discovery syndrome" is all too often the first step toward moral and ethical decline.

GRACELESS LAW

This is not to indict sincere people who learn about the marvelous depths of truth concerning God's loving grace toward us. Many Christians are formed in systems that can best be described as hotbeds of "graceless law." In these places, righteousness rests in obeying a set of general rules and regulations earmarked as standards for church membership. At times, zealots administer these rules in ways that destroy rather than save the sheep. Often these holiness codes become occasions for spiritual pride and the remorseless pursuit of those who fail to keep every jot and tittle of the law.

My dear friend Pauline Parham told of one of the most extreme cases of graceless law I have ever heard. In a little Kansas town, a local holiness church split over whether its male members should wear buttons or hooks and eyes on their shirts. A few members had come to believe buttons were symbols of pride, while the simpler hooks and eyes fell more in line with a holiness lifestyle. When the church split in two over the controversy, people in town called one group the "buttons church" and the other the "hooks-and-eyes church." Needless to say, the church became the laughingstock of the community.

To be sure, Jesus contended with the spiritual pride and arrogance of the scribes and Pharisees, who could "strain out a gnat and swallow a camel" (Matt. 23:24, NKJV) in their pursuit of the law. This type of graceless law would stone a woman caught in adultery and then leave her equally guilty accusers to go free. Jesus, who had no patience for this hypocritical legalism, denounced it every time it reared its ugly head.

The apostle Paul, who based his entire theology on the grace of God through Christ, had no patience for this theology of graceless law either. He said, "By grace you have been saved through faith, and this is not of yourselves. It is the gift of God, not of works, so that no one should boast" (Eph. 2:8–9, MEV). Certainly, no Christian living in the age of grace would base his eternal salvation on the dubious grounds of performing good works rather than accepting the sacrifice of Jesus Christ, who is the only Savior.

Truly, it is the amazing grace of God through Jesus Christ that will save us in the end. No one who reads the New Testament can deny this basic truth. Jesus saves. We do not save ourselves.

LAWLESS GRACE

At the other extreme are those who believe in a form of "lawless grace" that allows Christians to throw away the Ten Commandments and all the clear moral teachings of Christ and the apostles under the guise of living under grace and not under the law. Those who hold to this teaching can be in as grave an error as those who live under forms of graceless law.

I often hear people in this camp deride those who live by the "thou shalt nots" of the Bible and those who posit their salvation on the sins they avoid. They often label this as "works righteousness," a favorite phrase used by these proponents to dismiss those who attempt to maintain biblical standards of holiness and righteousness.

Certainly, avoiding sin will not save anyone. Nonbelievers who live moral lives above reproach are still lost, despite their good works and moral lives, because they do not believe in Jesus Christ as their personal Savior.

Often those who "discover grace" fall into the trap of rejecting all of the moral law given to us in the Scriptures and become laws unto themselves. This is called *antinomianism*, which means "against law," and is an error as old as the gnostic heresy of the first century. These "knowing ones" taught that the spirit could remain pure even as the body sinned—a form of dualism the church has always condemned. Those who find themselves freed from the chains of graceless law should remember the advice of Paul: "Stand fast therefore in the liberty by which Christ has made us free.... only do not use liberty as an opportunity for the flesh, but through love serve one another" (Gal. 5:1, 13, NKJV).

Another grave error is to believe that a person's anointing justifies any lifestyle. I was once told by a fallen televangelist that the anointing seemed to be present in his ministry despite the lewd sins he seemed unable to avoid in his secret private life. People were saved and healed after he preached. My answer to him was that the Lord anoints His Word and that any results are due to the faithfulness of God, not the anointing of the minister. Paul made this clear when he said, "I bring and keep my body under subjection, lest when preaching to others I myself should be disqualified" (1 Cor. 9:27, MEV).

After all, "God has not called us to uncleanness, but to holiness" (1 Thess. 4:7, MEV). The Scriptures are clear on this too. Paul teaches, "Do you not know that the unrighteous will not inherit the kingdom of God? Do not be deceived. Neither the sexually immoral, nor idolaters, nor adulterers, nor male prostitutes, nor homosexuals, nor thieves, nor covetous, nor drunkards, nor revilers, nor extortioners will inherit the kingdom of God" (1 Cor. 6:9–10, MEV). He then says, "Such were some of you. But you were washed, you were sanctified, and you were justified in the name of the Lord Jesus by the Spirit of our God" (v. 11, MEV). The only way God's grace can reach people who commit these sins is for them to confess, repent, and abandon the lifestyles of sin that place them outside the kingdom.

The crucial point is this. Your works of righteousness cannot save you, but your sinful works of unrighteousness can destroy you. The Scriptures are crystal clear on this point. Works of righteousness cannot save, but willful works of unrighteousness can damn a person in eternity, despite the grace of God, who stands ready to forgive, heal, and restore. In the end, those who practice lives of unrepented, unconfessed, and unforgiven sin will be lost, regardless of their theology of grace.

THE TIME IS NOW

Over the centuries, the pendulum has swung back and forth between graceless law and lawless grace. The nineteenth century saw a mighty revival of holiness preaching and teaching, which greatly blessed the church and the world. As historians know, the Pentecostal movement was born in a holiness cradle. Part of the success of the early Pentecostal movement was due to the godly lives of its leaders and members. In recent years, however, the pendulum seems to have swung in the other direction, toward an acceptance of lawless grace that excuses sin not only in the lives of the laity but also in the lives of leaders. This is surely the great tragedy of this hour.

The world has seen enough of pastors, priests, teachers, evangelists, televangelists, bishops, and other church leaders who have "discovered grace," only to fall into grievous and scandalous sin. Churches are suffering untold internal harm and a drastic loss of public credibility due to the spectacle of so-called Christian leaders caught in adultery, homosexuality, child abuse, pornography, alcoholism, financial dishonesty, and many other outrageous sins. Many times, these ministers started out sincerely following the Lord, leading lives of holiness and righteousness, but later "discovered grace."

Perhaps what is needed most is a rejection of both extremes, the graceless law of the Pharisees and legalists and the lawless grace of those who think God has repealed His own basic rules of Christian living. Perhaps the church should look again at Hebrews 12:14, as did John Wesley, and contemplate the Lord's command to "pursue peace with all men, and the holiness without which no one will see the Lord" (MEV).

Chapter 1

JACK HAYFORD, THE SECURITY OF THE BELIEVER, AND THE NEED FOR PENTECOSTAL PASTOR-THEOLOGIANS

S. David Moore

I WAS CONVERTED THROUGH the Jesus People movement in California in early 1972. Coming as I did from a thoroughly unchurched background, I was rather naïve about Christianity. The Charismatic Southern Baptists who oversaw the Jesus House, a Christian commune where I lived for nearly a year, talked to me about the eternal security of the believer in Christ. They proclaimed the idea with such certainty that it made me wonder if righteous living really mattered, since, according to their understanding, God's saving grace was not based on anything I did but on Christ's atoning work alone.

At about the same time, I started attending a local Church of the Nazarene because the church's pastor had befriended me, I think in part because he was intrigued to have met a genuine, long-haired hippie. Growing up outside the church as I had, I was totally unaware of the differences in belief among churches, thinking they were all the same. My Nazarene pastor quickly challenged my naiveté. He pointed out how wrong my Baptist friends were about eternal security and taught me the more Wesleyan understanding that holy living mattered because without it I might be lost.

What an introduction to Christianity.

Fortunately, I found my way to a measure of theological stability, though even that took some time. As part of my pilgrimage, I joined a classical Pentecostal denomination, the International Church of the Foursquare Gospel, better known as the Foursquare Church. I never imagined aligning myself with classical Pentecostalism, but I was impressed by the ministry of Jack Hayford, himself an unapologetic part of the Foursquare denomination. Like so many, I appreciated Hayford's sane, scriptural approach to empowered Christianity.

Today, forty years into my pastoral ministry, I can testify that the competing questions I faced in those early days of my faith are still relevant today. Over the years I have counseled many Christians who have doubted their salvation although they were striving to live faithfully. I have also encountered more than a few believers who were living utterly sinful lives yet believed they were saved because they had prayed to receive Christ at some point in the past. Of course, there is a spectrum between these two extremes that makes the security of the believer an important pastoral challenge. The issue raises many questions: Once a person is saved by Christ, are they then always saved? Can Christians lose their salvation through acts of sin that follow conversion? Do Christians need to confess post-conversion sins? What is the extent of God's saving grace in Christ?

The hyper-grace controversy has brought these questions to the forefront for many Pentecostals and Charismatics. Yet Christians have wrestled to understand the nature, extent, and limits of God's saving grace for twenty centuries, and this struggle has produced multiple positions across the major Christian traditions. In the Protestant tradition alone there is a considerable range of theological opinion regarding God's grace and its consequences. Calvinists and Arminians not only disagree with each other but carry on significant debate *within* their respective traditions.[1]

Notwithstanding these challenges, I will endeavor to show Jack Hayford as one who has given classical Pentecostals a clear and balanced understanding of God's grace as it relates to the security of the believer. I will highlight one particular message Hayford preached on the issue of suicide and the security of the believer, using it both to sketch his views on the extent and limits of God's saving grace and to demonstrate the value of practical, pastoral theologizing in the regular preaching and teaching ministries of the local church.[2]

But First, Some Background

Hayford, the longtime pastor of one of America's flagship congregations, The Church On The Way in Van Nuys, California, is arguably the most highly respected Pentecostal leader of his generation. Known for his integrity, Hayford is appreciated as one of classical Pentecostalism's most able communicators. His public ministry has defied Pentecostal stereotypes, at least in part because of his theological depth and generous ecumenism. Without question, he has been an ambassador for Pentecostalism, spreading the message of Spirit baptism and glossolalia—spiritual language, as he calls it—far beyond Pentecostal borders to evangelicals who have appreciated his clearly articulated approach to what some still see as controversial topics.

Hayford's theological clarity in his preaching and teaching has been invaluable in helping countless people and pastors discover a stable and durable understanding of Christian faithfulness. Hayford has also demonstrated considerable wisdom and grace in addressing theological and practical controversies that have arisen in both classical Pentecostalism and the modern Charismatic Renewal. For example, without vilifying or questioning the motives of individuals,

Hayford spoke openly and with theological wisdom about concerns and imbalances he saw in the both the Shepherding Movement, with its emphasis on discipleship and spiritual authority, and the Word of Faith movement's so-called "health and wealth" gospel. In critiquing both Renewal expressions, Hayford found things to commend as well.[3] Over sixty years of public ministry, Hayford has articulated his distinctive views on countless subjects through his preaching and teaching.

Accordingly, Hayford's example demonstrates the need for pastoral theologians who can lead the people of God through the morass of differing opinions to sort the good from the bad, the balanced from the extreme. With the multiplied media avenues that make controversial teaching themes readily available to believers, there has never been a greater need for the leadership of theologically astute pastors and practitioners in the local church.

Concerning our present study of grace and its implications on the security of the believer, where does Hayford come down on the issue? He preaches a strong message of God's amazing grace. Does this mean he is an advocate of the hyper-grace teaching? The answer is that Hayford is not an advocate and has privately expressed reservation about how some have applied the present grace emphasis in sectors of the Renewal movements.[4] Nevertheless, could Hayford strike a balance on this issue, highly respected as he is for his ability to find and forge balanced positions on difficult pastoral and theological issues?

The real question is this: Is it possible to affirm the extravagant grace God provides through Christ in a balanced and biblical manner while respecting the basic Arminianism of a classical Pentecostal denomination that acknowledged the possibility of apostasy for believers? As a classical Pentecostal, Jack Hayford, a man who has served the Pentecostal and Charismatic movements as a mediator and statesman in many of its controversies, has done just that.

THE SECURITY OF THE BELIEVER
AND "THE SIN OF SUICIDE"

In the fall of 1984 Hayford's Van Nuys congregation was shaken when one of its worship leaders committed suicide. Wanting to address the concerns and questions many people had regarding the worship leader's eternal fate, Hayford set aside a Sunday evening service on October 28 to address the matter.[5] His choice of a Sunday evening allowed for an extended time of teaching. The message, titled "The Sin of Suicide," lasted more than ninety minutes and addressed a number of theological themes. Prominent among them was the grace of God and the security of the believer.

Hayford wasted no time tackling the question head-on. "Is the sin of suicide automatically damning?" he asked. Then he continued:

> Answering this question is the whole purpose of this message. *Is the sin of suicide one for which there is no forgiveness?* ... I begin by saying, "no." ... I want to say it again: Because a person commits suicide and their last act was a violation of the revealed commandments of God does not mean they are damned.[6]

Hayford followed these opening statements with a carefully developed overview on the nature of God's saving grace in Christ, affirming that salvation is based on Christ's atoning work alone and not on any merit of the believer. Sounding almost Calvinistic at times, he presented the classic argument from Romans 3–5 on justification by faith in Christ. For Hayford, it

> is not within the power of man to either initiate or inaugurate his own salvation, or to perpetuate it by his own works. We are saved by the work of Jesus Christ on the Cross, and there are no works that we contribute to that saving process. Since there's nothing we contribute to our salvation, then the argument can be extrapolated that there are basically no works

that can alter our salvation, as long as abiding faith in Jesus Christ, the Son of God, is maintained intact.[7]

Hayford went on:

People don't lose their soul over a single act of sin or even some particular ongoing continual sin.... Salvation is through Jesus Christ alone. When a person who knows Jesus Christ takes his or her life, for whatever reason, they have not, by that single act, overreached the power of the Covenant of God to save their eternal soul.... It is a pusillanimous, small view of the Cross that would lock anyone into the chains of the eternal darkness because of one single act (or even a set of specific acts)...that on the grounds of those acts alone, a believer could have lost his or her eternal soul. A person who says that doesn't understand the bigness of the Cross.[8]

Although at first glance Hayford seems to affirm a view some might say is akin to "once saved, always saved," he in fact believes apostasy is possible for the believer, as we will soon see. Rather, the emphasis on God's saving grace was a conscious counter-message to what he believed was classical Pentecostalism's tendency to use fear and guilt as a means to motivate believers to live holy lives. In Hayford's view, although most Pentecostals affirm justification by faith alone, in practice the emphasis is not always focused sufficiently on Christ's saving work as much as it is on the importance of the believer's faithfulness to Christ.

He had learned another way in the 1950s while attending his denomination's L.I.F.E. Bible College. Influenced by a few Reformed-leaning professors, Hayford began to more fully appreciate the biblical emphasis on justification by faith alone distinct from the believer's works. It was at the college that Hayford discovered the "liberating truth upon which life and ministry could be built."[9] He said:

I was taught of God's sovereign love and gift in Christ, the solidarity of the believer's position before the Father through

Jesus' justifying work on the cross. I discovered the deep, securing peace that begets true personal identity, gained when a person learns to identify with Christ. I gained deliverance from the spectre of condemnation, finding in God's Word that my complete acquittal from sin's record and judgment was secured through the Cross.[10]

For Hayford, this understanding was the solid ground from which a believer could then develop the confidence to grow in grace and overcome sin.

After graduating from the college in 1956, Hayford learned to incorporate a message of grace into his ministry. By 1969, when he assumed an interim assignment pastoring the fading, eighteen-member First Foursquare Church of Van Nuys, he had learned how

to trust myself to proclaim His love, with an ever-deepening conviction about His desire toward and His overwhelming commitment to mankind—to me! It began to affect my thinking thoroughly, my teaching and my leading of others. My convictions about God and man provided a biblical and theological base for cultivating a ministry to the saints— a true loving, accepting, forgiving fellowship among the Lord's people. I was braced against humanistic and legalistic traditions, and grounded in a sense of God's majestic, condemnation-shattering provision for us all in the Lord Jesus' death and resurrection.[11]

Hayford made this grace emphasis a central theme of his Van Nuys pastorate, where he would go on to spend the next thirty years as the church's senior pastor, leading what became a ten-thousand-member congregation by 1999. The remarkable growth the church experienced was based on many factors, but Hayford's grace-filled message was no doubt one significant reason. Although his comments on God's grace in his message on suicide were not new to his congregation, putting the security of the believer in the context of suicide was.[12]

Decades later, in sessions at his School of Pastoral Nurture at The King's University, Hayford continued to emphasize that God's mercies endure forever, telling pastors there is too much focus in much of the conservative, contemporary church on God's displeasure with sinners. Hayford's comments revealed a more expansive view of the Atonement than simply the penal-substitution theory:

> When you explain...[that] Jesus' atoning death was to appease the anger of God—the violated part of a just God who could only be pacified if his son suffered on the cross and, on our behalf, did that to appease the fury of a God who had just had it "up to here" with mankind...I don't think there is anything in the Bible that requires that application of what the Atonement was about.[13]

For Hayford, the Atonement is about more than appeasing an angry God. Rather, it reflects the great love God has for humankind, in keeping with the declarations of John 3:16–17. Hayford's concern, as a pastor, was for people to hear the good news of God's redeeming love and grace demonstrated through the cross of Christ (Rom. 5:6–8). Grace, for Hayford, was the expression of the love of God that ought to characterize every dimension of Christian ministry.

Nevertheless, Hayford qualified his affirmations of the love of God and the sufficiency of grace. This is especially evident in his message on suicide. While affirming that salvation is based solely on Christ's atoning work, he told his listeners that a "delicate balance" needed to be addressed. He said he wanted "to talk about how people lose their salvation."[14]

His starting place was the texts that are commonly seen as affirming eternal security (John 6:37–40; 10:27–29) but which he used as an entrée to discuss what he termed "free will," the responsibility of the believer to remain in the state of grace. He raised the question, "So how can a person lose their soul?"[15] To answer, Hayford quoted Hebrews 10:26–29 (NKJV):

> For if we sin willfully after we have received the knowledge of the truth, there no longer remains a sacrifice for sins, but a certain fearful expectation of judgment, and fiery indignation which will devour the adversaries. Anyone who has rejected Moses' law dies without mercy on the testimony of two or three witnesses. Of how much worse punishment, do you suppose, will he be thought worthy who has trampled the Son of God underfoot, counted the blood of the covenant by which he was sanctified a common thing, and insulted the Spirit of grace?

He discussed the opening phrase, "if we sin willfully," in light of its tense in the original Greek, arguing that the author had in view "a pathway of ongoing sinning with indifference" when he said there "no longer remains a sacrifice for sins."[16]

Ultimately, Hayford proclaimed:

> People don't lose their salvation by accident. You don't lose your salvation because you had a flash of temper. I hate to even concede this ground because I've been very direct [in past messages] about the sin of immorality and its undesirability, its unrighteousness, and its evil, so let me go one step further and say what is the truth of God's Word: No more than the act of suicide is necessarily going to damn the soul of a person who has entered into the covenant of salvation with God and not denied that, an act of immorality isn't going to damn a soul either.

> The problem is that once people begin to presume on the grace of God, they move into territory in which their heart and conscience toward God become neutralized and numb. That's what the "willing sinning" of Hebrews 10 is talking about— people who, in a continuum, get on a path where they're moving more and more distantly away from true discipleship to Jesus Christ. They are living under the delusion that they

are disciples when, in fact, the Covenant is being dismantled
by their violation of it at point after point after point.[17]

Perhaps the best way to sum up Hayford's view of apostasy is
to note something he has said on many occasions: "If you are going
to lose your salvation, you are going to have to be very sincere
about losing it."[18] Hayford has also sometimes stated that while
he does not believe in the notion of "once saved, always saved," he
certainly does not believe in "once saved, *hardly* saved," referring to
the sense of insecurity produced by poor teaching among classical
Pentecostals on the conditional nature of salvation.

As his 1984 suicide message illustrates, Hayford readily acknowledges he would rather emphasize the security of the believer. Still,
he is unwilling to affirm absolute security of those saved by Christ
because of biblical texts he believes suggest some element of contin-
gency and personal responsibility. Hayford's "both/and" approach
on this issue is emblematic of his theological method and illustrates his willingness to yield to the tension between two truths in
Scripture rather than force one or the other into a prescribed theological system.

It is worth pointing out that Hayford's message was more than
a matter of articulating his views on the security of the believer
and the possibility of apostasy. He perceptively located the temptation of suicide within the broader societal and cultural issues of
1984.[19] He also suggested that the most important counter to suicide is for each and every Christian to discover and live within
God's high purpose. The message went on to become one of the
most widely distributed of Hayford's teachings.

OUR NEED FOR
MORE PASTOR-THEOLOGIANS

Whether or not one agrees with everything Hayford argued, his
message was an example of what pastors are called to do: address
biblically and theologically the concerns and challenges of living

out one's faith in the real world. For more than twenty years, Hayford spoke to more than twenty thousand pastors annually at various leaders' events and conferences around the world. He consistently called them to recognize that their call to equip the church required them to know their congregations well and that their preaching and teaching should boldly address the "real life" situations people face.

Hayford practiced what he preached. Over the years he dealt with topics that ranged from why prayers aren't answered to masturbation, or what he called "solo sex." After the deadly 1994 Northridge earthquake shook Van Nuys and the greater Southern California area, Hayford responded by sharing his own struggle with fear after the earthquake and by preaching about why bad things happen to good people. Those messages helped comfort and strengthen the quake-shaken congregation by giving them firm biblical ground on which to stand while the earth below them seemed less than certain.

Kevin Vanhoozer's recent book *The Pastor as Public Theologian*, written with Owen Strachan, calls for a recovery of the role of the parish pastor as a primary theologian for the people of God.[20] Vanhoozer laments the loss of "theological character"[21] in the pastoral office for so many churches. His metaphorical language is strong, putting special emphasis on his concern: "Theology is in exile and, as a result, the knowledge of God is in ecclesial eclipse. The promised land, the gathered people of God, has consequently come to resemble a parched land: a land of wasted opportunities that no longer cultivates disciples as it did in the past."[22] Vanhoozer believes the "idea of the pastor as a theologian—one who opens up the Scriptures to help people understand God, the world, and themselves—no longer causes the hearts of most church members to 'burn within' them."[23]

Noting the bifurcation between theologian and pastor, Vanhoozer calls this separation an "ugly (and embarrassing) ditch"[24] and believes it has severely injured the contemporary church. He flatly asserts, "Theologians and pastors have been torn asunder, relegated to separate publics (the academy and church, respectively)."[25] A professional theologian himself, Vanhoozer makes his concern ever so clear, stating that "theology is too important to be left to 'professionals.'"[26]

In a 2011 essay for the periodical *First Things*, Gerald Hiestand echoes Vanhoozer's concerns, speaking of the "chronic 'disconnect' between the academy and the church."[27] Hiestand challenges such a disconnect by noting:

> Historically, the church's most influential theologians were *church* men—pastors, priests, and bishops. Clerics such as Athanasius, Augustine (indeed, nearly all the church Fathers), Anselm, Luther, Calvin, Zwingli, Edwards, and Wesley functioned as the wider theologians of their day—shaping not only the theological vision of their own parishes, but that of the wider church. In their day, the pastoral community represented the most influential, most insightful, and most articulate body of theologians.[28]

Hiestand rightly points out the ultimate aim of theology ought to be the "edification of the church"[29] and that there is a need to see again the preaching event—the pulpit—as a primary place for theologizing with "a bare-fisted, take-no-prisoner, prophetic, pulpit voice."[30] He believes the church must see anew that the primary audience of theological reflection is not those in the academy but the "regular people."[31] This, he argues, was the way the church fathers, because of their parish locations, were forced to make "connections between their most profound thoughts and the lives of average people."[32]

Vanhoozer also believes that competing images of the pastoral vocation[33] have significantly contributed to a loss of vision of the pastor as a public theologian. The pastor today is seen as a CEO, therapist, moral coach, media personality, and so on, but seldom as an able theologian.[34] I could not agree more.

Alternatively, I have shown Hayford's preaching to be driven by practical pastoral concerns and a deep passion to communicate biblical truth that nourishes and sustains the people of God. He is not a systematic or theoretical theologian but a practical theologian whose articulations emerge from pastoral, congregational realities.

Although the term *pastor-theologian* is seldom used in Pentecostal circles, it is a worthy descriptor for use in a movement that from its beginnings has been shaped theologically by its pastors and practitioners. Douglas Jacobsen has observed that early Pentecostal thinkers, while most lacked advanced theological training, were nevertheless astute and able theologians whose theologizing was "theological reflection grounded in real life."[35] James K. A. Smith has noted that "Pentecostalism is a tradition of preachers and evangelists" and that Pentecostal theology is "forged at the pulpit and in prayer."[36] Though there are a number of elements that help mark a uniquely Pentecostal theological method, one thing is certain: the sermon has been and still is crucial in articulating Pentecostal pastoral theology, and no one has proven better at it than Jack Hayford.[37]

LEARNING FROM JACK HAYFORD

What elements from Jack Hayford's example can be replicated by all Pentecostal pastors? Although few have all the gifts Hayford possesses, several things can be learned from his life.

First, Hayford, although never going beyond the two undergraduate degrees he earned, is an example of someone who has long valued the importance of formal theological training and pursued it within the expectations of his denomination.[38] His appreciation of the value of theological education is no better illustrated than when in 1997 he founded The King's College and Seminary (today The King's University), where he continues today as the university's chancellor. Jack Hayford is not a scholar in the formal, professional sense but holds high regard for those who have earned advanced degrees and values the significant role professional scholars have in the academic arena.

Second, Hayford has striven to live within what Roger Olson calls "Great Tradition Christianity" by acknowledging the unity and diversity in the Christian faith.[39] Hayford situates himself within the Arminian tradition but acknowledges the blessings of the Reformed tradition. This has contributed to the theological balance he is known for, as well as his gracious and respectful tone in addressing differences.

Third, it is important to remember that Hayford interprets within an identifiable faith community that helps hold him accountable pastorally and theologically. In addition, beyond the Foursquare Church, Hayford has a significant number of trusted personal friends and colleagues he regularly consults for personal, pastoral, hermeneutical, and theological counsel, including a number of faculty at The King's University.

Following Hayford's example in just these three areas would serve all Pentecostal pastors and the larger church as well. Hayford's life and ministry point the way forward as the church contends to live faithfully in our challenging and complex times. The Christian church will always face doctrinal extremes and outright heresies. What is needed are more pastor-theologians like Jack Hayford to lead the church forward unto the "Day of the Lord."

S. DAVID MOORE, PHD, is the M. G. Robertson Professor of Pneumatology at The King's University and lead pastor of Jackson Avenue Church in Escalon, California. He is the author of *The Shepherding Movement: Controversy and Charismatic Ecclesiology*, *The Charismatic Century: The Enduring Impact of the Azusa Street Revival*, and *Renewal History and Theology: Essays in Honor of H. Vinson Synan*.

Chapter 2

ARE ALL OUR SINS—PAST, PRESENT, AND FUTURE— ALREADY FORGIVEN IN JESUS?

Michael L. Brown

ONE OF THE foundations of the modern grace message is that the moment we are saved, God forgives all of our sins, meaning past sins, present sins, and future sins. In fact, some hyper-grace teachers claim that God doesn't even see the sins we commit as believers since He sees us as completely sanctified and holy in His Son.[1] To back up this position they commonly quote the words of the new covenant prophecy spoken in Jeremiah 31:31–34 and repeated in Hebrews 8:8–12, culminating with these words: "For I will be merciful toward their iniquities, and *I will remember their sins no more*" (ESV, emphasis added), a phrase that is quoted again in Hebrews 10:17 (ESV)—"I will remember their sins and their lawless deeds no more."

It is true that when Jesus died on the cross, He paid for every sin that you and I and the rest of the human race would ever commit, from Adam's first sin until the very last sin that will be committed on this planet. But that doesn't mean God forgives our sins before we commit them. That is not taught anywhere in the Bible. When the Lord says He forgives us and remembers our sins no more, He's speaking of the sins we have committed at the time He forgives us.

The New Testament is totally clear on this. As it is written in 2 Peter 1, the believer who goes backward spiritually rather than forward "is nearsighted and blind, forgetting that they have been cleansed *from their past sins*" (2 Pet. 1:9, NIV, emphasis added; the English Standard Version reads, "...having forgotten that he was cleansed from his former sins").

What sins did God forgive when we asked Him to save and cleanse us? He forgave our past sins, our former sins, the sins we committed before we were born again. As Colossians 2 explains, when we put our faith in Jesus and became children of God, He canceled "the record of debt that stood against us with its legal demands. This he set aside, nailing it to the cross" (v. 14, ESV). The Complete Jewish Bible says, "He wiped away the bill of charges against us," and the New International Version puts it this way: "Having canceled the charge of our legal indebtedness, which stood against us and condemned us; he has taken it away, nailing it to the cross."

Under the law we accumulated a massive amount of spiritual debt, with each new sin we committed adding to that debt. And it was a debt we could never repay, especially since the standards of God's law continually reminded us of our failures and short-comings. But the moment God saved us, He forgave us that debt—some scholars refer to it as an IOU—and then He brought us into a new and better covenant, one in which His laws are written on our hearts, and He remembers our sins no more (Jer. 31:31–34).

So when we look to the Lord for salvation, He forgives every sin we have committed up to that point, and He even forgives us for who we are: lost, rebellious sinners. But He does not forgive us for our sins before we commit them. This is clearly stated in many passages, and it makes perfect spiritual sense as well.

Before we look at some additional scriptures, let me ask you a simple question. When you put your trust in Jesus as your Savior and Lord and you asked Him to forgive you for all your sins, what sins did you mean? Perhaps you said something like, "God, I confess to You that I am a sinner and have done many wrong things in my life, and I ask You to forgive me and wash me clean."

Is that how you prayed? I said something similar to the Lord, and He met me right where I was as a heroin-shooting, LSD-using, rebellious, hippie rock drummer. I was clean and forgiven and washed at that very moment. Totally! And all the guilt I had been feeling in previous weeks as the Holy Spirit was convicting me of my sins was totally gone as well. What amazing grace!

But it didn't dawn on me to say, "And Lord, while we're at it, could You please forgive me for all the sins I plan to commit tomorrow and for the rest of my life, along with the sins I don't plan to commit?"

I bet it didn't dawn on you to say that either. Why? It is because we understand that forgiveness is for what we have done, not for what we will do.

In the same way, if I sinned against my friend and let him down, I would go to him and say, "Please forgive me for being irresponsible and causing you pain. I was wrong, and I make no excuses." But I wouldn't say to him, "And since I'm confessing and you're forgiving, I ask you to forgive me in advance for every sin I will ever commit against you in the future as well." Of course not!

You might say, "But isn't it different with God, since He sees the future the way we see the past?" Not at all, even though He inhabits eternity (Isa. 57:15) and knows the beginning from the end (Isa. 46:8–10). When it comes to forgiveness, He forgives people only for what they have done, not what they will do. Consequently *there is not a single verse in the Bible where God forgives a person's sins before they commit those sins*. Not one.

To repeat: Jesus *paid for* all our sins when He hung on the cross, which means that for all of us living after the cross, He paid for our sins before we were ever born. But He does not forgive our sins until we come to Him asking for mercy, and when He forgives us, He forgives what we have done.

To give a simple analogy, let's say I put one million dollars into a special account for a person's education, telling the student that whenever he incurred a debt for tuition, textbooks, or living expenses while in college, he could just send me a text with the amount and I'd transfer the funds into his account. The funds are there and the provision is made in advance, but the money isn't transferred until the debt is incurred.

In the same way, forgiveness covers whatever "debt" we have incurred, which is why Jesus taught us to pray, "Forgive us our debts, as we forgive our debtors" (Matt. 6:12, MEV). We are not encouraged to forgive debts not yet incurred.

If you look at every single prayer for forgiveness recorded in the Bible, you will see that people (and nations) ask for forgiveness only for what they have done, not for what they will do. Then look at every single time God pronounces a person or nation forgiven in the Bible, and you will see that, without exception, it is for sins that person or nation has already committed, not for future sins.

GRACE IN ACTION

I know some teachers today say, "God doesn't forgive in install-ments," and it sounds very powerful. But that teaching has no basis in Scripture. In fact, the entire Bible is against it.

That being said, it *is* true that God doesn't *save* in installments, meaning that the moment He says, "I forgive you," you become a child of God and you pass from death to life, from the kingdom of Satan to the kingdom of God, from condemned to not guilty, from wicked to righteous, from lost to saved, from having a debt of sins bigger than Mount Everest to being totally and absolutely forgiven—all in a moment of time. That is grace in action. That is the power of the blood of Jesus. It is a free gift, and it is yours forever.

That also means that if you sin tomorrow and get upset with a coworker, you do not become unsaved and go back to death, back to the kingdom of Satan, back to being condemned, back to being wicked and lost. Instead, as a child of God who is still in the "forgiven" column—meaning God looks at you as His beloved child, a former guilty sinner whom He has pronounced forgiven—you now need to apply the blood of Jesus to your life and receive fresh cleansing. But you do *not* do this as a lost sinner being saved. Rather, you do it as a child of God who is in the "saved-righteous-holy-forgiven" column, freshly applying that source of forgiveness—the blood of Jesus—to your life again.

It is important to understand clearly that God does not forgive our sins before we commit them, since this false teaching opens the door to all kinds of deception and danger. You see, if I really believe that my future sins are already forgiven, in a time of weakness or temptation I might think to myself, "It's no big deal if I do that, since I'm already forgiven and therefore nothing could change my relationship with God, no matter what I do." I think you can see how dangerous that could be.

To explain this further, we know that God doesn't dredge up our past to condemn us, reminding us every day, "You were a terrible wretch before you were saved, and you did some really bad things. You should feel ashamed of yourself." That is not our Father! We *did* do terrible things before we were saved, and we *did* feel ashamed, but all that is forgiven and forgotten.

But what if I believed the same thing about my future sins? That would mean that when the Holy Spirit came to make me feel uncomfortable, warning me of danger, I would ignore the Spirit's loving work, thinking it was my own mind or, worse still, attributing it to the devil: "God already forgave me for this sin, so the Holy Spirit wouldn't convict me." And so, rather than heeding the

Spirit's rebuke—which is meant to be life-saving—I will plunge headlong into disaster.

It would be like a driver saying, "By faith I've already arrived at my destination, so I can ignore these warning signs on the road." In reality, we ignore them to our own peril.

The Price for Forgiveness Has Been Paid

That being said, modern grace teachers make a very good point when they remind us that God deals with us as His children, which means that we don't get saved one moment, become lost the next moment (the moment we commit a sin), and then get "resaved" the moment we ask for forgiveness. This kind of spiritual schizo-phrenia is not only totally unbiblical, but it is also totally mad-dening. Who can possibly live like this?

So it is crucial that we find a place of security in the Lord, remembering that we are saved by grace, not by works; by God's goodness, not by our goodness. It is also crucial to understand that when God forgives, He forgets—meaning He doesn't keep a record of wrongs against us—and that when we are forgiven, we are really forgiven. And it's crucial to understand that Jesus paid the price for every sin we will ever commit, and when we come to Him in sin-cerity, asking Him to wash us clean, He will do so without hesita-tion. The price has already been paid.

This means that if God isn't bringing up your past, you shouldn't bring it up either, and if He says you are forgiven, you really are forgiven. Receive it, no matter what you've done and no matter how far you've fallen. And shout it out for the world to hear: "I am God's child, and I am forgiven!"

You might grieve deeply over the sins you committed, and that is commendable. Could you imagine a husband who committed adultery not grieving deeply over his sin when he repents to God and to his wife? You might feel sorrowful when you think back to some foolish thing you did in the recent past, one that brought terrible hardship on you and others, and you might kick yourself, thinking, "How in the world could I have been so stupid?" That is totally understandable.

But at the same time you should know that God really has forgiven you, that He really does love you, that He doesn't put you in the doghouse, that you don't need to get saved again, and that He doesn't want you to wallow in guilt. Just consider the parable of the Pharisee and the tax collector in Luke 18:9–14. The Pharisee, a respected religious practitioner, boasted to the Lord about his own righteous works. In contrast, the tax collector, recognizing his guilt, wouldn't even lift his head when he prayed. Instead, he beat his breast and said, "God, be merciful to me a sinner" (v. 13, MEV).

Those simple words, "God, be merciful to me a sinner," were the only words that tax collector needed to pray. Jesus says it was this man—the sinful tax collector, not the religious Pharisee—who went home justified. Amazing!

That is the grace of God, and to repeat, when He forgives, He forgets. As the Scriptures declare:

> Blessed is he whose transgression is forgiven, whose sin is covered. Blessed is the man against whom the LORD does not count iniquity, and in whose spirit there is no deceit.
> —PSALM 32:1–2, MEV

> I have blotted out, as a thick cloud, your transgressions, and your sins, as a cloud. Return to Me, for I have redeemed you.
> —ISAIAH 44:22, MEV

> For I will forgive their iniquity, and I will remember their sin no more.
> —JEREMIAH 31:34, MEV

> Who is a God like You, bearing iniquity and passing over transgression for the remnant of His inheritance? He does not remain angry forever, because He delights in benevolence. He

will again have compassion upon us. He will tread down our
iniquities, and cast all of our sins into the depths of the sea.
—MICAH 7:18–19, MEV

And here is something remarkable: all the verses I just cited are
from the Old Testament, with the authors still looking forward to
the fullness of forgiveness that comes to us through the cross. How
much more, then, can we be confident that our own sins are forgiven in Jesus once and for all!

So you can rest assured that, as far as your salvation is concerned, you have been forgiven of your sins and God remembers them no more. How mind-boggling is that? And as for your
ongoing relationship with God, forgiveness is applied whenever we
need it and ask for it.

To illustrate this point, let me take you back to December
1971 when God graciously saved me from my sins. Although I
first made a profession of faith on November 12, 1971, this profession was more of an (unexpected) acknowledgment that I actually
believed Jesus died for me. Prior to that I would have dismissed the
idea. But when I professed my faith that Friday night in November,
it was only a first step, since I wasn't willing to follow Jesus or turn
away from my sinful lifestyle.

It was on December 17, 1971, that the breakthrough came, and
it was a glorious breakthrough I will never forget. The Lord met
me so wonderfully that night—it was also a Friday night—and I
knew beyond a doubt that my slate was clear and my heart was
clean. I was totally forgiven, even before I went home and threw
out my needles and the drugs I used to shoot into my veins. All
my guilt was gone, and in God's sight I was like a newborn child.

For me, the point of surrender was to say to the Lord, "I will
never put a needle in my arm again," since that was the principal
battle in my soul, the principal area where I had been unwilling to
say yes to the Lord. But on that glorious night in December, my
heart was so filled with the love and joy of the Lord that it was

easy for me to make that commitment, and by His grace I was free from that night on.

A couple of days later, while hanging out with some friends, I got high, smoking hash (hashish), and not really thinking much about it. But a few hours later, riding home alone on the bus, I felt convicted in my heart that this too was displeasing before God. I asked Him to forgive me and told Him I would give up all drugs, not just those I shot intravenously.

But this is what I want you to grasp: I was still saved and forgiven while smoking hash that day. I didn't ask God to forgive me for getting high that day because I needed to get saved all over again. It was because I realized that my actions were displeasing in His sight, and more than anything I wanted to honor Jesus with the way I lived.

It took some weeks before I realized that profanity was sinful (to be perfectly honest with you, I was such a rebel and so full of ugliness that there were quite a few other things the Lord dealt with me about before He began to convict me of my foul speech), and thankfully I haven't used profanity in more than forty-four years. It's really the last thing on my mind. But, to use this as an example, if, God forbid, I uttered a profane word today, of course I would be instantly convicted by the Spirit, and of course I would instantly apologize to the Lord (and anyone who heard me utter the word), asking for immediate forgiveness. But I would not need to get saved all over again.

Why then would I ask for forgiveness? Once again, this would be the forgiveness of relationship, not the forgiveness of salvation. I received that once and for all the night Jesus saved me from my sins, and it is only by rejecting Him as Lord and turning my back on that forgiveness that I could forfeit His precious gift.[2]

MICHAEL L. BROWN, PHD, is the founder and president of FIRE School of Ministry, a leadership training institute birthed out of the fires of revival that is called to equip authentic and devoted disciples of Jesus. With a PhD from New York University in Near Eastern Languages and Literatures, he is recognized as one of the leading Messianic Jewish scholars in the world today. He hosts the nationally syndicated daily talk radio show *The Line of Fire* and is the author of more than twenty-five books, including *The Grace Controversy*, from which this chapter is drawn.

Chapter 3

THE HYPER-GRACE GOSPEL

Trevor Grizzle

THE DECADE OF the seventies ushered in a brand of Christianity popularly called the *hyper-faith movement*. *Positive confession*, *health and wealth*, and *word-of-faith gospel* are other monikers by which it has been known. This "gospel" created a stir in theological circles and is still regarded as an illegitimate child by most evangelicals. Purveyors of this teaching believe words have the power to create reality, good or bad, such that "what you say is what you get."

To state an oft-quoted biblical verse its proponents employ in support of their claim, "Death and life are in the power of the tongue" (Prov. 18:21, MEV). Consequently, positive outcomes depend on positive confession. The opposite is also true for this group: negative confession leads to negative outcomes. Positive spoken words are the means by which "faith force" is activated, thus clearing the path for one to claim whatever one wants.

Though still a force to reckon with today, the hyper-faith movement in the United States has shown signs of tempering, mellowing, and maturing theologically. But a relatively new theological belief system has emerged on the Christian stage in recent years and is troubling biblical waters. It has been dubbed the *hyper-grace movement.*[1]

If the hyper-faith movement developed in reaction to a passive and powerless Christianity whose God was distant and inaccessible, hyper-grace Christianity emerged largely in reaction to a legalistic religion that eviscerated the life-giving gospel, corroded and toxified Christianity, and brought people under the thralldom of rules and regulations that were impossible to keep and resulted only in spiritual death.

According to the promoters of the hyper-grace movement, the sixteenth-century Reformers fell short in reforming the church, particularly in the area of sanctification, or the believer's perfected status in Christ. They believe "Luther and Calvin both drew up rigid rules of conduct in their churches"[2] for Christians to live by. Thus, from Luther until now, a form of "legalistic leaven" has "leavened the modern Church's doctrine," bringing about "tragic results" to the Christian faith.[3] Hyper-grace teachers believe that no matter the strain of Protestant Christianity that exists today, "at the end of the day, almost all are presenting a version of the Gospel leavened with law."[4] In the words of Steve McVey, "Law is the Trojan horse that has infiltrated contemporary Christendom, with devastating results."[5] Thus, according to them, a grace reformation is desperately needed. Hyper-grace propagandists believe they are bringing this grace reformation about to a degree that will make Luther's teachings on grace and faith appear "utterly primitive."[6]

It can surely be said that through the modern grace movement, untold thousands have left behind the chafing and constricting shackles of legalistic religion and have found glorious freedom and spiritual transformation in the unearned and undeserved favor of God. And it would be wondrous news if the "movie" ended there. However, Michael Brown, in his painstaking study of the movement, came to this penetrating conclusion:

The truth is that the modern grace message is quite mixed, combining life-changing, Jesus-exalting revelation with serious misinterpretation of Scripture, bad theology, divisive and destructive rhetoric, and even fleshly reaction. And, in all too many cases, it is being embraced by believers who are not just looking for freedom from legalism but also freedom from God's standards.[7]

Deny it though they may, hyper-grace teachers inadvertently pave the way with velvet toward a Christianity that gives no regard to sanctified life. What are we to make of the following statements by McVey? "I highly recommend that you give up your Christian values,"[8] and "The desire to live right is an improper goal for the Christian."[9]

Are hyper-grace teachers correct in saying a person's salvation should not be judged by his or her conduct and that Christians cannot increase in holiness? This chapter will seek to answer that question.

THE MOVEMENT'S TEACHERS

Scholars though some are, I know of not a single hyper-grace teacher of repute who is merely an academic sitting in an ivory tower creating and refining arguments that have no practical value to the Christian life and the kingdom of God. As I have read their writings, listened to their sermons, heard them teach, and explored their ministries, I have come away fully convinced that these are people who sincerely love God, are passionate about His kingdom, are Christ centered theologically, exalt Christ, and want to see people become transformed by the power of divine grace.

Additionally, the modern grace movement is not a monolith. Not all hyper-grace exponents subscribe to every tenet of the movement, nor is everyone equally persuaded by and passionately committed to all the teachings for which it is known.

Let's take a look at some of this movement's most influential teachers.

Joseph Prince, probably the movement's most prominent voice, is cofounder and senior pastor of New Creation Church in Singapore, one of Asia's largest churches, with 31,000 members and adherents. He is also founder and CEO of Joseph Prince Ministries, Inc., which reaches out to the less fortunate of Asia, and host of *Destined to Reign*, a weekly TV broadcast seen in 150 countries.[10]

Clark Whitten has been in ministry for forty years and has pastored three megachurches. The first, Gateway Baptist Church in Roswell, New Mexico, which he founded in 1978, two years after he graduated from seminary, grew to 2,500 attendees within six years. His church led the entire Southern Baptist Convention in 1982–1983 with 1,350 baptisms. After his pastorate, a three-year stint in revivals and evangelistic conferences brought spiritual awakening to many churches across America. His superlative gift as pastor was again evidenced at MetroChurch, Edmond, Oklahoma, and later at the 4,000-member Calvary Assembly of God in Winter Park, Florida, where he liquidated an $11.5 million debt in five years. While continuing to be a featured speaker in churches and conferences, Whitten currently pastors Grace Church Orlando in Longwood, Florida, a flourishing church of his founding and one that exemplifies his lifetime message.[11]

An engaging speaker and prolific author, Steve McVey transitioned from a term as a pastor to become host of both a radio and TV ministry called *Grace Walk* and founder of Grace Walk Ministries, located in Atlanta, Georgia. Many of his books have been translated into multiple languages. Grace Walk Ministries has offices in at least seven countries.[12]

Paul Ellis is an award-winning author and scholar and makes his home in Auckland, New Zealand, with his family. For ten years he shepherded a multicultural congregation in Hong Kong.

He is said to be "one of the world's most prolific scholars in the field of international business" and was a full professor at one of Asia's finest business schools.[13]

THE MOVEMENT'S CHARACTERISTICS

The hyper-grace movement is bereft of denominational identity, as its leadership is drawn from both the Calvinist and Arminian traditions and its membership derives from a heterogeneous mosaic of churches and ministries. The absence of a centralized structure of authority and theological uniformity is reflected in the disparities in the message peddled by its "marketers." While proclaiming a message of grace, many do so with a tone that is shrill, jarring, and condemning of Christians who embrace a faith persuasion different from their own.[14] Rob Rufus, for example, says, "Grace haters are the legalists who will try to intimidate, manipulate and dominate people with a spirit of witchcraft."[15]

Further, they hold to no doctrinal unanimity on crucial tenets of belief. For example, not a few believe the Old Testament laws are obsolete and have no value whatever for the Christian. One proponent is aghast that both Testaments are included under the same cover.[16] Andrew Wommack, in an ad in the back of his book *Grace, The Power of the Gospel*, unmasks his belief by posing the question, "Are you confused about the nature of God? Is He the God of judgment found in the Old Testament, or the God of mercy and grace found in the New Testament?"[17] Andrew Farley concedes that while the New Testament is superior to the Old Testament, "it's important to read and teach from the Old Testament while keeping it in context."[18] He acknowledges that the law still has a purpose but warns that "it's not designed for Christians as a tool or guide for daily living. Its sole purpose is to convict the ungodly of their spiritually dead state."[19]

When referenced, the Old Testament is routinely used to set in stark relief the superiority of the new covenant (grace) to the old (law). For the hyper-grace advocate, the New Testament, or new covenant, began with the death of Christ, not with His birth. Many exponents view Jesus as having lived under the law, or old covenant, and therefore disregard His pre-cross teachings in the Gospels as old wine for old wineskins—outmoded instruction addressed to Jewish people and not meant for Christians to adopt today.

Farley says:

> We often attempt to apply directly to our lives every word Jesus said, without considering his audience and purpose. But the context of Jesus' harsh teachings must be seen in the light of the dividing line between the Old [covenant] and the New. Remember that Christ was born and lived during the Old Covenant (law) era.[20]

Farley remarks in another of his books, "Jesus wasn't preaching to a new covenant crowd when he said those harsh things [in Matthew 5–6]. Instead, he was showing an old covenant crowd *why they desperately needed something different.*"[21] He continues elsewhere in a similar vein, "Peter, James, John, and Paul wrote epistles about life under the New Covenant," whereas Jesus taught "hopelessness under the Old. The audience wasn't the same. The covenant wasn't the same. And the teachings aren't the same."[22]

Since Jesus was speaking to an old covenant audience, Ryan Rufus says this of the Sermon on the Mount:

> Is this sermon intended for the church? Absolutely not!...It's a pre-salvation preach [*sic*] that exposes self-righteous pride and performance...Unless you really understand grace, don't go near the Beatitudes. They will mess you up! Teaching the Beatitudes to Christians produces legalism and religious pride or condemnation in them.[23]

AN EXAMINATION OF "LAW"

The relation of the Old Testament law to the Christian life is a highly controversial topic. One of the first points of contention among scholars is determining in what sense "law" is used in different contexts in the New Testament, particularly in Paul's writings. A second is the purpose and function of the law. While it may be conceded that in the majority of cases "law" refers to the Mosaic code, its compass truly comprehends a vast range—from the totality of the Old Testament scriptures to the single idea of a governing principle (Rom. 7:21), and much in between! This fact urges caution and careful attention to context—attention which modern grace teachers do not always give.

So, let's examine this idea in greater depth.

In what sense is Christ both the end (*telos*) of the law, as Paul names Him in Romans 10:4, and fulfiller of the law, as He describes Himself in Matthew 5:17–19? The Greek word for *end* used in Romans 10:4, *telos*, is hotly debated among scholars and can mean both "end" and "goal." In the first instance, it can be understood in the sense of termination, Christ bringing an end to the period of the Torah, the age and reign of the law. The second refers to a goal or aim, that Christ is the goal of the law, "that at which it was aimed or for which it was intended."[24]

Drawing upon athletic imagery of a race with a finish line, Colin Kruse reconciles both in Christ:

> Christ brings to an end the era of the law's jurisdiction, while
> at the same time recognizing that Christ is the goal of the law
> insofar as he is the one to whom it testifies...[and who by]
> the sending of the Spirit makes it possible for the "righteous
> requirement" of the law to be fulfilled in believers.[25]

The Matthew passage, which speaks of Christ having come to fulfill the law, is consistent with the Gospel writer's portrayal of Jesus as the Jewish Messiah who came not to abolish the Old Testament scriptures but to fulfill them. The fulfillment note struck in that passage harmonizes with Matthew's repeated use of it some twelve times in his Gospel. Abolishing the law and the prophets, or the Jewish scriptures, was not the mission of Jesus.

But what does it mean, then, that He came to fulfill the law? Some take this to mean that His coming validated, established, or confirmed the law.[26] Others believe it meant that He would "fill up" the law by giving it its full and divinely intended meaning. Another plausible meaning is that Jesus "fulfills the Law and the Prophets in that they point to him, and he is their fulfillment."[27]

Though he takes what may seem a contradictory position regarding the law, Paul is not at odds with it. He urges that God's law—by which he means the Mosaic law—is holy, righteous, good, and spiritual (Rom. 7:12, 14). But as an external code, it cannot make one righteous, which renders it inadequate in God's redemptive plan. As a Christian, Paul reinterprets the law. As a Jew, he does not see it as abolished. At no time does he commend it as a means to salvation (justification) or condemn it as a guide to ethical living (sanctification).

George Ladd notes:

> In as much as Paul always regards the Law as holy and just and good, he never thinks of the Law as being abolished. It remains the expression of the will of God....The permanence of the Law is reflected further in the fact that Paul appeals to specific commandments (*entolai*) of the Decalogue that are fulfilled by love.[28]

Paul sees Christ's death not as renunciation of the law but as condemnation of sin "in order that the righteous requirement of the law might be fully met in us, who do not live according to the flesh but according to the Spirit" (Rom. 8:4, NIV). Paul's opposition to the law finds its strongest response when the Mosaic code is used in an attempt to achieve justification before God or when the Torah is turned into a perverted system of legal restrictions that leads to bondage rather than freedom.

The hyper-grace protagonists' separation of law and grace is unwarranted. The two are not mutually exclusive. It can be argued that the law was and is a gift of grace. Law is not "something that is opposed to grace," says D. Martyn Lloyd-Jones. It conflicts with grace only "in the sense that there was once a covenant of law, and we are now under the covenant of grace."[29]

THE IMPLICATIONS OF THE CROSS

One of the central weight-bearing pillars of the hyper-grace doctrine is the once-for-all finished work of Christ on the cross. It is a natural and expected corollary, then, that much use is made of the Book of Hebrews and the Pauline epistles, especially Romans and Galatians, in their teachings. John 19:30 is another verse that receives much attention, as it holds one of the last sayings of the dying Savior on the cross: "It is finished."

Regrettably, hyper-grace proponents take the teaching of Christ's finished work on the cross to an untenable extreme, concluding that both salvation and sanctification are complete, finished works that have made Christians perfect before God. Like shrapnel from an explosion, this belief has flung destructive fragments far and wide across the Christian landscape.

This conflation of salvation and sanctification into one finished, perfected, and purifying act at the cross has, for instance, led one hyper-grace teacher to the conclusion, "In this one man, in this one event [the cross], all sin of all men and in all time would be dealt with, with such finality that God would never think of sin again!"[30] It has also emboldened Joseph Prince to declare:

> There is no scripture in the new covenant for new covenant believers that tells you, you have got to continually confess your sins and repent of your sins and ask forgiveness for all your sins. Why? Because *one* sacrifice for *all* time for *all* of your sins has already dealt with *every* single one of your sins![31]

With this same assurance, Clark Whitten boldly exclaims, "You are like Him [Jesus], my friend, and are in a permanent and unchangeable state of being of holiness. It cannot be any other way."[32] If this is the case, how should we understand 2 Corinthians 7:1, which reads, "Since we have these promises, dear friends, let us purify ourselves from everything that contaminates body and spirit, perfecting holiness out of reverence for God" (NIV)?

It follows from their belief that there is no need for a believer to repent, confess sin,[33] or try to do anything that may aid and advance personal holiness. Christ's sacrifice has made that unnecessary and, like Him, believers live in a permanent state of holiness. The existential payoff is effortless spirituality for the Christian.

Indeed, Paul Ellis asserts, "Repentance isn't doing something about your sin. Repentance is responding positively to God's kindness and grace."[34] He remarks in another place, "We don't repent and confess to get God to forgive us. We repent and confess *because* God has forgiven us."[35] This tune is picked up by Steve McVey, but with a new stanza added:

> What if repentance doesn't have anything to do with emotional or mental upheavals accompanied by heartfelt commitments to change our evil ways? What if, like obedience, repentance is a gift we possess by virtue of the life of Jesus Christ?...Repentance isn't something we work up and use to get right with God. That has already happened for us through Jesus.[36]

Paul Ellis further observes that because of performance-based indoctrination, many Christians pursue what they already possess, unmindful that forgiveness precedes repentance. "There is nothing you can do to make God forgive you because He's already done it,"[37] he says. Modern grace advocates believe the human will is passive in the work of sanctification.

That Christ's work at the cross is universal in its scope and final in its historical enactment is a tenet no orthodox Christian will deny. But exactly what was the saving transaction Jesus conducted at the cross? What did Jesus mean when He said, "It is finished"? What did the writer of Hebrews have in mind by saying, "We have been made holy through the sacrifice of the body of Jesus Christ once for all" (Heb. 10:10, NIV), and, "By one sacrifice he has made perfect forever those who are being made holy" (Heb. 10:14, NIV)?

Concerning "It is finished," one commentator says it "signifies full completion of Jesus' work...Nothing further needed to be done."[38] The cry, adds another, "is the triumphant recognition that [Jesus] has now fully accomplished the work that He came to do."[39] It therefore informs us that sin has been dealt with once for all, one for all—not that "the battle against sin is decisively over" the moment a person is saved.[40] Furthermore, the original Greek depicts the historical and objective fact of Christ's death whereby He completed God's assignment to accomplish universal salvation. It says nothing about the appropriation of benefits that makes the work of the cross personally and individually effectual.

Concerning the Hebrews 10 passages, hyper-grace teachers put much stock in these verses to support the notion of the finished work of Christ and its once-for-all perfecting of believers. But what did the writer of Hebrews mean when he penned the verses? Verses 5–10 form the immediate context and draw our attention to the inefficacy of the sacrifices of the old covenant, which have been replaced by the sufficient sacrifice of Christ. The Levitical system, with its cultic practices and provisions for atonement, has been annulled, and the unrepeatable sacrifice of Christ in obedience to God and in fulfillment of Holy Scripture is the only basis by which the new covenant community can be consecrated for divine service. Viewing Psalm 40:6–8, from which the writer of Hebrews borrows, as a prophetic window into God's displeasure with and future displacement of the old sacrificial system, the writer determines that the one who replaces that system is none other than the Son of God by whom "we have been made holy...once for all" (Heb. 10:10, NIV).

How should that statement in verse 10 be understood? Thankfully, it is largely explained in verses 11–12, in which a comparison is made between the old covenant priest who stood daily to minister and the new covenant priest who sat down after He had offered the one sacrifice of Himself. The priest standing daily and day after day speaks both of the ineffectiveness of the sacrificial system and its inability to remove sin. Sacrifices under the old covenant "covered" sin; they did not "take away" sin. Impurity remained—covered and out of sight, but not removed!

Christ as priest, however, sat down, signaling the perpetual efficacy of His offering and the cessation of His sacrificial duties. Sin has been dealt with—removed—once for all, not merely covered. Believers are, therefore, made holy. No more sacrifice is needed or is possible.

The verse in question (v. 10) also speaks to the position and privilege of the new covenant worshippers before God. Old covenant worshippers had to be purified of all ceremonial defilement each time they appeared for worship. This is certainly not the case with new covenant worshippers. For them, no sacrifice has to be made to remove defilement. Because they have already been "made holy," they have been made worthy of unhindered access into the presence of God. Sinless perfection and the need for confession and repentance of sin are another matter altogether and are not the intent of the author of Hebrews.

Modern grace advocates believe Hebrews 10:14 (in addition to verse 10) teaches the permanent and sinless perfection of Christians. Not only does such a claim contradict clear teaching to the contrary in other books of the New Testament, but vendors of that message overlook the end statement in the verse regarding new covenant believers who were, in verse 10, said to "have been made holy" (NIV); in verse 14, they "are being made holy" (NIV).

The writer of Hebrews uses two different tenses of the same verb in two separate verses to describe the spiritual state of believers. In verse 10, he uses the perfect participle, "emphasizing the completed state or condition"[41] they enjoy. In verse 14, the present participle describes believers as "the ones who are being sanctified" or "being made holy." The present tense indicates an ongoing process.

Michael Brown sees no contradiction in the use of the perfect and present tenses to describe the Christian life and experience: "We *have been sanctified* [perfect tense] by the death of Christ and the work of the Spirit, and we *are being sanctified* [present tense] by the application of what Jesus has done, with the help of the Spirit."[42] Albert Barnes agrees, stating that Christ's offering of Himself

> secures their [believers'] final freedom from sin, and will make them forever holy. It cannot mean that those for whom he died are made at once perfectly holy, for that is not true; but the idea is, that the offering was complete, and did not need to be repeated; and that it was of such a nature as entirely to remove the penalty due to sin, and to lay the foundation for their final and eternal holiness.[43]

The perfect and present tenses in verses 10 and 14 capture the ongoing rival strivings in the Christian life between salvation and the ongoing sanctification that attends it. It illustrates the tension between being and becoming, the struggle between the already and not yet, the competing tug of the two ages for the allegiance of every believer. At no time should the claim be made that these verses teach sinless perfection. Not only does such a notion conflict with teaching to the contrary in the New Testament and orthodox Christian belief over the centuries. It is also incompatible with Christian experience.

AN UNTENABLE "GRACE"

Beyond the law and the cross, grace forms an undoubtable pillar of the hyper-grace teaching. McVey correctly asserts, "New Testament Christianity is not grounded in what we do, but in what He [Christ] has already done,"[44] a biblical truth no true evangelical will deny! That indeed is amazing grace that tunes our hearts to heavenly praise.

The grace movement feels it finds ample biblical justification in Paul for its teaching. He exhorts, "But where sin increased, grace increased all the more" (Rom. 5:20, NIV). The phrase "increased all the more" translates a Greek word (*hyperperisseuō*) that could be rendered "super-increase" and is used in a variety of contexts to convey "overflow" or "lavish increase." No one dare disagree with Paul!

What can be confidently affirmed, however, is that much of Paul's teaching on grace has been exaggerated and misrepresented by the modern grace camp. The grace reformers have morphed grace into "hyper-grace," putting grace on steroids, taking a vital biblical truth to an extreme. Their theology is off balance and out of balance.

McVey, for example, struggling to balance God's justice and love, concludes, "There is no side to God the Father that looks different from the compassionate grace demonstrated by God the Son."[45] Farley adds, "You're already as close to God as you'll ever be....Stop trying to get close. Stop trying to stay close. Relax. Practice the art of doing nothing—nothing to achieve *more* forgiveness, nothing to achieve *more* acceptance, and nothing to achieve *more closeness*."[46]

The hyper-grace movement is like a runaway train that has jumped track, is out of control, and is careening headlong downhill to sure disaster. While its teachers may urge that Christians do not need the law and are "governed by the King of kings and Lord of lords" under whose rule "love is the law of the land,"[47] the unintended consequence of the teaching, to a large degree, has been the removing of the moral guardrails, resulting in unbridled sin among many of its adherents. As Michael Brown notes:

> Some of this new grace teaching is unbalanced, overstated, at times unbiblical, and sometimes downright dangerous—and I

mean dangerous to the well-being of the body of Christ....I believe we are witnessing the rise of a hyper-grace movement, filled with its own brand of legalistic judgmentalism, mixing some life-giving truth from the Word with some destructive error.[48]

There is a grace that is cheap; it costs nothing and demands nothing. And there is a grace that is costly, demanding a costly Christian discipleship. In his famous work *The Cost of Discipleship*, Dietrich Bonhoeffer, writing from a prison cell, spoke on these two radically different types of grace. Of cheap grace he penned:

> Cheap grace means grace sold on the market like cheapjacks' wares. The sacraments, the forgiveness of sin, and the consolations of religion are thrown away at cut prices. Grace is represented as the Church's inexhaustible treasury, from which she showers blessings with generous hands, without asking questions or fixing limits. Grace without price; grace without cost! The essence of grace, we suppose, is that the account has been paid in advance; and, because it has been paid, everything can be had for nothing.[49]

Bonhoeffer continues in the same vein:

> Cheap grace means the justification of sin without the justification of the sinner. Grace alone does everything, they say, and so everything can remain as it was before....Cheap grace is grace without discipleship, grace without the cross, grace without Jesus Christ, living and incarnate.[50]

Has the modern grace camp unwittingly become culpable of this charge?

But then there is costly grace, Bonhoeffer points out:

> Such grace is *costly* because it calls us to follow, and it is *grace* because it calls us to follow *Jesus Christ*. It is costly because it costs a man his life, and it is grace because it gives a man the only true life. It is costly because it condemns sin, and grace

because it justifies the sinner. Above all, it is *costly* because it cost God the life of his Son.[51]

Cheap grace, not costly grace, threads through hyper-grace teaching.

Hyper-grace theology has driven a false and unnecessary wedge between law and grace, yet law and grace are not polar opposites. Not grace only, but law also was a gift from God. Thomas Oden calls the terms God enacted at Sinai to govern the relationship between Him and Israel the "gracious covenant." He states further, "The covenant is a gift, hence grace. The blessing of the covenant is promised on the simple condition that recipients are willing trustingly and joyfully to receive it."[52]

Proponents of modern grace Christianity, in their zeal to promote grace, have pitted Paul against Jesus. Though "grace and truth came through Jesus Christ" (John 1:17, NIV), according to modern grace advocates, all Jesus preached and taught prior to His death is old covenant and has little or no relevance to the Christian today. Paul, the new covenant man of grace, is the champion of their Christianity. His teaching of superabounding grace, in their view, is God's fresh revelation for the church. This divergence grossly misrepresents the teachings of both Jesus and Paul.

A CONCERNING MOVEMENT

Hyper-grace teachers' theological approach has resulted in a misrepresentation of the truth, especially as it deals with the atonement and grace. Through their view, the progressive work of sanctification is all but jettisoned, leaving the sluice gate wide open to lawless living. Further, a glaring weakness of the movement is its tunnel vision. Its methodological approach to theology and exegesis is superficial, subjective, and truncated. Little attention is given to biblical context and intertextual study, resulting in a cherry-picking or omission of passages that appear to oppose its theology and a knee-jerk dismissal of interpretations and arguments that are in conflict with its teaching.

The soft stance on sin in the Christian life in the hyper-grace view is a natural corollary of its belief in the obsolescence of the law, for where there is no law, there is no sin. Radical grace's myopic view of grace fails to take into account that neither grace nor the Spirit can bring about growth or maturity in the Christian apart from the standards of the law. It further fails to understand that grace does not permit what the moral law condemns, for love is the fulfillment of the law (Rom. 13:8–10).

The modern grace gospel is a mirroring of the present Zeitgeist in which individual rights, individual freedom, self-determination, and contempt are flaunted, and recalcitrance to moral norms and a meta-narrative to life is pooh-poohed. It panders to and massages a lustful self-gratification of the flesh and resonates with a narcissistic generation that sets its own standards and celebrates and rewards itself not for accomplishing much but for accomplishing little or nothing at all. Demanding little, it expects little—or nothing—of its adherents. It finds a ready audience with many today whose cry is, "Lord, bless me but don't change me." Is the hyper-grace movement a reformation, as it claims? Or is it a fad that will ultimately fade?

TREVOR GRIZZLE, PhD, is a professor of New Testament at the Oral Roberts University Graduate School of Theology and Ministry.

Chapter 4

JOHN WESLEY'S FULLER UNDERSTANDING OF GRACE

Henry H. Knight III

J OHN WESLEY HAS been called both a theologian of grace and a theologian of love. The terms are apt. For Wesley, the "Scripture way of salvation"[1] has as its goal the renewal of human hearts in love. This renewal is accomplished by the grace of God, understood not only as divine favor but most centrally as the power of the Holy Spirit.

The linkage of the renewal in love as God's goal in salvation with grace as the transforming power of God is at the heart of Wesley's theological vision. It has been rightly called his optimism of grace, and in this essay it will be shown to be a fuller understanding of grace than some, past and present, have held.

LOVE DIVINE

For Wesley, the most succinct statement of the nature of God is found in 1 John 4:8: "God is love." Commenting on this verse, he says:

> God is often styled holy, righteous, wise; but not holiness, righteousness, or wisdom . . . as he is said to be love; intimating

that this is...his reigning attribute, the attribute that sheds an amiable glory on all his other perfections.[2]

This "reigning attribute" governs all other aspects of God's nature. It is in love that God's justice and mercy find their unity. God's judgment and even God's wrath are in service to God's love. Thus Wesley rejects any depiction of God as sometimes loving, sometimes judging. For Wesley, God judges sin, but God *is* love.

We can misunderstand Wesley's theology at this point if we are not clear about what he means by *love*. For Wesley, God's love is defined by God's actions and promises in Scripture, and most fully and deeply in the life and especially the death of Jesus Christ. It is the cross that Wesley calls "that amazing display of the Son of God's love to mankind."[3] His brother Charles Wesley describes it this way:

> O Love divine, what hast thou done!
>   The immortal God hath died for me!
> The Father's coeternal Son
>   Bore all my sins upon the tree.
> Th' immortal God for me hath died:
>   My Lord, my Love, is crucified![4]

It is this understanding of "God is love" that informs the content of salvation in Wesley's theology and the operation of the grace that makes it possible.

NEW LIFE THAT IMPACTS LIFE NOW

Wesley describes salvation as "a present deliverance from sin, a restoration of the soul to its primitive health, its original purity; a recovery of the divine nature."[5] Our problem is that we are fallen into sin and no longer have the image of God in which we were created. For Wesley, salvation is the means by which God restores us to that image so that we love as God loves.

This means salvation is not essentially about life after death.

Commenting on Ephesians 2:8, which says, "For by grace you have been saved through faith" (MEV), he argues that the "salvation which is here spoken of is not what is frequently understood by that word, the going to heaven, eternal happiness."[6] The words "You *have been* saved" make this clear. He says, "It is not something at a distance: it is a present thing, a blessing which, through the free mercy of God, ye are now in possession of."[7] Salvation is a new life which we now receive and continues into eternity. "Whoever will reign with Christ in heaven," Wesley says, "must have Christ reigning in him on earth."[8]

New life, new birth, new creation—the New Testament abounds with language that promises transformation of human hearts. Wesley links this language with that of Jesus in the Sermon on the Mount, which clearly shows God's concern not only with our external behavior but with the desires, motivations, and dispositions of our hearts.

In a real sense, this was what the eighteenth-century awakening was all about. Calvinists like George Whitefield and Jonathan Edwards preached just as fervently the promise of a new birth as did the Wesley brothers and their colleague John Fletcher. All of them spoke of the new birth as initiating growth in sanctification. But the Wesleyans took this much further. They proclaimed the promise of the full restoration of the image of God in human hearts in this life, which they called *entire sanctification* or *Christian perfection.*

Here is how John Wesley defined it: "Entire sanctification, or Christian perfection, is neither more or less than pure love—love expelling sin and governing both the heart and life of a child of God."[9] Wesley was quite clear that Christian perfection does not mean everything we do is in agreement with the will of God. We continue to make misjudgments and mistakes, which some would term sins but Wesley believed could be more precisely called "involuntary transgressions."[10] It is because of these involuntary transgressions that love remains humble and those who attain Christian perfection continue to pray for forgiveness of their sins.

What Christian perfection does mean is that our intentions and desires are fully governed by love for God and neighbor. Put differently, it means living in full obedience to the two great commandments of Jesus through a disposition of the heart toward love. What God commands us to do, Wesley argues, God will enable us to do by grace.

EMPOWERED BY THE HOLY SPIRIT

The Wesleyan teaching on Christian perfection faces an immediate theological difficulty in the doctrine of original sin. If Wesley were Roman Catholic or Eastern Orthodox, the problem would not be so severe, because for those traditions the fall into sin severely damages the image of God in humans but does not erase it. Grace, as taught in those traditions, can work on nature to move persons back to their original condition.

But Wesley is a Protestant who subscribes to the same understanding of original sin as Martin Luther and John Calvin. For Wesley, original sin is "total corruption,"[11] the loss of the moral image of God, which is love. Sin governs the heart and life, and there is no portion of our hearts and lives untouched by sin. It would be possible to envision our being forgiven sinners, our growing in external obedience, or even receiving a new nature that remains in conflict with the old nature. But how can there be the thoroughgoing change Wesley believes God has promised? How does one move from total corruption to Christian perfection?

The answer lies in Wesley's theology of grace. Certainly he agrees with the common Protestant understanding of grace as a declaration of our forgiveness. But that is not the heart of grace. For Wesley, grace is fundamentally transformative. Commenting on 2 Corinthians 1:12, Wesley says:

> By "the grace of God" is sometimes to be understood that free love, that unmerited mercy, by which I a sinner, through the merits of Christ, am now reconciled to God. But in this place it rather means that power of God the Holy Ghost, "which worketh in us both to will and to do His good pleasure." As soon as ever the grace of God in the former sense, His pardoning love, is manifested to our souls, the grace of God in the latter sense, the power of his Spirit, takes place therein. And now we can perform, through God, what to man was impossible.[12]

In other words, the grace of God goes beyond eternal salvation. It empowers us also to live holy lives of love, which is accomplished through the Holy Spirit living in us.

We see this transformative work of the Spirit throughout the way of salvation. It begins with prevenient (or preventing) grace, in which God counteracts the total corruption of original sin by giving every person a measure of liberty to act against their sinful desires and a conscience to awaken them to the need to do so. This conscience, says Wesley, "properly speaking...is not *natural*, but a supernatural gift of God."[13] Wesley, as a true Arminian, rejects any claims of natural free will, arguing that original sin requires salvation to be a work of grace. But he also insists that God loves all and Christ died for all, and therefore grace is extended universally, to all humanity.

This does not imply universal salvation. Unlike the Calvinists of his day, Wesley did not believe grace to be what the Calvinists called "irresistible." If grace were irresistible, then persons would no longer be human—their "inmost nature would be changed."[14] A person "would no longer be a moral agent, any more than the sun or the wind."[15] Such a person "would no longer be endued with liberty,—a power of choosing, or self-determination."[16] Ultimately, irresistible grace would mean that a person could never be restored to the image of God because they would never be able to love in freedom, as God loves.

Grace, for Wesley, does not overcome us but enables us to respond to God. It does this by restoring in us a capacity to respond, initially through restoring to us a slight measure of liberty and giving us a conscience, and much more thoroughly in the new birth. It is as we respond to grace that we receive more grace and grow in the knowledge and love of God. "First," Wesley says, "God worketh in you; therefore you can work: otherwise it would be impossible."[17] But then, "Secondly, God worketh in you; therefore, you *must* work: you must be 'workers together with him,' (they are the very words of the Apostle,) otherwise he will cease working."[18]

Prevenient grace creates the condition for growth in the Christian life, which is fueled by our knowing, not just knowing about, God. We know God by faith, which is itself a work of the Spirit, given to those who are open to receive it. The awakened sinner has the faith of a servant, the justified believer the faith of a child of God. Of this latter faith Wesley says:

> "It is the gift of God" [Eph. 2:8]. No man is able to work it, in himself. It is a work of omnipotence. It requires no less power thus to quicken a dead soul, than to raise a body that lies in the grave. It is a new creation, and none can create a soul anew but He who at first created the heavens and the earth.[19]

Through this faith one is able to know and trust in Jesus Christ, thereby receiving justification and a new birth. Justification, or pardon, reconciles us to God. With this new birth, we begin to love God, which initiates our sanctification. Our love for God and neighbor grows through a gradual work of grace, until, in a second instantaneous act of grace, we are perfected in love. Christian perfection is the goal of salvation.

A CHRISTIAN FAITH BEYOND MORALISM

Wesley's teaching was controversial. Of course, his Arminian understanding of grace was rejected by mainstream Calvinists who were otherwise his colleagues in the eighteenth-century awakening. Wesley believed there were serious problems with their portrayal of a God who predestines some to heaven and some to damnation, as well as their understanding of grace as irresistible. Major conflict between Wesleyans and Calvinists erupted twice during Wesley's ministry. What they had in common was proclamation centered on the new birth.

Apart from this disagreement, there were two sorts of teaching that were positively fatal to seeking and receiving the salvation promised by God and which Wesley therefore opposed with all his strength. These were legalism and antinomianism.

The legalism of Wesley's day might better be described as a mild sort of moralism taught from many Church of England pulpits. Wesley notes that for many in his church,

> by a religious man is commonly meant, one that is honest, just, and fair in his dealings; that is constantly at church and sacrament; and that gives much alms, or (as it is usually termed) does much good.[20]

Being a Christian by this definition is basically being a respectable person as defined by the culture: minimal morality, minimal belief, minimal generosity, and faithful church attendance. Such a person would then have a happy afterlife in heaven.

Such a portrayal of the Christian life is a weak substitute for that promised by God in Scripture. Wesley says he and his Methodists are "grieved at the sight" of "on every side, either men of no religion at all, or men of a lifeless, formal religion." The Wesleyans would "greatly rejoice" in convincing them

> that there is a better religion to be attained,—a religion worthy of God that gave it. And this we conceive to be no other than love; the love of God and of all mankind; the loving God with all our heart, and soul, and strength, as having first loved *us*, as the fountain of all the good we have received, and

of all we ever hope to enjoy; and the loving every soul which God hath made…as our own soul.[21]

Against the tepid moralism of his day, Wesley and his movement lifted up God's promise of a new life of love.

A CHRISTIAN FAITH BEYOND ANTINOMIANISM

But this promise of a changed heart was threatened by another danger to the Christian life that arose out of the awakening itself, and that was the danger of *antinomianism*. Rather than a cure for the disease of moralism, Wesley saw antinomianism as a poison that brought spiritual death in place of the new life in Christ.

Antinomianism literally means "against law." It seeks to uphold the Protestant principle that we are justified by grace and not by works but does so by severing justification from sanctification. It considers justification the entirety of salvation, and sanctification unnecessary. The new birth, which begins sanctification, is thus minimized. It also understands grace to solely mean the favor of God, denying the Wesleyan emphasis on grace as the power of the Holy Spirit. Today, this view continues to hold sway in what has been coined the "hyper-grace movement."

Combating antinomianism was a lifelong concern of John Wesley's. In the final year of his life, he said, "The imagination, that faith *supersedes* holiness, is the marrow of Antinomianism."[22] This is identical to his description of it in his two earlier sermons on "The Law Established through Faith," which is one of his more extended arguments against antinomianism. There he says we can make void the law through faith (Rom. 3:31) by not preaching it, by teaching that faith supersedes holiness, or by believing in holiness in principle while not living it out in practice.

In these sermons he makes two important claims. First, while we are justified by faith purely through the merits of Christ, without any preceding righteousness of our own, it does not follow that there is no need for holiness after our justification.[23] Indeed, Paul in his letters argues just the opposite.

Second, faith, "as glorious and honourable as it is," is "still only the handmaid of love."[24] So "those who magnify faith beyond all proportion, so as to swallow up all things else, and who so totally misapprehend the nature of it as to imagine it stands in the place of love"[25] have failed to understand its purpose. It is to enable us to be born into a new life of holiness governed by love: "Love is the end, the sole end, of every dispensation of God, from the beginning of the world to the consummation of all things."[26]

Connected to these is a third point Wesley makes in numerous places. It is often said that the righteousness of Christ is imputed to us by grace through faith, such that God sees not our sins but the righteousness of Christ. Wesley agrees that imputed righteousness is the ground of our forgiveness and acceptance by God, but he says this does not "imply, that God is *deceived* in those whom he justifies; that he thinks them to be what in fact they are not."[27] Again, justification is not the goal but a means to the greater end of sanctification.

What both moralism and antinomianism have in common is an understanding of salvation as obtaining a happy afterlife and a concern to delineate the minimal conditions for going there. As Wesley reads Scripture, he finds a much richer understanding of salvation. Salvation is the gracious gift of a new life through the power of the Holy Spirit, ultimately restoring us to the image of God so that we love as God has loved us in Christ. Grace and faith are the means by which God accomplishes this end; justification is not the goal but the doorway to sanctification. Salvation is for this life as well as the life to come.

HENRY H. KNIGHT III, PhD, is the Donald and Pearl Wright Professor of Wesleyan Studies and E. Stanley Jones Professor of Evangelism at Saint Paul School of Theology in Overland

Park, Kansas. He is an ordained elder in the United Methodist Church and teaches in the areas of Wesleyan theology, history, and evangelical theology. He is the author of *Anticipating Heaven Below: Optimism of Grace from Wesley to the Pentecostals* and editor of *From Aldersgate to Azusa Street: Wesleyan, Holiness, and Pentecostal Visions of the New Creation.*

Chapter 5

THE GRACE REVOLUTION[1] AND PERSON-CENTERED THERAPY: A COMPARATIVE ANALYSIS FROM A PASTORAL CARE PERSPECTIVE

Thomson K. Mathew

I RECEIVED AN EMAIL not long ago from an individual who said he was born again as a teenager at a church I pastored in New Haven, Connecticut, three decades ago. He had found my contact information online in order to share that the time he spent under my teaching was a blessing and that he currently enjoyed listening to the teachings of Joseph Prince. "I'm sure you are aware of his teachings," he said. Then he asked, "Do you agree with his Grace Revolution?"[2]

Do I agree with the Grace Revolution, as led by Joseph Prince? As a student of pastoral care, I took an interest in this question, primarily as it relates to current trends in pastoral care.

It has been shown historically that ministry adapts to cultural trends, often adopting models that are based on dominant contemporary social characters.[3] For instance, during the seventeenth and eighteenth centuries, the educated *master/teacher* was the dominant social character; consequently, ministry adopted this model for itself. In the nineteenth century, society replaced the character of master with that of *orator*, and oration replaced teaching; the church produced "princes of the pulpit," and the dominant ministry model became revivalist or pulpiteer. During the late nineteenth and early twentieth centuries, the concept of *profession* emerged, and the church adopted the professional model of ministry; ministers began to receive professional training in university settings.

During the 1930s and 1940s, according to H. Richard Niebuhr, there was no single model of ministry.[4] The minister functioned as *pastoral director*, maintaining institutions already built by others. The roles of preacher, teacher, and priest diminished during this period, while the roles of manager and counselor increased. During the 1960s, the dominant social character was the *manager/therapist*; as a result, the church adopted a similar model of ministry; the minister functioned as organizational problem solver (therapist) as well as counselor of church members.

To the best of my knowledge, no one has formally defined the dominant social characters of the 1980s, 1990s, and beyond. In my discussions with colleagues and students, we note that due to major developments in technology, multimedia, and communications, we might claim media personalities and corporate executives (CEOs) as the dominant social characters during this period. It is not difficult to demonstrate that ministry has adopted these models. Could it be that the twenty-first century is fusing the concepts of CEO, media personality, and therapist as a contemporary model of ministry?

There is also evidence that the theological focus of pastoral care has changed with shifting historical and cultural contexts, at least in the West. For instance, William A. Clebsch and Charles R. Jaekle, in their classic work *Pastoral Care in Historical Perspective*, demonstrate that certain theological themes relating to pastoral care dominated during particular historical periods. These themes expressed the main theological thrusts of pastoral ministry. They claim that the focus alternated between healing, sustaining, guiding, and reconciling, depending on the needs of different historical periods.[5]

Jaekle and Clebsch describe *healing* as the main goal of pastoral care. They consider Christian education and preservation of traditions as defining the ministry of *sustaining*, whereas *guiding* involves devotional life, spiritual direction, leadership training, and discipleship. According to these authors, *reconciliation* deals with evangelism and the issues of social structure.[6] Howard Clinebell claims there has been a fifth emphasis in recent years: *nurturing*.[7]

If social and historical contexts influenced the theological emphasis of pastoral care in the past, could this be happening again, this time expanding the concept of guiding or reconciling to include *"revolutionary" grace*? Could the "grace revolution" be a response to the needs of the postmodern generation? Could current trends in therapy reflect similar correlations? How do these play out in current approaches to pastoral care?

Let's explore the trend of person-centered therapy as a mode of healing in recent times and then see how it compares to modern grace preaching to test this hypothesis.

MAJOR TENETS OF PERSON-CENTERED THERAPY

Carl Rogers, the father of person-centered therapy and the major architect of humanistic psychology, was born in 1902 and was raised in a Protestant home by parents who were described as fundamentalist Christians. His family was deeply committed to a Protestant Christian faith and work ethic.

With a bachelor's degree from the University of Wisconsin and a desire to be a clergyman, Rogers entered Union Theological Seminary in New York City in 1924. Feeling that orthodox Christian dogma would prevent him from a free search for truth, Rogers left the seminary to earn a PhD in clinical psychology at

Columbia University. He wrote, "I felt that questions as to the meaning of life, and...of the...improvement of life for individuals, would probably always interest me, but I could not work in a field where I would be required to believe in some specified religious doctrine."[8]

Rogers trusted his own experience above any dogma. In *On Becoming a Person*, Rogers asserts, *"Experience is, for me, the highest authority....* Neither the Bible nor the prophets—neither Freud nor research—neither revelations of God nor man—can take precedence over my own direct experience."[9]

After a period of teaching at the University of Rochester, Rogers moved to Ohio State University, where he began to develop a form of therapy distinct from Freudian psychotherapy. His approach was first called nondirective, then client-centered, and, more recently, person-centered.[10]

In Rogers's system, the patient is considered a client. Establishing a warm and friendly relationship between client and therapist is crucial to the client's process of becoming. According to Ralph W. Lundin, in person-centered therapy, "the therapist may never make any critical and punishing statement."[11] Following the footsteps of Abraham Maslow, who had introduced the concept of self-actualization as the final inherent human goal, Rogers became an architect of humanistic psychology. He did not approve of advice-giving or exhortation by counselors.

Person-centered therapy stands in contrast to the more traditional forms of psychotherapy. According to Rogers, "it definitely rejects the medical model which involves looking for pathology and developing a specific diagnosis, or thinking of treatment in terms of cure."[12] Person-centered therapy, according to Tracy A. Knight, "was designed to provide the conditions that encourage natural human growth and development toward the realization of the individual's potentials."[13]

Rogers's theory is based on a hypothesis that claims everything in the universe tends toward greater differentiation and integration.[14] This principle expresses itself as an actualizing tendency in humans. It is the primary motivating force that moves persons toward growth and adaptation, maintaining and enhancing themselves.

This actualizing tendency is the essential restorative factor in psychotherapy. Person-centered therapy attempts to provide the ideal relational conditions where this motivating force tendency can be fully expressed. Rogers finds this potential biological in nature.

Rogerian person-centered therapy's main "doctrines" are *unconditional positive regard*, *empathy*, and *congruence*. Unconditional positive regard refers to the therapist's genuine care for the client. The therapist has the highest regard for the client's experiences without judgment. No specific conditions or expectations are placed on the client. Rogerians hypothesize that conditional caring and expectations of conformity are causing the client's problems in the first place.

Empathy is not sympathy. It is defined as perceiving the internal frame of reference of the client accurately. It is the capacity to perceive from the client's frame of reference without losing one's own sense of self.[15] Congruence refers to the therapist being consistently aware of his own ongoing experience and remaining genuine in his relationship with the client. Congruence is defined as the "accurate matching of experience with awareness."[16]

Maureen O'Hara reports that research has demonstrated that clients move toward health and integration when the relationship between the therapist and client has the following characteristics: 1) it is non-authoritarian; 2) the therapist is authentic and warm; 3) the therapist listens well; 4) the client experiences basic acceptance by the therapist; and 5) the client is acknowledged as being essentially competent.[17]

The goal of therapy in Rogers's model is not just to address presenting problems and reduce symptoms but to assist the client in his journey toward self-actualization. A self-actualizing person is a fully functioning person. Therapy enhances the actualizing tendency that is in every human being. The therapist does not teach, coach, direct, or prohibit. This part of Rogers's theory came under criticism, and others have recommended remedies to its perceived weakness. In pastoral counseling, for example, Howard Clinebell recommends adding a more direct approach.[18]

Person-centered therapy assumes that "behavioral changes evolve from within the individual rather than through the manipulation of external contingencies."[19] Other assumptions include the following: 1) human beings are experiencing beings; 2) behavior can be understood only from a person's internal frame of reference; 3) the value of life resides in the present; 4) humans are innately good and trustworthy; 5) humans tend toward self-actualization; 6) people do the best thing possible given the right conditions; and 7) human capacity for evil results from negative "conditions of worth" imposed on children by family and society.[20] Rogerian therapy clients leave "with an impression about their own thoughts rather than the practitioner's suggestions."[21]

Leroy Aden remarks on the impact of Rogerian counseling theory on the church and pastoral counseling:

> Rogers was introduced (by Seward Hiltner and Carroll Wise) into the church's pastoral ministry, and he has exerted an almost normative influence on it ever since. He has given it a method, has defined its purpose, and has even lent it a basic understanding of human nature. In a word, his becoming became the hallmark of pastoral counseling's becoming.[22]

Aden goes on to say that Rogers maintains that individuals are accepted because they are unique and significant human beings. "In contrast," Aden says, "forgiveness means that individuals are accepted *in spite of* their being unacceptable."[23] According to Aden, Rogers supplies an "optimistic promise of self-evolved becoming and stands in danger of giving us a sense of failure and despair to the extent that we do not achieve it."[24]

THEOLOGICAL THEMES OF
MODERN GRACE PREACHING

Now let us consider the major tenets of modern grace teaching. It appears that the following are its major theological themes: "1) Nothing you do will negatively affect your relationship with God. 2) As a believer, you never need to confess your sins to God or repent of your sins. 3) God doesn't see your sins; He always sees you as perfect through the blood of Jesus. 4) You can follow Jesus effortlessly."[25]

From these themes, grace teachers call the doctrine of progressive sanctification a "spiritually murderous lie." They say a believer's future sins have already been forgiven and that the teachings of Jesus before the cross do not apply to today's Christians. Self-examination should be discouraged to prevent believers from taking their eyes off the finished work of Christ. Sins past, present, and future are already forgiven, so Christians do not have to repent. The Holy Spirit does not convict believers; He only convinces them of their righteousness.[26]

Already we can find potential overlap between modern grace teaching and person-centered therapy, especially in the area of unconditional positive regard. Prohibitions against advice-giving (correction) and affirmation of a built-in human tendency for self-actualization are also shared themes. But let's dig deeper into modern grace teaching and see what else its leaders have to say.

Clark Whitten, a pastor, believes that the Protestant church teaches a doctrine of "saved by grace but perfected by human effort," producing "a Church that is judgmental, angry, hopeless, helpless, dependent, fearful, uninspired, ineffective, and perpetually spiritually immature."[27] Martin Luther's concept of grace and faith is "utterly primitive,"[28] according to John Crowder. But Michael Brown finds this unbalanced, unbiblical, and spiritually dangerous theology.[29]

Andrew Farley is among the grace teachers who believe

the sayings of Jesus before the cross are not applicable to post-resurrection Christians. He says his opponents exaggerate his position on this, stating that some of Jesus's commands regarding anger, adultery, selling everything, and so forth were only meant to teach His hearers about the true spirit of the law and that He is only recognizing "this plain and obvious purpose of some of Jesus's teachings."[30]

Concerning the lack of any need for confession of sin for believers, Colin Dye, pastor of Kensington Temple in London, says others are mistaken when they teach that sins, in order to be forgiven, must be confessed to God: "God has already forgiven all our sins at the cross! We have received judicial forgiveness once for all."[31] Dye argues there is no need for "the kind of morbid introspection some religious teachers demand."[32] Just as we were not born when Jesus died on the cross and yet our sins are forgiven after our birth, the same principle applies for our future sins. "God has totally forgiven and forgotten all our sins—past, present and future," he says.[33]

Jeremy White states that hyper-grace preachers are not soft on sin but rather "extremely big on Jesus."[34] Repentance is needed only for the initial experience of getting saved. After that, we are meant to experience a daily lifestyle in which an ongoing "renewal of the mind" process is taking place within us. According to White, "Confession does not trigger any transaction between us and God that would issue forth more forgiveness, as though God were dispensing forgiveness in various doses based upon our confessions. Confession of sin, then, is about humility and walking in agreement with God."[35] It is not "based upon a humanly-invented two-tiered approach to somehow 'maintaining close relationship' with Him."[36] Salvation and sanctification are "either completely by law or completely by grace, but cannot be a result of mixing the two."[37] There is no need to balance grace with anything else in spite of the possibility of abuse by those who might misunderstand it or misrepresent it as a license to sin.[38]

Clark Whitten agrees. "Sin...is a violation of friendship—relationship—not a violation of the law. Christians are not under the jurisdiction of the...law."[39] Christians don't have to be "perpetual spiritual babes dismissing sinful behavior with the proper behavioral repentance."[40]

Nobody needs a license to sin, says D. R. Silva, another leading voice in the movement.[41] Silva states:

> Now listen. I could *potentially* do anything I want and God won't hold it against me (1 Cor. 6:12)...I'm not waiting on 'more of God,' I'm not begging to be purified and forgiven, I'm waiting on myself to discover and accept what God has already given, and what it truly means to have all of His fullness (Col. 2:9–10) and all of His kingdom (Luke 17:21) within me.[42]

"We are not called to ask for forgiveness even after we have sinned," declared Ryan Rufus at the Glory and Grace Conference held in Manila, Philippines, in 2011.[43] "God doesn't want guilt-ridden and introspective focusing on our sins—He wants us in Him."[44] Sinning does not make Christians "unholy and unrighteous."[45] Sanctification isn't a process, he stated. "[Christians] do not become more and more holy—no—we become holy once and for all!...You can't lose your salvation!"[46] The spirit has received full perfection at new birth. Believers should not be encouraged to repent or confess; instead, they should be taught to activate their spirits.[47]

According to Simon Yap, grieving the Holy Spirit has nothing to do with the believer's sinful life. He says that the Holy Spirit is actually grieved when "speaking words and messages that teach God has only partially [forgiven] you of your sins."[48] Yap states that the sin that easily entangles us is "the sin of thinking Jesus' blood is not enough to satisfy God of your sins past, present, and future."[49]

Michael Reyes says that the Holy Spirit never convicts believers of sin. He only convinces them of their righteousness. Therefore, there is no need for Christians to confess their sins to God or repent.[50] Bill Snell of Grace Church, Florida, adds, "The corrupting power of sin in the flesh is powerless to affect the inward, invisible reality of the 'new creation.'"[51]

A CRITIQUE AND COMPARISON

According to Joseph Mattera, Joseph Prince's classic work *Destined to Reign* contains many good points but makes the mistake of considering grace and the person of Christ to be synonymous.[52] Mattera finds that Prince is trying to fit all Scripture within his narrow system, basing all of his theology of grace on the writings of Paul alone. Prince makes a simple dichotomy, Mattera says, between two covenants without making "allowance for the need for the moral law of God (the Ten Commandments) [Decalogue], except to show us how sinful and lost we are."[53] Mattera says Prince "lumps the moral law (the Ten Commandments) with the ceremonial law of God and says both have been done away with and are not relevant to the church."[54]

David Kowalski provides a focused theological critique of Prince's grace theology too. He believes Prince confounds the notions of faith and repentance and that Prince fails to note that "though justification and sanctification are distinct in concept (a very important truth!), they are inseparable in experience."[55] Prince claims, according to Kowalski, that all concept of law is Mosaic Law. Although Paul issues the most specific exhortations to godly living in the New Testament, Prince considers those exhortations "legalistic ministration of death."[56]

Kowalski calls Prince's position *quietism*, defined as "a passive approach to sanctified living that ignores a massive amount of Scripture that tells us we must, in dependence upon the Spirit, 'strive'... [and] *actively* walk by the Spirit...with 'diligence' and 'perseverance.'"[57] He also finds shades of Kenneth Hagin's teaching in Prince, especially as it concerns confession. To Kowalski, Princianism is a blend of theology that "falls outside the boundaries of biblical and historic orthodoxy."[58] He calls it a "harmful rebellion rather than a beneficial revolution."[59]

Ultimately, current-day grace teachers seem to equate justification with sanctification. They seem to interpret the New Testament concept of law as meaning only Mosaic Law. Any active engagement with the Spirit to "press on," "strive," "walk," "work out," "follow," "abstain," "run," or "fight" is seen as mixing law with grace. Any exhortation to live a holy life is seen as legalism.

Person-centered therapy, in comparison, places its focus on experience, because Rogers did not trust dogma. To him, experience was more reliable. Salvation in therapy is seen as self-actualization, and therapy promotes the process of self-actualization.

In the end, person-centered therapy and hyper-grace teaching are at odds because person-centered therapy is humanistic. It is a psychological theory-based practice. It is based on experience. It is built on evolutionary human potential. Its aim is self-actualization based on the theory that all beings move toward differentiation and integration.

Hyper-grace, on the other hand, is theistic. It is a theological position. It is based on a particular understanding of the biblical concept of grace. Potential for growth, in this doctrinal position, is resident in believers who have confessed Christ as their Savior once. As past sins were forgiven long before one was born, so are present and future sins. They have already been forgiven, requiring no more sacrifices, or repentance, or request for forgiveness. Andrew Wilson's analysis may be right when he says that contemporary grace theology "is a heavily encultured phenomenon, resulting from a fusion of hyper-Lutheranism and Western therapeutic individualism."[60]

A careful comparison of person-centered therapy and hyper-grace reveals several common underlying humanistic themes and noticeable conceptual overlap. Priority given to the individual's self-sufficiency and the diminished capacity assigned to divine provisions remain problematic. To the extent that sanctification is seen as independent of the Word of God and the community of faith, hyper-grace remains theologically wanting.

WHERE DO WE GO FROM HERE?

Is the overemphasis on grace today a response to the needs of the burnt-out workaholic evangelicals and wounded postmodernists of the twenty-first century?

The truth is that genuine legalism is being preached and practiced within evangelicalism. Many within evangelical churches are living with guilt and condemnation and not reaching their potential to live abundant lives. Toxic faith is a real thing. Current grace preaching seems to be a theological effort to respond to this desperate need, but it fails due to its own legalistic and unbalanced application of God's liberating grace. By pushing some important biblical concepts to the extreme, serious theological error is preached and practiced.

Joseph Prince and others who preach the modern grace message occasionally admit that the potential exists for some followers to make serious mistakes, but they still maintain their overemphasis on one biblical truth. They seem unable to grant the possibility that justification is by faith, by grace alone, and that sanctification is the work of the Spirit in our lives that has instant and gradual dimensions. Practically speaking, sanctification involves both divine and human cooperation, empowered by the Holy Spirit. This cooperation cannot be summarily labeled legalism.

Person-centered therapy based on humanistic psychology has helped countless counselees deal with the issues of their lives. Even its critics admit that it has revolutionized psychotherapy. Person-centered therapy was a reaction to authoritarian approaches to psychotherapy, and its appeal to both modern and postmodern generations remains strong. It is also clear that the Princian version of grace preaching as a reaction to legalism is attracting a great number of people to Jesus Christ. It is leading many to salvation as justification by faith, by grace alone.

It is unclear, however, if this teaching is necessary and sufficient for converts to fulfill God's call on their lives to be holy as He is holy. What is abundantly clear is that the great attraction of the "grace revolution" is a strong indication that evangelical and Spirit-empowered churches and ministries must faithfully preach with clarity and conviction the amazing grace of God that fully saves, sustains, and sanctifies, according to the whole counsel of God.

THOMSON K. MATHEW, DMIN, EDD, is Professor of Pastoral Care and former Dean of the College of Theology and Ministry at Oral Roberts University in Tulsa, Oklahoma.

Chapter 6

REFORMED THEOLOGY AND GRACE IN NEWFRONTIERS CHURCHES

William K. Kay

A GROUP CALLED NEWFRONTIERS came into existence through the ministry of Terry Virgo and eventually became one of the most successful neo-Pentecostal groups in the United Kingdom. Remarkably, under Virgo's leadership, Newfrontiers churches came to offer a balance of Reformed theology and grace that can benefit the broader church today. In this essay we will follow Virgo's theological development, notice how his teachings are founded in Scripture, and discover what his teachings can offer the church, particularly in its conversation about grace, today.

THE BEGINNINGS OF FAITH

Terry Virgo came to Christ in a Baptist church and later received an experience of Spirit baptism and speaking in tongues at a Pentecostal church. He attended a Baptist congregation and saw Baptist church polity firsthand. For a number of years as a young Christian, he experienced a heavy burden of evangelical legalism that left him unable to enjoy either his church attendance or his salvation. His faith pilgrimage led first to an intense private reading of missionary biographies and Reformed theology and then through a degree course at the interdenominational London Bible College, now London School of Theology. Newfrontiers comprises around twelve hundred churches worldwide.[1]

While Virgo was training at London Bible College, he adopted the practice of attending a Charismatic congregation in London on Sunday mornings where spiritual gifts were powerfully manifested. There were utterances in tongues, prophecies, healings, and a desire to shape the church as closely as possible along the lines described by Paul in 1 Corinthians 14:26: "When you come together, each of you has a hymn, or a word of instruction, a revelation, a tongue or an interpretation" (NIV). After attending this participatory Charismatic fellowship in the morning, Virgo attended Westminster Chapel, where Dr. Martyn Lloyd-Jones preached in the evenings. There, up to two thousand people would gather to listen to a service almost entirely directed by Lloyd-Jones's hands— it was anything but participatory. He would announce the hymns, pray the prayers, and then deliver a sermon of expository power, often focused on a few words of Scripture as he made his slow and majestic way through a particular book of the Bible verse by verse, taking many months, sometimes even years, to do it.[2]

By common consent, Martyn Lloyd-Jones was one of the greatest preachers of his day. He spoke with logic and clarity, and his theology was unashamedly Reformed. Indeed, he revived interest in the Puritans and held an annual conference on their writings. He was Calvinistic in his theological outlook and yet, as a Welshman, had knowledge of the Welsh revival, perhaps only at secondhand, and was aware of the validity and importance of spiritual experience.

In addition to his intellectual gifts, it was this combination of spiritual experience and Reformed theology that marked Martyn

Lloyd-Jones out from many of his contemporaries. Although he was perfectly capable of constructing theological treatises and a rationalistic defense of Reformed theology, which he appreciated, to him theology remained a desiccated theoretical discourse, powerless to move the heart or regenerate the soul without an infusion of the Spirit.

In short, Terry Virgo, by combining Charismatic experience with the theology of Martyn Lloyd-Jones, created a rare Reformed-Charismatic synthesis soon embodied in congregations in Britain and then across the world through the churches connected with Newfrontiers.

REFORMED THEOLOGY IN NEWFRONTIERS

Reformed theology permeated Newfrontiers without becoming a shibboleth, in the sense that it was possible to belong to a Newfrontiers congregation without being expected to subscribe to the five points of Calvinism—or, indeed, any of them.

The most obvious influence of Reformed theology in the normal activity of a Newfrontiers congregation was the emphasis given to expository preaching. After the flowing Charismatic worship at the start of a meeting, congregations would sit down to listen to a sermon of anything up to an hour in length and could expect to hear a passage or theme of Scripture explained and applied without any more adornment than the occasional PowerPoint slide. This prominence given to expository preaching, so far as one can tell, was common to Newfrontiers churches all over the world. In keeping with Reformed tradition, the preaching was almost invariably given by male leaders, even if female preaching at conferences and other settings did take place.

Teaching about election might occur, but a more usual way of presenting that doctrine took place through the assumptions that might underlie Bible study. So, for instance, when the life of Joseph in the Old Testament was considered, the notion that the final outcome of Joseph's life was foreknown might be highlighted, and the phrase "God meant it for good" (Gen. 50:20, NKJV) would be seen as an evidence of divine sovereignty overruling a human situation whose turbulent events appeared merely contingent. While Newfrontiers did not shy away from teaching election when the topic came up during the exposition of Scripture, and while from time to time election was seen as the key to the invisible formation of an individual's Christian identity, it never barred believers from offering humanitarian help to unbelievers or issuing a gospel invitation. Ideally, the church's message of grace mirrored the great generosity of God to sinners.[3]

Additionally, Virgo focused upon grace as fundamental to the teaching of the New Testament. But in doing so he noticed topics that had hitherto been underemphasized in Pentecostal preaching. He saw that grace, not works, made an apostle. He wrote:

> Paul's authority was not derived from a special title, position or office. It was the fruit of two things. First, the grace of God in calling and equipping him with a particular gift of "apostoling," and secondly, the working relationship he had with any particular church or individual.[4]

It was the notion of the "grace of God in calling" that underlined Virgo's connection between grace and apostolic ministry. It was by grace that Paul was called to apostolic labor, and it was grace that enabled him to succeed in that enormously challenging task. In Ephesians 4:11 (NASB), Paul wrote:

> He gave some as apostles, and some as prophets, and some as evangelists, and some as pastors and teachers.

Virgo affirmed:

> These grace gifts were distributed from a victorious king. He ascended through the heavens triumphantly and received from the Father the Spirit and distributed these gifts to his church. Paul happened to receive the grace of the apostle.[5]

GRACE IN NEWFRONTIERS

In relation to the ordinary life of the church, grace became a much-preached-upon theme. It functioned as a topic that inspired the transformation of Christian lives and in other hands might have settled to become primarily a discipleship course. Newfrontiers, in its engagement with grace, found a theme that released individuals from fruitless legalism—something that was relevant to those who had come across into the neo-Pentecostal movement from an evangelical background and at the same time welcomed the unconverted to the new world of biblical Christianity.

This teaching of grace helped to shape congregations so that, together with a teaching of individual empowerment through the work of the Holy Spirit, energetic activity followed. Indeed, it might be argued that the expectations put upon congregational members in Newfrontiers churches would have created excessive pressure on individuals apart from the countervailing effect of the doctrine of grace. Grace removed the sense that congregations were being driven too hard or being expected to make financial contributions above and beyond what they could properly afford.

Grace and legalism

The frustration of Christians who were constantly attempting to live better, more moral, more spiritual lives and constantly found themselves defeated was something Terry Virgo could identify with. He knew what it was to make resolutions and then to fall flat upon his face. He had been through the experience described by Paul of someone who could say that the good he wanted to do, he failed to do, and the evil he wanted to avoid, he did (Rom. 7:19).

The perpetual failure of the human being to live up to an internal moral law or external regulation was one that immediately raised the question of the purpose of moral law, a question addressed in the letters to the Galatians and Romans. Virgo illuminated the subject with power and clarity. He taught that the law was a schoolmaster to lead the believer to Christ. It was a standard to reveal human sinfulness. It was a taskmaster that led to "dead works" and mind-numbing church routines without any benefit to God or fellow human beings. This treadmill of legalism, found in the New Testament and preached by destructive legalists to the Galatian church, must at all costs be resisted. Grace tells the individual that he or she is completely accepted by God and completely justified on the basis of Christ's life and sacrifice, and this alone. Law is good, but it is powerless to convert the sinner. Grace provides a free gift of righteousness and authorizes identification with Christ, thus breaking the cycle of failure, enabling a new freedom and purpose in the will of God, and so transforming the frustrated sinner.

Conscience, identity, and culture

The law is a great provoker of bad conscience whereas the blood of Christ cleans the Christian conscience and removes a lingering sense of obligation to quite unnecessary activities. The purified conscience is able to make a correct judgement as to the will of God in any set of circumstances and in this way unbind the Christian from perpetual obligation to pointless duties. The believer may now serve the living God and not an agenda set by tradition or custom. Obligation changes to allow the believer to step out and accomplish truly God-given tasks.[6]

Grace, acting with this newly liberated conscience, defies understanding and breaks the inner sense that says you get what you deserve. By grace, you get exactly what you do not deserve. That is the miracle of grace, and it is found in God's choices for unexpected heroes, whether Jacob or Joseph or David. Grace removes confidence in the flesh, in natural ability or race or birth, and explains why God chooses the weak—the lowest caste, the smallest tribe, the youngest child out in the fields looking after the sheep—to confound the strong.

By grace a new identity is given. Paul can become a different man and no longer insist upon his Israelite pedigree but instead say, "By the grace of God I am what I am" (1 Cor. 15:10, NASB). Grace takes the embittered legalist and sets him free so that his past is left behind and his failures haunt him no more. It is grace that makes Paul "a wise master builder" (1 Cor. 3:10, NASB) and grace that provides gifts, charismatic gifts, to Christians so that they may serve one another "as good stewards of the manifold grace of God" (1 Pet. 4:10, NASB). Gifts are not and cannot be rewards, since if they were, they would not be gifts. Gifts are given, and the recipient may then say, "His grace toward me was not in vain" (1 Cor. 15:10, NKJV).

Grace is not cheap or an excuse for license. It does not provide freedom as "an opportunity for the flesh" but rather as a means by which Christians may "through love serve one another" (Gal. 5:13, NKJV). Grace resists legalism: "I do not nullify the grace of God, for if righteousness comes through the Law, then Christ died needlessly" (Gal. 2:21, NASB).

Yet hard work is no enemy of grace, because the recipient of grace can say, "I worked harder than any of them." Beyond this, grace paradoxically makes us what we are not, so Paul can say after speaking of his work, "Yet not I," and marvel at the new identity which is his. Grace is given to make us fruitful. In this respect, we retain a responsibility not to let grace be given in vain in our lives.[7]

Denial, discipline, and keeping in step with the Spirit

Grace teaches us to say no to the "downward gravitational pull of human society,"[8] to compromise with the opposite sex, or to use drugs. It teaches us to say no by assuring us that we are "totally acceptable to God through our faith in Christ"[9] and have no need to swim with the tide. Grace teaches us God's goal is for people to be "red-hot for good deeds"[10] and ready for good works foreordained for us.

Grace teaches us to aim higher and to do so without compromising. It acknowledges that God may discipline us as children and that this discipline, however unpleasant it might be at the time, is to "[yield] the peaceable fruit of righteousness" (Heb. 12:11, NASB). We are not to lose heart at discipline or become bitter. Again Joseph in the Old Testament is an exemplary figure. Grace assures us that we were not forgotten by God and that God has not ceased to care.

More than this, grace assures us we have been brought into a new covenant through the fresh activity of the Spirit of the Lord (Ezek. 37). The new covenant is fortified by the Holy Spirit, who was poured out on the Day of Pentecost and now revolutionizes Christian lives from within. The Spirit is the key to the new relationship with God so that we may walk by the Spirit and enjoy the new energy given to us from within. The essential basis of our new covenant life is the Spirit, as is the Spirit the secret of our success even as we await the new glorified earth and newly glorified bodies.[11] Exhortations to us in the New Testament spring from grace, and "Spirit-Christians who are enjoying God's grace still need to be exhorted and will need such exhortation until 'the perfect comes.'"[12]

Giving, maintenance, and security

Grace overflows, and the overflow results in giving. After the outpouring of the Holy Spirit on the Day of Pentecost, grace transformed individual lives so that people "relinquished their exclusive right to their own possessions"[13] and shared with others in need. Later the churches enjoying the grace of God, as they did in Macedonia (2 Cor. 8:1), gave extravagantly so that other churches in Asia would benefit. Before they gave of their possessions, the Macedonians gave themselves to God (2 Cor. 8:5). Grace in the life of the Corinthians resulted in extraordinary spiritual gifting, knowledge, and power, but also in simple giving. Jesus Himself noted the motivation for giving by those who donated to the temple treasury (Mark 12:41). Such giving often leads to many benefits, so that those who give may end up receiving resources that enable them to give even more.

Although self-effort might seem the very antithesis of grace,[14] it is important for those who enjoy grace to keep themselves in the love of God (Jude 21). They may do this by building themselves up in their faith by speaking with tongues, by purifying their hearts, and by cultivating good habits through practical choices and realizing that "His divine power has given us everything we need for life and godliness" (2 Pet. 1:3, isv) with the result that we avoid laziness:

> Grace is not meant to produce horizontal Christians fond of their beds. Grace is meant to liberate. Grace is meant to motivate. Grace is meant to put a spring in our step and hope in our heart...Grace sets you free to take action.[15]

Grace is found in the life of Elijah, who confronted the evils of his day in a climactic trial of strength on Mount Carmel. At the end of the contest, Elijah was deeply disappointed that the nation had not returned to God and so he ran "into a physical and spiritual desert,"[16] sat down under a tree, and prayed that he might die. His sense of purpose had vanished, and he condemned himself as worthless. It was here the grace of God met him and provided natural refreshment, rest, and food, and eventually, after an awesome display of divine power, he received a new purpose in life.[17]

It is grace that reestablishes the disappointed believer who has reached the end of hope or resources. "God has a wonderful way of working healing into weary people...This is what grace is all about."[18]

Future grace

As if this is not sufficient, there is greater grace in the future ages. We may be groaning and waiting for the completion of the present age, but in prospect is the translation of the individual into the image of Christ so that "the culmination of our salvation is not sanctification but glorification."[19] The whole of creation stands on tiptoe, waiting to see the full revelation of the sons of God. The pains of the present age, wars, and earthquakes will liberate the universe and "set [it] free from its slavery to corruption into the freedom of the glory of the children of God" (Rom. 8:21, NASB). The sufferings of the present world are not worth comparing to the glories to come. Furthermore:

> No doubt it has been the certainty of future grace that has released glorious faith and overcoming joy in the hearts of the martyrs throughout the ages.[20]

God's grace will not only lead us safely home, it will also bring us into future glory. The earth will be filled with the knowledge of the glory of the Lord. Grace will flow at the marriage supper of the Lamb.[21]

A Needed Balance

The doctrine of grace enunciated by Terry Virgo and implemented within Newfrontiers congregations is a doctrine that grows out of biblical study and is enunciated in preaching and relevant to practical Christian living. It is not a doctrine that finds its origin in systematic theology or a philosophical consideration of God's mode of action in the world. Nor does it originate from historical considerations or any Roman Catholic perspective on the transmission of grace through sacraments.

Equally, although there are Calvinistic foundations to Virgo's theology, his doctrine of grace does not center around election, at least not in its preached form. He does not attempt to unravel the metaphysical linkage between grace and election or peer into what might be revealed as divine foreknowledge. These matters are left alone. The purpose of Virgo's ministry, rather than to satisfy the intellectual queries of philosophically minded academics, is to produce mature and fruitful Christians.

What is clear about the practical nature of this exposition of grace is that it neither veers in the direction of antinomianism nor ignores the importance of traditional holiness. This is a grace that flows from the character and love of God to the individual and to the church. It is a doctrine of grace that, when it is first preached, may be rejected on the grounds that it is too good to be true and that God could not possibly be as generous with human beings as Scripture reveals is the case. Virgo encountered this reaction to his preaching, especially at the hands of evangelical legalists who gave lip service to the doctrine of grace while effectively seeking salvation by works. Virgo's teaching and preaching appear to be far closer to the scandal of Pauline doctrine than is heard in many evangelical circles. Its efficacy is tested against the fruitfulness of churches in mission, humanitarian activity, and plentiful charismata.

WILLIAM K. KAY, DD, is professor of theology at Glyndŵr University, Wrexham, Wales.

Chapter 7

A SPIRIT OF UNITY AND GRACE: LEARNING FROM THE ASSEMBLIES OF GOD IRELAND

Miriam (Mimi) A. Kelly

W HEN ATTEMPTING TO define the word *grace* through a brief examination of the Scriptures, we find that the Bible does not give a one-statement definition of the word—and yet grace appears throughout its pages. Jesus lived a life full of grace. He demonstrated it daily. He was presence-led by the Holy Spirit to live a fully human life. He stood beside the woman caught in adultery and demonstrated grace. The parable of the prodigal son demonstrates God's grace. When Jesus died on the cross, grace won out, and that same grace has been defined as "unmerited favor," God's free gift to humanity. Even so, He seems never to have used the word.

And so we look to what others have taught us about grace. Donald Barnhouse declared, "Love that gives upward is worship, love that goes outward is affection; love that stoops is grace."[1] And Charles R. Swindoll suggests that grace comes to us in two dimensions, vertical and horizontal. "Vertical grace centers on our relationship with God....It announces hope to the sinner [and] the gift of eternal life, along with all its benefits."[2] On the other hand, horizontal grace focuses on our relationships with other people. It can free us from the tyranny of people pleasing and of adjusting our lives to the demands of other people's opinions. It is non-judgmental and reaches out.

This essay concerns itself with that second kind of grace—the horizontal kind. What does it mean to show grace to our neighbors? To understand this horizontal kind of grace—a grace that is both Spirit-led and promotes unity in the Spirit—we will learn from the experience of the Assemblies of God Ireland, which in recent years has had opportunity to wrestle with this question.

A MULTIDIMENSIONAL LANDSCAPE

Since 2008, Ireland has undergone momentous changes in its economic, social, demographic, and religious landscapes. The economic crisis that occurred in Ireland in 2008 has had a dramatic effect on the Irish people, and many church organizations have been reflecting on their culture and the possible implications for the present and the future.

The monoculture that was prevalent in the Republic of Ireland has changed to become a multicultural landscape. The population stands at four and a half million, with no less than 10 percent of the Irish population being the "New Irish." The term is used to describe the diversity of people who have migrated into Ireland—in particular, individuals from Eastern Europe, the African nations, and the Philippines.

The most recent census published in 2012 in the Republic of Ireland found that 84.2 percent of the Irish population (3.86 million) consider themselves Roman Catholic, while the second-fastest-growing religion, in percentage terms, is the Apostolic and Pentecostal community.[3]

Begin by Reflecting on Culture

One of the foremost indigenous Pentecostal-Charismatic organizations in Ireland is the Assemblies of God Ireland (AGI).[4] The AGI is an all-Ireland movement that encompasses the twenty-six counties in the Republic and the six counties in Northern Ireland. Presently the AGI has approximately forty congregations in Ireland, and the vast majority of these communities are becoming more multicultural.

Although the AGI national leadership team meets regularly and holds an annual conference, they long desired to organize a series of regional gatherings to critique the culture of the movement and its church communities. These meetings can provide an opportunity for people on the ground to share what the Lord is doing in their churches.

To initiate its support of this vision, the AGI launched an e-magazine, titled *Connect*, in 2015. Its inaugural issue stated:

> Assemblies of God Ireland exists for meaningful connection. We long to connect people with God, connecting the lost to a saviour and the broken to a healer. We also seek to connect pastors to pastors, leaders to leaders, churches to churches and churches to a National movement. Our movement is all about connection.[5]

In conjunction with the launch of the magazine, the AGI organized a series of meetings around the country under the heading "The Power of Connection" to bring together leaders and ministry workers in the way it had long wanted to do. St. Mark's Church in the heart of Dublin city was one of the venues, and approximately eighty to one hundred people from across Dublin attended.

The national director opened the meeting by stating, "We all have a culture in our churches, and I would like us to begin to reflect on what types of culture we have from the standpoint of a newcomer."[6]

The AGI national leader further said:

> The Kingdom of God, his rule and reign is increasing, so the
> Word tells us. It is exciting to partner with God in what he
> is building; his Church. That is our heart at AG Ireland, to
> champion you and your local church and see you go from
> strength to strength. AG Ireland is a movement of churches
> with Christ at the centre, united in purpose to see a nation
> won to Christ.[7]

A series of questions were asked: What would an outsider's
first impression be? What values are communicated when someone
approaches your church from the outside? What would an outsider,
after sitting through several worship services, say that your church
values most? How would an outsider describe the spirit, or attitudes, most prevalent in your church? Who would you see as the
culture setters in your church (leaders, church staff, volunteer ministry leaders)?

Everyone was asked to reflect on these questions, write down
their thoughts, and discuss them with the other people who were
present. As individuals shared about their church communities,
an article by Veli-Matti Kärkkäinen came to mind, in which he
quoted Emil Brunner:

> The Body of Christ is nothing other than a fellowship of
> persons. It is "the fellowship of Jesus Christ" or "fellowship
> of the Holy Ghost," where fellowship or *koinonia* signifies
> a common participation, a togetherness, a community life.
> The faithful are bound to each other through their common
> sharing in Christ and in the Holy Ghost, but that which they
> have in common is precisely no "thing," no "it," but a "he,"
> Christ and His Holy Spirit.[8]

Being bound to each other through our common sharing in
Christ and His Holy Spirit was one of the core findings of the
meeting, and this unity in the Spirit, this sense of connectedness,

has been one of the foundational characteristics of the AGI since its launch in 2005.

UNITY WITHIN DIVERSITY

Each community represented at the meeting demonstrated great diversity, yet all had a deep desire to share the gospel of Christ in their churches and the communities they serve. It was evident each church had its distinctive DNA, own location, unique social context, and diverse church membership, yet all were members of the AGI. The manifold diversity was so evident, and people began to see and hear all that God was doing in and through the churches and the AGI as a whole. The grace to acknowledge and appreciate differences and diversity through unity of the Spirit through the bonds of peace came to the fore, together with a real and tangible sense of connectedness.

Perhaps what God desires from the Pentecostal-Charismatic movement in Ireland is not so much religious practice but a deep, personal relationship that transforms our lives so that we radiate the grace of God and His truth and beauty more clearly. Throughout history many have grappled with the issue of the one and the many—the relationship between unity and diversity. But perhaps this is not so much a problem as a richness that reflects the abundance of God and our human struggle to understand or grasp that overabundance.[9] Unity is not unanimity or uniformity. Unity is the bond that exists between people who know the things that unite them are deeper and more important than the things that might separate them. Solidarity does not equal sameness.

In 2014 Pope Francis met with members of the Catholic Fraternity of Charismatic Covenant Communities and Fellowships and delivered a speech in which he declared:

> [Unity] does not necessarily mean doing everything together
> or thinking in the same way. Nor does it signify a loss of iden-
> tity. Unity in diversity is actually the opposite: it involves the

joyful recognition and acceptance of the various gifts which the Holy Spirit gives to each one and the placing of these gifts at the service of all members of the Church....Unity is knowing how to listen, to accept differences, and having the freedom to think differently and express oneself with complete respect towards the other.[10]

Pope Francis also spoke about the church's need for the Holy Spirit:

The Church needs the Holy Spirit! How could we do without it! Every Christian in his or her life requires a heart open to the sanctifying action of the Holy Spirit. The Spirit, promised by the Father, is he who reveals Jesus Christ to us, but who makes us...gives us the possibility to say: Jesus! Without the Spirit, we could not say this. He reveals Jesus Christ, who leads us to a personal encounter with him, and who, in so doing, changes our life. A question: Is this your experience? Share it with others! In order to share this experience, you must live it and witness to it![11]

Having the grace to cultivate and grow in the unity of the Spirit through the bonds of peace in the AGI and its members is a noble aspiration. And as a result of these meetings, the foundation stones have been laid to nurture and facilitate ongoing unity within the AGI in Ireland and to promote a deeper sense of connectedness to each other in advancing the gospel of Christ throughout the nation.

OPENNESS TO THE OTHER

What are the challenges and opportunities that face the AGI within their movement? How do we begin to nurture and cultivate this sense of unity in the body with a genuine attitude of grace?

In a homily Dr. Mel Robeck gave in 2013 at the "Week of Prayer for Christian Unity," he suggested:

There are many things that we can do to bring about changes that reflect the kind of unity for which Jesus prayed. It would be dishonest if we did not admit right up front that we all too often speak disparagingly about one another. One very simple suggestion would be that we agree not to call one another names, or label one another with slurs of any kind. When we do not respect one another, when we speak evil of one another or simply dismiss one another without attempting to resolve our differences, when we belittle one another, we do not do justice to the vision of unity that Jesus had for His followers....

It is also the case that genuine unity is built upon solid relationships. A third suggestion, then, would be for all of us to reach out to other Christians who are different from us and develop relationships that can lead to changes in the status quo. Strong relationships help us better to understand and love the other. We become much more concerned about their welfare than we were before. Genuine relationships require that we be concerned about considering the hurt that we inflict upon our sisters and brothers when we charge ahead with unilateral actions. It is this type of thinking that is the beginning of real Christian unity.[12]

Being or becoming aware of our biases and attitudes toward others is something we all need to do. We all have prejudices, whether conscious or unconscious, and we all can prejudge a person or group before an encounter takes place.

Our prejudices may be based on a belief or arise from a person's appearance, age, sex, ethnicity, culture, origin, or status. It is an attitude that colors our view of the world. These attitudes and beliefs often lead to action and can be displayed through intolerance or rejection of the other. The more we reflect upon these ideas and acknowledge our prejudices, the more we can begin to change them in a spirit of humility and grace.

Additionally, utilizing grace to encourage the unity of the Spirit requires that we do not compare ourselves with others. Why are we uneasy with differences? Why do we prefer sameness? Why do we place so much weight on externals—on appearance, taste, clothing, or music styles? Do we compare spirituality on the basis of externals at times too? Who wrote the "let's compare" rulebook? As Chuck Swindoll says, "Comparisons fuels the fire of envy within people. It prompts the tendency to judge...Grace finds pleasure in differences, encourages individuality, smiles on variety, and leaves plenty of room for disagreement."[13]

LOVING OUR NEW NEIGHBORS

The New Irish, or migrant-led, Pentecostal and Charismatic communities have grown steadily in Ireland over the past fifteen years. These relatively new Christian communities in the Republic have helped to change the Pentecostal-Charismatic landscape in various ways. For example, the way they praise and worship, the way they dress in their native attire to attend church, and the manner in which they perceive church as an extension of their community give the migrant-led churches a sense of belonging and cohesion.

Understanding the differences between various faith expressions may help to promote unity in the Spirit. For instance, we can learn from our new African neighbors that African spirituality is not restricted to outward practices, beliefs, and behaviors associated with religious conviction, but also involves the internal personal and emotional expressions of joy, peace, confidence, comfort, or sorrow resulting from faith in and connectedness to the transcendent.[14]

African spirituality is expressed through song, art, literature, myth, parables, dreams, visions, trances, music, and dance. It does not create dichotomies between the material and the spiritual, between the sacred and the secular. It does not separate physical and spiritual, natural and supernatural, personal and social. All are interconnected. African spirituality emphasizes oneness over categories, commonality over individuality, enchantment over materiality, wholeness over separation.

Another aspect of African spirituality is the bold conviction that God continues to work in the church through supernatural means. The notion of power is crucial, and the emphasis on the power of the Holy Spirit to heal, to save, and to protect one's life in this world and the next is another core feature of the migrant-led churches in Ireland.

Abel Ugba's research suggests that the migrant-led churches believe they are part of God's plan to reintroduce the gospel to Europeans. The idea of reverse mission may in some way motivate the activities of many African Pentecostal migrant-led churches in Ireland.[15]

As Dr. Livingstone Thompson aptly states:

> The Pentecostal churches in Ireland are not only migrant-led; they are also Holy Spirit–led. This missionary impulse which has fired the ambition of the African Pentecostal churches is similar to the impulse that guided the European missionary enterprise in Africa, Asia and the Americas. This reverse flow of the Christian message, on the wings of the African Pentecostal evangelistic thrust, to the lands from whence it came, is bringing about a reform of Christianity to the benefit of the Irish church. The challenge then is to see this Pentecostal experience as more than just a socio-cultural curiosity. The migrant-led planting in Ireland of African style Pentecostalism, which is expected to sustain growth over decades, not only presents the churches with an ecumenical challenge but is also initiating a transformation of the Irish Christian landscape.[16]

This ecumenical challenge begins by welcoming strangers; this is an act of affirmation that says we value the other prior to making any judgment about them. Welcome is based on the recognition of our fundamental relatedness prior to any specific knowledge we have of who each other is.

Jean Vanier, founder of the L'Arche communities, writes, "Welcome is one of the signs that a community is alive. To invite others to live with us is a sign that we aren't afraid, that we have a treasure of truth and of peace to share."[17] He also offers an important warning: "A community which refuses to welcome—whether through fear, weariness, insecurity, a desire to cling to comfort, or just because it is fed up with visitors—is dying spiritually."[18]

Understanding the church as God's household has significant implications for hospitality and promoting and nurturing unity in the Spirit. When we come together as a Christian community, we ought to demonstrate God's love, grace, and hospitality.

The concept of hospitality is a long-established tradition in the Irish context. Given the unprecedented movement of people into the Republic, the challenge to the Pentecostal community and the AGI is to appreciate difference and with hearts filled with hospitality to welcome all who come to reside in Ireland. Hospitality is a way of life. Sharing it with others, because it is a way of life, must be nurtured and cultivated over time.

CHURCHES WORKING TOGETHER

The AGI needs to accept the fact that migrant-led churches are part of the new landscape in Ireland. Jesus demonstrated by word and action how all individuals, without exception, belong to the family of God, and the new migrant-led communities are equal allies in this family. Learning to recognize and appreciate cultural and ethnic diversity as gracious gifts of God is a core matter that needs to be acted on while working toward unity in the Spirit.

A challenge for the migrant-led churches is being open to understanding and appreciating the Irish culture in which they now live. There is a measure of responsibility on the part of migrant-led churches to be alert to what approaches are applicable and acceptable in twenty-first-century Ireland and perhaps shape their church culture in light of the new context. Churches learning to work together have a responsibility to educate their faith communities of each other's cultural differences so they can begin to grow together in a spirit of grace and love. Becoming aware of the local context, especially in rural Ireland, may prove advantageous and help migrant-led churches become more integrated into the communities in which they live today.

PROMOTING INTERCULTURAL DIALOGUE

Dialogue means witnessing to our deepest convictions while listening to those of our neighbors in a two-way exchange. Without such commitment, dialogue becomes mere chatter or empty words. Dialogue is possible if the AGI comes with an expectation of meeting the God who has preceded us and has been relating to people within the context of their own culture and conviction all along. Dialogue is a way of taking seriously the truth that all humans are created in God's image. It means venturing outside our safety zone and making ourselves vulnerable. Dialogue aims at holding hands and developing relationships across the barriers of faith, ethnicity, gender, and cultural background.[19]

A document authored by the Irish Inter-Church Committee entitled "Irish Churches' Affirmations on Migration, Diversity and Interculturalism" states:

> Cultural diversity is one of the most visible changes migration has brought to Irish Churches and society. This reality calls for a response by the Churches based on an appreciation of richness and vibrancy inherent in such diversity.
>
> Parishes and congregations can provide forums for intercultural dialogue…Public celebration is an important element in recognising and valuing cultural diversity: cultural events and initiatives can serve to enhance the visibility of local new communities, as well as foster better understanding between different communities. The Churches have an important role also in promoting inclusive concepts of culture, and

facilitating the participation of people with a migrant background in cultural events and activities.[20]

WE LOVE AS HE LOVED

Horizontal grace focuses on the relationships we cultivate with other people, other groups, other communities, and other churches. When Christians come together in the unity of the Spirit, this can present a powerful witness to the lost.

God first loved us when we were unlovely and unattractive. Because He continues to love us, we in turn should love one another. God also gave to us, and continues to give to us, in spite of our weaknesses. In turn, this kind of grace giving ought to flow from our hands to others' hearts.

To truly embody grace, we need to grow in grace. None of us has arrived, but with the Spirit's help we are being transformed, and this transformation needs to be lived daily and be extended to others when promoting and cultivating unity of the Spirit. Grace that is really amazing is grace that is truly accepting.

MIRIAM (MIMI) A. KELLY, PHD, is a lecturer of Pentecostal-Charismatic history and Irish church history at the Irish Bible Institute in Dublin, Ireland.

Chapter 8

GRACE, SANCTIFICATION, AND ITALIAN PENTECOSTALISM

Paolo Mauriello

THE ORIGINS OF the Italian Pentecostal movement can be traced back to the beginning of the twentieth century, when William H. Durham came into contact with Luigi Francescon, an Italian immigrant from the province of Udine. Durham had recently returned from Los Angeles, where he had participated in the events of Azusa Street, had spoken in tongues, and was now leading the church on North Avenue in Chicago. Soon after Francescon met Durham, he was invited to attend Durham's Pentecostal meetings. After a few months, he received the Pentecostal experience of the baptism in the Spirit and started the first Italian Pentecostal church in America.[1]

This encounter laid the foundation for the development and growth of the Italian Pentecostal movement. In fact, Francescon became convinced that the revival should expand beyond Chicago and reach all the Italian immigrants, even to his Italian homeland. He was apparently encouraged in this by Durham. Therefore, in the following years, this missionary activity began to spread the Pentecostal experience among the Italians in many parts of the world.

The fact that Francescon received the Pentecostal message, among other important elements, from Durham meant that this most important wing of Italian Pentecostalism was linked to the current of the so-called Baptist Pentecostalism. Durham, in fact, was the first advocate of the Pentecostal "finished work" theology as opposed to the second work of grace for sanctification.

THE FIRST MAJOR SCHISM

There followed a strong dispute that caused the Wesleyan wing of the Pentecostal movement to separate and strongly oppose Durham's view on sanctification. The major historical leaders of Pentecostalism, such as Seymour and Parham, opposed Durham's theory. As a matter of fact, from 1906 to 1914, the emerging Pentecostal movement had to face the most important doctrinal division the movement would ever experience: the schism over sanctification as a second work of grace.[2]

The "finished work" believers argued that sanctification occurs at the time of conversion, and then the believer grows in grace. The Wesleyan Pentecostals argued that sanctification occurred as a second work of grace that must precede baptism in the Spirit— indeed, that it is a prerequisite to receiving it. The two-step account of the Christian life as supported by Durham did not diminish the importance of sanctification, but it did deny that sanctification is a second work of grace distinct from and subsequent to conversion. According to this view, sanctification is included with conversion in the completed work of Christ at Calvary.

Most probably it was because of its link with the Pentecostal church of Chicago that Italian Pentecostals "understand sanctification as a process by which the believer experiences transformation and a growing commitment to Christ, the church and the world."[3] They also identified the doctrine of grace as God's gracious gift, where "the sinner is in no way able to receive a new life in Christ based on any human merits."[4] As a matter of fact, Ephesians 2:8–9 was one of their favorite quotations for salvation, as it says, "For it is by grace you have been saved, through faith—and this is not from yourselves, it is the gift of God" (NIV).

It was not uncommon as Pentecostalism began to spread in Italy to hear Pentecostal preachers mentioning such verses to talk about the grace of God as a gift for salvation, as opposed to the need of works being required by the predominant and domineering Catholic Church. With very simple words, a Pentecostal would preach the gospel to the unbeliever who was under the deception of a salvation that came by pilgrimage, by placing money on the statue of a saint while in procession along the streets of the town, and by other peculiar traditions of the Catholic Church in Italy. This was the strength of the Pentecostal preaching—that salvation was by grace through faith with the intent of living a renewed holy life full of good works.

A SIMPLE MESSAGE

Now, if the doctrine of sanctification had produced the first initial schism among Pentecostals, it must be recognized that the doctrine of grace, at least in the Italian context, had a unifying effect. The first generation of Pentecostals had a simple but effective theological conception of sanctification and grace.

However, it was hard to define it strictly as a theological position, because *theology* was almost a bad word among the first Italian Pentecostals. They had an aversion to any theological or cultural expressions, and to culture in general. It was common to hear sermons from the pulpit advocating the "no culture" idea, making it, ironically, almost a doctrine and typical form of Pentecostal teaching.

"The letter kills, but the Spirit gives life" (2 Cor. 3:6, NIV) was a phrase that often sounded imperiously from the pulpit. This was a frequently cited passage of Scripture in the first Pentecostal communities, for whom it was a source of pride not to have proper theological training. According to Pentecostals, the words *theology* and *theologian* were synonymous with a cold and stale reading of the Scriptures, which certainly increased the cognitive aspect of learning but did not transfer into daily practice what had been learned. Theology was seen as an enemy of the Bible and of the knowledge of God since it focused mainly on generating "an infinity of words and discussions"[5] distant from the experience of the individual believer.

Therefore, the early Italian Pentecostal movement firmly believed in the doctrine of salvation by God's grace alone through faith, which would ultimately lead to a sanctified life full of good works.

ITERATIONS OF GRACE

But grace was not only related to salvation. From an analysis of written testimonies and biblical studies reported in the Pentecostal magazine published in Italy since 1946, *Risveglio Pentecostale* (Pentecostal revival), which for many years was the only voice of the Pentecostal circles in Italy, it can be inferred that the word *grace* was used in the most varied contexts connected to Christian life. *Grace* was defined as the "law of God manifested in Christ which repeats to us one word: Love. It is the law of freedom that cannot be bound to formality and that finds its application only in the Lord's saving grace."[6] But even more, the word *grace* would be associated with concepts related to mission and missionaries ("with the word of grace missionaries are recommended to the grace of God"), to testimonies ("we testified of God's grace and power"), to the ministry of the Word of God ("the Lord gave us grace to minister His word"), to the help of God ("being supported by the grace of God"), to the fight against the devil ("with the grace of God we overcame the battle against…"), to proclaim the childhood of God ("by the grace of God we are His children"), and to thank God for the growth and perseverance in the faith ("with the grace of God we continue our Christian walk in which the Lord called us").

But we could go a bit further, saying that grace was seen as the opposite of formalism and dogmatism, as we read:

> Christ, the Living Word, has dwelt among us as the "manifestation of grace and truth." First grace, then truth....Many of us would do well to seek to possess more grace before attacking furiously some argument of truth, because only the fact to place truth before grace differentiates us already from Jesus...Defense of Christianity! Defense of the truth! It is a vain speaking that comes to our ear, it is a vain and absurd claim of those who still today, puffed up of learning and carnal knowledge, and perhaps for this looking at others with an awkward and contemptuous look, continue to mortify the Grace,...Christians, do not strive in vain arguments and words, look for Grace, always Grace, if you want that Christianity shines in the purity of the early centuries! There is no other way![7]

Even from an analysis of the word *sanctification*, we can infer that it was not seen as a rigid, normative way of life. It is emblematic that in 1949 an article appeared in *Risveglio Pentecostale* in which S. L. Brengle defined *holiness* as pure love: "Do you want to know what holiness is? It is pure love. Do you want to know what is the baptism of the Holy Spirit? It is not a vain sentiment. It is a baptism of love."[8]

The denunciation of formalism and illusory sanctification was strong and conceived as opposite to practical sanctification: "Practical sanctification has to heal the condition of the illusory sanctification, which proceeds from the ego. This tends to exalt the creature, to expose it to the admiration of the world."[9]

A SLOW DESCENT INTO LEGALISM

The process that brought the Italian Pentecostal movement to regard sanctification as moralism, with a whole set of rules to follow, was progressive and slow. In 1947, an article against fashion appeared in

Risveglio Pentecostale, a translation of an article by Charles Finney taken from the *Pentecostal Evangel.* But it was especially in the fifties that we see the first reports, articles, and testimonies that show a shift in the concept of sanctification and grace.

Actually, it was a shift that had been progressively imposing itself over the last two decades in almost all the Pentecostal churches in Italy. In fact, in a report about the Conference of the Churches of Puglia and Lucania, when speaking about the order to keep during the worship service, it was written:

> It is once again reminded to all the churches, and especially to the leaders, that it is necessary to impart teachings in order that all the believers manifest simplicity, modesty and bashfulness (1 Timothy 2:9) in their clothing (clothes, socks, hair, etc.) and participate to worship services with clothing that sets an example to the unconverted.[10]

In September 1953, another article in the same magazine, with no signature at the end of it, and given the significant title of "A Happy Experiment," the church of Rome was presented as an example (a happy experiment) of a Catholic holiness dress code because a "common assembly" was organized and had decided, among other things, the following:

a) Clothing—the sisters are forbidden to enter the worship premises wearing clothes with a low neckline or with short sleeves. The brothers are forbidden to show up without a jacket.

b) Stockings—The sisters must always wear socks with visible stitching.

c) Hair—The sisters must wear long hair, not loose and gathered up in a bun.

d) Veil—the veil must cover their heads and therefore it is not permissible to use handkerchiefs and veils of tulle, but nontransparent veils must be used.[11]

Other decisions were made on that occasion, such as those concerning weddings:

> The betrothal between believers should be short and with a healthy testimony, and thus deprived of all worldliness and carnality...It is disapproved the tendency to make worldly wedding ceremonies...The church will not allow in the future, according to the principles always advocated, engagements and marriages of believers with unconverted. The disobedient will be considered outside the church fellowship.[12]

In 1954, in an article with the meaningful title of "Salvati per Grazia?" (Saved by grace?), R. Bracco, one of the most intelligent and enlightened men of the time, attacked those who did not practically show their salvation and only proclaimed a salvation by grace that allowed them to do whatever they liked. His words against women were particularly strong: "We should not be scandalized if we encounter Christian women dominated by vanity: short hair or with their hair permed; lipstick or going to the cinema; the passionate novels or furtive love affairs can destroy the salvation which was purchased by Christ for us."[13]

Bracco's attacks against fashion and vanity continued in later articles:

> The code is precise and detailed. It states that the believer must have no relationship with "fashion" because it has to move within the limits of honesty, of modesty and economy. Not luxurious clothes, not flashy ornaments, no nudity, no unnecessary eccentricity. The ornament and the clothing of the Christian must be represented by the *holiness* [italics mine] of his/her life.[14]

From these citations we can understand that clothing, ornaments, short hair, permed hair, stockings, lipstick, and the cinema
were all related to holiness—or, better, to unholiness.

In the following year, the above-mentioned "code" became even
more strict, then including the forbidding of watching the recently
invented television. As to women, it was prohibited for them to
wear trousers (as those were distinctive of men) or any jewels or
similar ornaments, or to have makeup or dyed hair.[15] Later on,
many churches went so far as to prohibit the singing of hymns that
were not in the official hymnbook. During Christmas celebrations,
it was forbidden to eat the typical Italian Christmas cake called
panettone. Similarly, during the Easter holidays, it was not allowed
to eat another typical Italian cake called the *colomba*. The list of dos
and don'ts could easily continue.

Now, if an enlightened and intelligent person such as R. Bracco
could write those words, it can be easily imagined what the rest of
the Pentecostal churches thought on these themes. The pure love
of sanctification of the early days had grown directly into sterile
moralism and, at the end, into a desolate formalism, and finally
legalism.

The early Pentecostal Italian movement emphasized the need
for sanctification but in the context of spiritual renewal and of a
committed Christian life. That kind of preaching derived from
the missional tension early Pentecostals felt was their priority in
life and brought many people to salvation. But when sanctification
becomes only a formal exercise for not doing things or doing other
things, this ends up first in a sterile moralism and then in pure
legalism, and at the end it will bring in a lot of pain. Such an idea
of sanctification inevitably leads to many forms of criticism, where
accusations of bad conduct come against even the slightest act of
nonconformism with the predominant idea of holiness.

As a matter of fact, on the basis of this idea of sanctification,
Italian Pentecostalism experienced its first division. The radical

group known as the *zaccardiani* did not want anything to do with other Pentecostals because they felt too sanctified to mingle with them and thus started their own movement of "most holy" people, as they were subsequently nicknamed.[16] Nowadays this group of "most holy" people has almost disappeared, but the remaining members still hold the same conviction that holiness is based on a heap of unreasonable restrictions.

We can certainly assert that after that first generation of passionate pioneers in Italy, there was a comfortable settling of "doctrinal" positions with a strong emphasis not on salvation by grace and subsequent progressive sanctification but on a series of dos and don'ts that have caused the Pentecostals in Italy to be known as the "those who do not."

The legalistic reduction of sanctification, as opposed to liberal grace, further caused the Italian Pentecostal movement to close itself up—the extreme conclusion of separation from the world. Perhaps Italy was the only nation in which Pentecostals would not celebrate Christmas or Easter just because those holidays include pagan elements derived from the Roman Catholic Church. In fact, the justification for all the rules was "We do not do as the world— read: the Catholic Church—does."

But if many of the rules of the aforesaid "code" were stated in opposition to the Catholic Church, others sprang up from an evangelical moralistic view that created a lot of confusion and division in the Pentecostal world. Many churches passed through the terrible pain of splits and divisions because some of their members would have liked to sing new songs that were not in the hymnbook or because some women would not wear the veil on their head or because they were more sympathetic and tolerant regarding women's clothing. Once sanctification was seen as a moral code and legalism ruled in many churches, it opened up a season of conflicts, especially between the new and older generations.

A SERIES OF NEW BEGINNINGS

At the end of 1958, an American missionary, John McTernan, felt it was not possible to continue with such an idea of holiness. Therefore, he started a new church where most of the things that were prohibited in almost all of the Italian Pentecostal churches of the time were easily admitted. For example, there was no division between males and females during the worship service. There was freedom to wear or not wear the veil for women. It was possible to freely use television and radio and even the Christmas tree. Also, the eating of the *panettone* and the *colomba* was permitted. It was a new church that attracted a lot of criticism from almost all of the Pentecostal world. However, it was likely easy for McTernan to make such decisions, being himself an American without the peculiar heritage of Italian Pentecostalism.[17]

If the sixties and the seventies were the years of immobilism and substantial incapacity to face new challenges, the eighties were years in which several movements started with a new vision not bound to the former norms and petty rules. For example, in 1985, in Palermo, Lirio Porrello, a young man who had just gotten his master's degree in medicine, decided with a small group of young people to start a new movement called Parola della Grazia (word of grace) that today counts more than five thousand members in the city of Palermo alone, plus twenty-one churches and fifteen missions in other parts of Italy. It was a movement that was birthed out of a traditional church through the desire for a strong renewal based on a new concept of grace and sanctification.

Pastor Porrello, recalling that experience, affirms:

> At the time there was a strong desire of freedom with a strong emphasis on grace in order to reduce legalism, it was the freedom of grace. We were tired of that rampant legalism and hypocrisy, because people lived a double life, with opposite behaviors in the society and in the church. One cannot be a Christian in the church and another person outside the

church. The work of grace brings a transformation of our way of life that is based on the truth. We chose to call our movement "Word of Grace" because until then we could only listen to the word of the law. You walked into the church hoping for restoration, but you would come out of it even more condemned than when you walked in, because there was only the preaching of the law, of doing and not doing things. The radical message of grace means the denial of yourself because grace induces you to give up your ego, while legalism, misperceived as sanctification, gives you the presumption of earning salvation with your own strength. Legalism generates hypocrisy and hypocrisy destroys the awakening. Our movement fought this attitude which is actually nothing more than a disguised Catholicism, trying to save yourself by your own efforts, and certainly the Catholic culture does not go away in a generation. True holiness is the genuineness and authenticity that comes from a new attitude which accelerates the need to live in a missiological church and therefore stimulates the Church to grow.[18]

A TRUE GRACE

The focus on a radical gospel does not involve petty rules but proposes a concept of grace that does not mean you do whatever you want. Grace means having the capacity and the power to do what you cannot naturally do. It means being radical with yourself—and this cannot be achieved without the power of the Holy Spirit. It is therefore this powerful triad that must lead the life of a Christian: a *Spirit*-empowered people saved by *grace* with the ability to live *holy* lives.

There is no mission if there is only permission theology. The grace of God urges us to sanctification. We can affirm that grace is based on Galatians 2:20: "I have been crucified with Christ and I no longer live, but Christ lives in me" (NIV). It is the opposite of legalism, which is the exaltation of one's ego. Grace is the denial of the ego. It is an embrace of the cross and following Jesus with joy and a heart full of hope and grace.

We can, therefore, agree with those who believe it is impossible to understand the meaning of Wesleyan sanctification except in the context of a Spirit-led revival movement. Some may begin to feel the inadequacy, the superficiality, and the sterility of the Christian life up to that point, and sanctification, understood as Christian perfection, becomes not a closure or an imposition, but rather a liberation and an opening up to the other. "Far from conveying the weight of a law, articulated in various codes, it rather represents the one, undivided, fruit of the Spirit, a work of enrichment, of deepening and of good use of a gift."[19]

This missiological tension is central to the Pentecostal perspective; it is the announcement that asserts the exclusivity of salvation in Christ. The Charismatic experience and the emphasis on the guidance of the Spirit are functional to this primary task. It is in this synthesis that Pentecostalism reveals its intimate Trinitarian structure that encompasses the wider Christian tradition. In turn, this necessarily leads to a concept of mission as an essential part of the Christian faith.[20]

Pentecostalism encompasses a missiological vision of the church, identifying in the tension between grace and sanctification the possibility of change through the action of the Spirit that involves ethical implications with missiological significance. For Pentecostals, conversion and sanctification mean the adoption of reasonable and consequent behaviors. If you add to the equation the experience in the Spirit, especially the baptism in the Holy Spirit, which is often seen as an inner cleansing experience, you understand how for Pentecostals it is important to draw lines between the current morality in a sort of nonconformist attitude.

We could, therefore, look at the history of the Italian Pentecostal church on the theme of grace and sanctification as a paradigm for churches and movements, even on a global scale, that have faced the same doctrinal issues or are still facing them today. Often doctrinal rigidity, excessive concerns about the dominant culture, and the difficulty of combining individual freedoms and community guidelines have made true for Pentecostal churches what has been said for Christian churches in general:

> In the life and growth of every young church there seems to be a perennial disappointment that more than anything else grieves and surprises both the missionary and the student of church history. Even before the first generation of converts disappears, the Gospel is transformed into law. The first wonderful charm of a new discovery deteriorates until it becomes a sad tale of rules of conduct, apostasy and ecclesiastical disciplines. In the eyes of non-Christians, the church thus appears not as a community with a new way of life, but a sect with a heap of many unreasonable restrictions. The second generation, therefore, knows much more about the gospel and understands more clearly the obligations arising therefrom.[21]

I am utterly convinced we can look to the future for a new generation of mature Pentecostals, conscious that grace is the foundation ground for a sanctified life in the power of the Holy Spirit.

PAOLO MAURIELLO, MA, is professor of missiology, homiletics, and faith communication at the Facoltà Pentecostale di Teologia e Studi Religiosi in Bellizzi (SA), Italy.

Chapter 9

MANIFESTATIONS OF GRACE: A LATIN AMERICAN WITNESS

Miguel Álvarez

WHAT IS GRACE? In the New Testament, *grace* means God's love in action toward men and women who merited the opposite of love. As a matter of fact, J. I. Packer once said, "Grace means God moving heaven and earth to save sinners who could not lift a finger to save themselves."[1] In light of that, by grace God sent His only Son to descend and die on the cross so that we guilty ones might be reconciled to God and be received into heaven. Truly, God "made him to be sin for us, who knew no sin; that we might be made the righteousness of God in him" (2 Cor. 5:21, KJV). Therefore, Paul Enns says *grace* may well be defined as "the unmerited or undeserving favor of God to those who are under condemnation."[2]

In Western theology, grace is known as that love and mercy granted by God to humanity because He wants men, women, and creation to have it. Randy Maddox sees grace as the condescension or benevolence shown by God toward the world that He so loved.[3]

In the biblical point of view, Western scholars take grace as unmerited favor.[4] It is God's free action granted to benefit humanity. They see grace as different from justice and mercy. A simple way to explain it is this: Justice is getting what one deserves. Mercy is not getting what one deserves. Grace is getting what one does not deserve.[5] In that case, grace is the benevolent act of God by which He grants salvation; it is something no one deserves, but because of God's love and kindness manifested in Jesus, a person receives the blessing of redemption.

A good definition of *grace* in the theology of the apostle Paul is found in *Baker's Evangelical Dictionary of Biblical Theology*. In the entry for grace, Andrew H. Trotter Jr. notes that in the letter to the Ephesians, Paul explains the free character of grace and offers simply a message of salvation. Trotter further explains:

> We are told that we have been saved "by grace" but "through faith" [Eph. 2:8–9, NIV]. Grace is seen here as the means by which we are saved, a free gift; faith is seen as the mechanism by which that salvation or grace is appropriated. Paul must then go on to argue that even faith is "not by works so that no one can boast" (v. 9).
>
> This does not mean that Paul keeps grace separate from works in sanctification, for he goes right on to speak of us being God's workmanship created in Christ Jesus to do good works (v. 10). Similarly, grace is seen as being in the midst of our present Christian life. In Romans 5:2 Paul speaks of gaining "access by faith into this grace in which we now stand" and in 5:21 of grace reigning "through righteousness to bring eternal life through Jesus Christ our Lord."[6]

Although these statements could lead one to think that I am overemphasizing works here, that is not the case. The idea is to see grace as the source of balance in the pursuit of holiness.

Moreover, in this context grace is viewed as reigning even as one lives in Christ.

> Hence the argument of Romans 6 that we are not to go on sinning so that grace may increase, but we are to "count [ourselves] dead to sin but alive to God in Christ Jesus for sin shall

not be [our] master, because [we] are not under law, but under grace" (vv. 11–14). The key metaphor used in this chapter to describe this "work" of sanctification is "offer." Hence we are not to "offer the parts of [our] body to sin as instruments of wickedness," but rather offer ourselves to God, "as those who have been brought from death to life" (v. 13).[7]

This definition of *grace* is important in the context of Latin America. This is so because there are two streams clearly identified in the region. One is the Catholic Church, and the other is the Reformed stream, mostly identified by historical, evangelical, and Pentecostal movements operating in the continent. In this presentation we will see how these Christian streams interact with each other and how they consider grace in their theology.

CONSIDERING GRACE IN LATIN AMERICA

With that theological understanding as our foundation, let us now consider the manifestations of God's grace that have been present in Latin America both historically and up to the present day.

Some scholars believe that even as early as the 1600s God's grace was manifested in favor of Latin Americans during the colonization and exploitation of foreign forces.[8] For more than five centuries Latin America was dominated by political forces foreign to the land. The domination was over political, economic, and cultural realities.[9] So God's grace began to be manifested first through the solidarity and compassion of the Catholic friars and then, three centuries later, through the independent movements of every country. Self-determination formed new societies that struggled to survive but gave a new starting point to the people of the continent.

During the colonial times, foreign policies empowered the conquerors to exterminate any resistance from the natives.[10] In many cases the use of force led to the annihilation of the natives. But even in those dark days, God raised Catholic friars who defended the rights of the natives. Keep in mind that at this point in history there were no Protestant missions in Latin America. Incidentally, the first Protestant missionaries did not arrive until the late nineteenth century, some three hundred years after these events took place.[11] What is important here is to remark that even in the midst of violence and inhuman treatment against the natives, God's grace was there. The Dominican order, for instance, took a decisive stand in favor of the natives, defending their rights even to the point of risking their own lives.[12]

These actions took place in several heavily populated locations across Latin America. It was not until the early nineteenth century that most Latin American colonies recovered their independence from foreign political powers.[13] Thus, it is fair to argue that even the declaration of independence was the result of divine providence granted by the grace of God upon the leaders that called for the self-determination of the peoples of Latin America.

Moreover, that struggle for self-determination continued even after the nations had achieved their political independence.[14] Hence, it was during these early days of rebuilding that foreign capital from North America and Europe was invested in the local economies, generating new controlling mechanisms over the sovereignty and the economy of the Latin American nations.

It was at that time that new Christian leaders emerged, bringing new ideas about freedom to the political, social, and economic arena.[15] This was the time when liberating movements arose and proposed a nationalistic approach to those fields mentioned here. In this essay, we will consider freedom to be that gift of God graciously granted to those who long for progress and prosperity. It is part of human nature and has been bestowed upon people so they can live freely and enjoy life in their own society. Such desire for freedom is a sovereign act of grace granted by God to the peoples of Latin America.

GRACE IN THE CATHOLIC
CHURCH OF LATIN AMERICA

The Catholic Church was instrumental in bringing Christianity for the first time to Latin America, although there are clear evidences that the church was used by the conquerors to exercise power and control over the natives. For some this was an unfortunate event that affected negatively the work and ministry of the church. However, at that point in history the Catholic Church was the only source of evangelization for Latin America.[16] As was already mentioned, the first Protestant missionaries did not arrive until the nineteenth century. In fairness to the Catholic Church, it is important to acknowledge that for about three hundred years this was the only Christian movement known in Latin America.

When the Catholic Church first encountered the Protestant movements, this generated a new approach to evangelization, which brought drastic changes to the mission in ministry practices of the Catholic Church during the colonial times.[17] Arguably, most Protestant movements were inspired by the new winds of freedom proposed by the French and the American revolutions.[18] There were liberal ideals that furthered science and philosophy as well as human growth and transformation in the new societies. Unfortunately, the struggle between conservatives, who wanted to preserve the status quo, and the liberals, who proposed a new model of society, continues even to this day.

Traditional Catholic stand

As we have seen, the Catholic Church brought a Christianity of the Middle Ages to Latin America that had not yet been confronted by the Reformation movement. This observation is particularly important because of the religious practices that took place during the time of the colonies.[19] The conquerors practiced domination over the natives, modeled after the conquests that took place during medieval times. The natives were enslaved in their own land,

111

and the conquerors took possession of everything that belonged to the natives.[20] They used inhuman methods of domination and control so severely that soon the friars intervened on behalf of the natives.

Some Dominican friars such as Antonio Montesinos, Pedro de Córdoba, and Bartolomé de las Casas took a stand against slavery and oppression.[21] They advocated for the rights and dignity of the natives. Those friars were concerned for the well-being of the local people.[22] Therefore, for our purposes, these actions are regarded as acts of divine grace on behalf of the people of Latin America.

The stand of liberation theology

Even liberation theology in the 1970s should be considered an act of divine grace, whereby Catholic priests took a stand against poverty and oppression in the region.[23] This seed of liberation may have been planted as early as the sixteenth century by Dominican friars such as Montesinos, de Córdoba, and de las Casas, who took a stand to protect the natives from the atrocities of the conquerors in the Caribbean, Mexico, and Central America.

More than a spiritual movement, liberation theology was a social and political action that was born from the commitment of Catholic priests and lay leaders who took a prophetic stand against social and political injustice across the continent. From the pulpits of their parishes they were able to raise consciousness against financial exploitation, human oppression, social injustice, and political domination.[24] Gustavo Gutiérrez continues to insist that the poor are human beings with a dignity that must be recognized. In a recent interview he said:

> We referred to the poor as non-persons, but not in philosophical sense, because it is obvious that each human being is a person, rather in a sociological sense; the poor, that is, are not accepted as persons in our society. They are invisible and have not rights, their dignity is not recognized.[25]

GRACE IN THE EVANGELICAL WORLD
OF LATIN AMERICA

The arrival of the evangelical churches in Latin America could also be considered an act of the grace of God. Their first arrivals happened at the end of the nineteenth century. Those early expeditions, mostly from North America and Western Europe, established their bases on Latin American soil supported by the ideals of the French and American revolutions. Evangelicals were concerned about the evangelization of the continent. At the beginning they experienced certain animosity from the Roman Catholic communities, but they were able to establish their ministries mostly among the poor.

Evangelical missions

Early in the twentieth century, evangelical missions became the first manifestations of spiritual grace in favor of the people of Latin America. Not only did they plant churches, but they also established elementary schools, hospitals, and homes for children and the elderly.[26] Evangelicals were committed to nurture the spiritual and the physical nature of their adherents.

Integral mission and grace

One of the most outstanding contributions of the evangelical movement was the induction of the theology of integral mission into the Latin American church and beyond. Samuel Escobar, C. Rene Padilla, and other evangelical leaders were able to introduce this new theology of mission that proposed a holistic approach to evangelism in Latin America.[27]

Integral mission is also known as transformational development, Christian development, or holistic mission. The Spanish term *misión integral* was coined in the 1970s by members of the Fraternidad Teológica Latinoamericana (Latin American Theological Fellowship). It describes Christian mission as the proclamation and demonstration of the gospel. Samuel Escobar, for instance, uses integral mission to affirm the importance of expressing the love of God through every means possible.[28] Proponents of integral mission emphasize Christian mission by using the word *integral* to propose a mission that embraces both evangelism and social involvement in the practice of the gospel.

The proponents of integral mission argue that the concept is rooted in Scripture and clearly exemplified in the ministry of Jesus. For some, like Chris Sugden, integral mission is synonymous with holistic mission.[29] In essence, integral mission stands against the traditional dualistic approach to evangelism or social responsibility.

In Latin America, a commitment to integral mission is reflected through intentional concern for the poor and the pursuit of justice. The concept of integral mission is largely advocated by the evangelical movement. However, in most recent years, Pentecostal scholars have studied it with significant interest, which may broaden the scope of integral mission among the Pentecostal movements.

Contrary to liberation theology, which embraces social and political action against the sociopolitical structures of domination and oppression, motivated by religious principles of social justice, integral mission embraces both the proclamation of the gospel and solidarity with the poor as modeled by Jesus Christ, who is the giver of the good news to all people. Integral mission reaches the spiritual and physical needs of the person and his or her environment in a holistic way. Therefore, integral mission has become another act of divine grace given to Latin America by way of evangelical scholarship.

GRACE IN THE PENTECOSTAL MOVEMENTS OF LATIN AMERICA

In Latin America, Pentecostalism became a movement of the poor. In Pentecostal congregations the poor found hope and support, which led them to overcome not only their spiritual struggles but also their social and economic limitations.

With its approach to the poor and marginalized, the Pentecostal message found fertile ground in the region. At some point, Pentecostals were able to capitalize on what was earlier initiated by the evangelical movements in the area.[30] According to Calixto Salvatierra Moreno:

> The twentieth century witnessed the rise and development of Pentecostalism. This religious movement generated the formation of new expressions of religion worldwide, which had sociological, anthropological and spiritual influence on contemporary societies. Pentecostalism innovated and created various ways to express the religious beliefs that affected significantly the culture and spiritual ethos of humanity in Latin America.[31]

The Pentecostal lifestyle brought explosive numerical growth in most depressed and marginalized areas of large cities. Pentecostalism made the message of the gospel relevant to the poor, the sick, the depressed, and the weak. The message was simple yet powerful enough to convince people about the relevance of the gospel. The implementation of the supernatural was observed in most congregations. Pentecostalism became instrumental in finding a solution to civil war, natural disasters, disease, and the need for spiritual deliverance.

Pentecostals in Latin America speak of grace as the intervention of God on behalf of the poor. In the power of the Holy Spirit, the persecuted may obtain deliverance from their enemies and find a solution to any source of affliction or adversity.[32] For Pentecostals, living in the Spirit denotes spiritual enablement, daily guidance, forgiveness, and protection in the midst of trouble.

Pentecostals also emphasize the importance of simplicity. For them, living in community and sharing their lives with other people is the testimony of the grace of God actively operating in the congregation.

This kind of Christianity shook the religious establishment that already existed in the area. Churches and Christian leaders had never seen this church model before. Naturally, the first reaction was to oppose it. The Pentecostal worship style made them nervous. The impartation of spiritual gifts among the congregants was completely different to the order in the church they had experienced before.

Eventually, Pentecostal worship and ministration permeated most evangelical, Protestant, and Catholic churches. Thus, this influence could also be interpreted as an act of the grace of God to revitalize the church in Latin America. Through the imprints of Pentecostalism, churches have become more dynamic in evangelism, social action, and development of the laity in ministry.

GRACE IN THE CHARISMATIC MOVEMENT OF LATIN AMERICA

In the 1960s, a new wave of spiritual revival reached Latin America. Lutheran minister Harald Bredesen[33] called this new awakening a Charismatic movement. The Charismatic movement may also be identified as an act of grace that reached out to the Catholic middle class of Latin America that otherwise would have remained alienated from the gospel.

Charismatics rallied businessmen and professional women to meet the gospel of Jesus Christ. Incidentally, most political leaders of future generations were led to Christ through Charismatic gatherings.[34] Young professionals were also affected by the Charismatic message of that time.

This message also made Pentecostals nervous. The difference between these two movements was that Pentecostals ministered to the poor and Charismatics ministered to the middle class and the leadership of the countries. It was not until recent years that both movements have been able to dialogue and accept each other's role in the evangelization of Latin America.

It seems that over the course of time, spiritual revivals tend to reach a plateau. Leaders become comfortable, self-gratifying, and satisfied with their ministry. As a result, their passion for evangelism weakens and the thrust for expansion loses momentum.[35] That is the time when the Holy Spirit begins to work new revivals among His people. This awakening is an act of divine grace.

GRACE IN THE NEO-PENTECOSTAL MOVEMENT OF LATIN AMERICA

Evidently the Lord foresaw the difficulties of the coming days among the different societies of Latin America. The second half of the twentieth century witnessed times of war, political unrest, extreme poverty, corruption, and different sources of violence. Thus, through the neo-Pentecostal movement that emerged, it seemed the Holy Spirit was preparing the church to face all of these adversities with the proper attitude and the efficiency of God's people. This was an act of grace to revitalize the movement of the Spirit.

According to Bernardo Campos, Pentecostals and Charismatics had become comfortable and institutionalized, so a new wave of spiritual revival was ignited by the Holy Spirit in order to revitalize the church and start new movements in the area.[36] The time that was coming was critical for the church, and the Lord wanted to prepare for such.

HAS HYPER-GRACE ARRIVED IN LATIN AMERICA?

There is no clear evidence that the hyper-grace movement has openly entered Latin America. Some leading pastors of megachurches may have aligned themselves to this kind of thinking, with their preaching styles and the order of ideas reflected in the message.[37] However, out of the eight signs of a hyper-grace church proposed by Joseph Mattera,[38] it is possible to find certain tendencies pointing in that direction. For instance, some pastors have no clear intention to preach against sin and they allow people living immoral lives into ministry. Also, some leading pastors speak against the so-called institutional church.

Although there is no leader or entity already identified with the hyper-grace stream in Latin America, some leading pastors in the Apostolic and Prophetic Movement in Latin America concur with the presentation of the gospel as modeled by hyper-grace teachers.[39] For instance, some Latino pastors affirm that when God looks at us, He sees only a holy and righteous people. They conclude that we are not bound by Jesus's teaching, even as we are not under the law; that believers are not responsible for their sin; and that anyone who disagrees is a pharisaical legalist. They also maintain that all sin—past, present, and future—has already been forgiven, so there is no need for a believer to ever confess it.[40]

We have yet to see what will happen in the near future, but as of right now, hyper-grace does not seem to be a problematic issue in Latin America.

GRACE AND SOCIAL CONCERN IN LATIN AMERICA

As we have seen, integral mission was studied and implemented at the influence of the evangelical movement and later adopted by the Pentecostal churches of Latin America, thus generating fresh ideas for the advancement of social and political justice on behalf of the poor.[41]

In 1970, the Fraternidad Teológica Latinoamericana (FTL) was created. This fellowship was instrumental in raising consciousness in favor of a holistic approach to the gospel. FTL also initiated the Congreso Latinoamericano de Evangelización—CLADE (Latin American Congress on Evangelization). These movements were able to join other initiatives that were taking place in other Christian organizations in different sites of the continent. As a result, a new model of evangelism emerged, and an explosive expansion of the church happened in the region. This time evangelicals, Pentecostals, Charismatics, Catholics, and all the Christian movements had peace and justice in mind for the presentation of the gospel.

Grace in human rights

Most Christian movements are now involved in the promotion of human growth and transformation. This effort has not been easy due to the diversity of the body of Christ. Because of that, multiple efforts took place.

Liberation theology, from its Catholic point of view,[42] and integral mission, from its evangelical perspective,[43] helped Christians across Latin America confront social evils and injustice with theological, biblical, and spiritual authority.[44] There were many mistakes made and unfortunate circumstances during the process of evangelization, but Christians were able to preach the good news and reach out to the poor.

When civil wars took place in Cuba, Central America, and South America, many people suffered violence, expatriation, extreme poverty, and even death.[45] There were also natural disasters that hurt many Latin American nations. Some may argue that the church failed to meet these disasters properly. This could be the case of isolated situations, but in general, Christians were prepared for adversity and were able to respond according to the principles of the gospel. Therefore, the credibility of the churches drew people in need into the congregations. Typically, after a natural disaster, large crowds would gather in the churches, so these had to enlarge their facilities to welcome all kinds of people.

Grace, peace, and justice

Although there are still challenging high levels of injustice, Christians in Latin America are making every possible effort to influence transformation in their communities. They know that this can be possible through the implementation of the principles of the gospel.

In recent years, violence has claimed thousands of lives. Many young people have died or been mistreated at the hands of the gangs and drug trafficking.[46] Insecurity causes people to migrate to safer places. Weak economies cause the search for better options in other areas of the world. Political instability has forced people to flee for safety. Administrative corruption has driven people against political authority. All of these social evils hurt society and raise a legitimate demand for social justice and peace that can only happen when civil authority is held accountable under civil law.

As Christianity grows in Latin America, a new generation of leaders has begun to lead the church. They are aware of the challenges ahead of them. Therefore, in order to respond to the social needs of the countries, they are preparing solid discipleship programs with the principles of the gospel to prepare the church for the future. They also know transformation will eventually happen over the course of time. They will have to strategically invest in younger generations.[47] True peace and justice will occur under the lordship of Christ in the new societies.

ALL ARE PENTECOSTALS

We have seen a historical approach to the manifestation of God's grace in Latin America. Christian leaders of this region seem to understand there is more work to be done by the church in order to reach true transformation in society. They realize that the initiative of grace comes from God Himself. He loves the Latin American people and wants all of them to experience redemption through Christ. Many people have responded to God's offer, yet the work of redemption and transformation remains unfinished.

Fortunately, the implementation of the grace of God among the Latin American people continues to expand. God's gift of grace faces opposition from the forces of evil that have been in positions of authority and in control of the economy. Nonetheless, God's people continue to take a stand against all of them in the power of the Holy Spirit, which makes that grace relevant to communities. At this point, I think that the key to success in this endeavor is to endure hardship, be patient, and trust God and His grace on behalf of the people He so loves in Latin America.

One cannot refer to the Pentecostal tradition of grace without considering the roots of Pentecost in the Latin American church. Although the subject of this essay is grace, some elements of history may reveal some indicators of the operation of grace in the region.

As a matter of fact, Peruvian scholar Bernardo Campos has coined the term *pentecostalidad* [pentecostality], which he defines as "the universal experience that expresses the occurrence of Pentecost"[48] in the body of Christ. Campos argues that this pentecostality of the church must be understood as "a pluralist and diverse action of the Spirit."[49] Pentecostality is the strength of the Spirit that enables the church to operate as a body and to engage *missio dei* as modeled by Christ.

In principle, pentecostality becomes the act of grace that surpasses any historical Pentecostal event that would claim to be the only model of Pentecost, denying others the uniqueness of their own Pentecostal experience.[50] According to Campos, the pentecostality of the church refers to the mission of all believers, who, after being filled with the Holy Spirit, by God's grace, operate in the world, showing the marks of the incarnate Christ who holistically redeems human beings and their world.

The work of Campos is significant because it makes pentecostality the common experience of all believers throughout history. Every person who follows Christ Jesus and obeys His commands can show the marks of Pentecost in private and in public service. That pentecostality is an act of grace granted to the church that can be seen in its nature and mission.

Since the Holy Spirit is the initiator of Pentecost, then all who are led to Christ by the Spirit are Pentecostals. This notion of pentecostality deconstructs the classic Pentecostal exclusivity of the reception and implementation of the gifts of the Spirit. Therefore, all Christians are potentially Pentecostals because all are brought by and follow the same Spirit, who is the initiator of the Pentecostal experience. This insight should foster cooperation and stimulate works of grace among Christians as they engage *missio dei*.

Miguel Álvarez, PhD, is a missionary from Honduras. He is associate representative of CBN's *Superbook* and adjunct professor of theology and mission at Regent University in Virginia Beach, Virginia. He also serves as Director of Hispanic Ministries for the Church of God in Virginia.

Chapter 10

STILL AND STILL MOVING: GRACE IN THE ANGLICAN TRADITION

Andy Lord

G RACE IS A way of describing the way the love of God is embodied in Jesus, the One "full of grace and truth" (John 1:14, NIV). This is both a deeply theological way of describing the nature of God and a practical way of exploring how this nature is lived out in the world. Grace is both diverse and yet always personal.

Furthermore, living traditions, such as that of the Anglican tradition, draw people together from diverse backgrounds into communities that share some common experience and understanding of grace. They are hard to define with complete clarity yet form a helpful way of considering shared ways of living in grace.

Simon Barrington-Ward, an Anglican mission leader, bishop, and writer on spirituality, finds a way into these experiences related to grace, particularly as they concern questions of mission and spirituality commonly raised in contemporary Western contexts. I suggest that Barrington-Ward articulates an Anglican understanding of grace that is rooted in our need to be "still and still moving," as the Anglican convert T. S. Eliot put it.[1]

A DISTINCT TRADITION

Anglicanism finds its roots in Reformation England, though it has now spread across the world, largely due to missionary efforts. There are many strands to Anglicanism, and it has been suggested that Anglicanism is marked by an internal pluralism alongside a commitment to be located in particular cultures.[2] Historically, the strands usually labeled Catholic and Reformed are considered most significant within the Church of England's branch of Anglicanism, which sees itself as both Catholic *and* Reformed.[3] This is a reflection of its original development in contrast to both Roman Catholicism and nonconformism.

The diverse makeup of Anglicanism means it is not easy to articulate a distinctly Anglican theology, although it is assumed to exist. Rowan Williams, the former archbishop of Canterbury, suggests that to discern such a theology, what is needed is a "passionate patience" that takes account of the different historical strands through a patient reading of differing understandings.[4] He stresses the Reformed nature of Anglicanism that is yet shaped by Catholic realities.

Yet Anglicanism is more than simply an approach to theology. Williams describes the tradition as a way of inhabiting Christian orthodoxy.[5] This fits the wider understanding of Anglicanism as a tradition that finds its shape in Christian life more than doctrinal structures. Doctrine is important within the "sense of what a human life looks like when it is in the process of being transformed by God in Christ."[6] In this, Anglicans "show in their lives the grace and the glory of God."[7] This is not grace simply in terms of understanding or external objects or structures but rather God's grace at work in shaping lives—the hidden working of God made visible in life.[8]

Anglicanism is particularly suitable for the study of grace inasmuch as its identity is tied to the ways God's grace is at work in human life. It also draws together the Catholic and Reformed traditions in a way that illustrates how seemingly different approaches might enrich one another.

Yet we cannot remain abstract in this. The nature of grace requires us to seek a personal study. Many Anglicans are suitable for such a study. Historically, John Wesley looms large in this regard, and Ken Collins's recent study of Wesley's theology brings to the fore the themes of holiness and grace. In terms of grace, Wesley is seen to combine a Protestant emphasis on "free grace" that is the work of God alone with the Catholic emphasis on "cooperant grace," in which there is a process of divine-human cooperation. This gives equal weight to God's sovereign and instantaneous bestowal of grace as a favor received by believers with the need for empowered human cooperation with God over time in response to God's initiative.[9]

However, in this chapter we will look at a more contemporary example. Simon Barrington-Ward's work reflects this same twofold approach to grace within a framework shaped by his long involvement in world mission and his desire to encourage spirituality. He was also significantly impacted by the Charismatic Renewal and African revival movements, which provide important contributions alongside the Reformed and Catholic traditions.

In this chapter, therefore, we will explore Barrington-Ward's understanding of grace against the background of his life and ministry. This will provide a fresh perspective on contemporary debates related to grace. Though we will not begin by naming a specific definition of grace, in order to allow engagement with how Barrington-Ward uses the term, it needs to be noted that themes of grace, love, and the Holy Spirit are often used interchangeably in Barrington-Ward's writings while relating to the person of Jesus Christ in different ways. So we will be on the lookout for the ways in which Barrington-Ward considers the grace or love of God that is often embodied through the work of the Holy Spirit to draw people to Jesus to be transformed.

ENTERING THE STILLNESS OF GRACE

Barrington-Ward was born in London, entered national service during World War II, and then studied at Cambridge. In the 1950s he went to Berlin and met with a radical group of Lutheran Christians before returning to England to train for Anglican ministry. After working as a chaplain, he taught in Nigeria, where he encountered a revival movement. Upon returning to Cambridge, he encountered the Charismatic movement and was filled afresh with the Holy Spirit when David du Plessis prayed for him.

He moved to oversee the Church Mission Society training center with a vision for agape revival. During the 1980s and '90s he served as the bishop of Coventry before retiring once more to Cambridge. In his later years he became a regular retreat leader of the Jesus Prayer, which has roots in the Orthodox tradition.

Barrington-Ward's life contains both the settled focus on ministry within the Anglican Church and also a global movement that embraced different traditions in mission. His is a life that has been both "still and still moving" within God's grace. This twofold pattern reflects something of the Anglican history noted above and is described by Barrington-Ward through the Orthodox theme of exchange.[10] He speaks of three kinds of exchange, the first two relating to two aspects of grace we will consider here and the third relating to how those two aspects might be integrated in life.

The first exchange relates to personal salvation and justification as individuals call out to God for His mercy. This is the call of the tax collector in Luke 18 who humbly relies on the mercy of God and whose "appeal for an atoning grace is most certainly met fully in the cross."[11] This is understood, for Barrington-Ward, through 2 Corinthians 5:21, which is seen as the heart of Christian life:

It is saying that in the man Jesus Christ, God entered, as nowhere else, into the depths of our human tragedy, our utter frustration, and brokenness. In Jesus Christ also, we could enter into our true destiny, our freedom, our fulfilment, our ultimate joy, our final transformation, beyond death, to be made part of the new creation to come. This is "*der süsse Austausch,*" the "*sweet exchange.*"[12]

Here we have an objective appreciation of the cross that is never separate from the subjective implications for those of faith. In other words, grace is both atoning and transforming as we come in faith, in stillness, before Jesus at the cross. This is an inherently participative approach, in line with those that have become more common in recent theology.[13]

Such an encounter with God is deeply personal and attractive to people seeking a personal God. Barrington-Ward sees

a pressure gradually building up, in scattered places, here concentrated, there diffused, fragmentary, ambiguous and yet taken as a whole I believe unmistakable, towards the person of the crucified and risen Christ, the personal God. There is a universal search for One who is truly personal.[14]

There is a "flow of the Spirit" through which the grace of God is drawing people to Jesus that they may be transformed by a personal encounter. Barrington-Ward sees this happening in places of crisis and pain and of pressure and difficulty. It happens beyond the church, which is often seen as an obstacle rather than a help.[15]

Barrington-Ward is more likely to share stories of such grace than to provide nuanced theological reflections on it, and such stories fill his writings. Personal grace is discovered in the complex lives of those who travel the journey to faith in Jesus, the crucified and risen One. Such people often experience the "joy of the first apprehension of grace" that comes from this meeting with Jesus.[16] Over time this needs to work into the personal mix of life so that grace touches the whole person.

This is a very personal grace, yet because it is personal it "is never merely individual."[17] To be a person is to be in relationship with others. Thus, an encounter with God's grace will draw people into community, particularly small groups that gather around the crucified and risen Jesus. This is what inspired Barrington-Ward's faith in Berlin after the war and continued to guide him afterward, when he says he discovered "an atmosphere of what I can only describe as 'forgiven-ness'…a deep mutual acceptance and openness to each other, and an even deeper sense of the presence of God. A divine spirit seemed here to be at work within us and amongst us."[18] Such communities make up the church, which is

> becoming in modest, minor, broken ways something of a paradigm, a model, a showpiece of what grace can bring about—a fellowship of the *unlike* able "to speak to the world of the possibility of genuine reconciliation and justice" because its members have begun to realise in their own life together the radical implications of God's reconciliation.[19]

Christian communities touched by grace draw people from many backgrounds, whether from East and West Berlin or from the differing tribes in Nigeria, which Barrington-Ward saw drawn together in a "new society" that showed a taste of heaven on earth.[20] Despite such differences, these communities are formed alike by grace in the way of Jesus Christ. There is a kind of "family likeness" that is about "that lovely balance, the equipoise of grace" that comes through the "energy of the Spirit."[21] Lives touched by grace in community illustrate a "juxtaposition of opposed qualities miraculously fused," a meeting point of universal and particular, distance and nearness, strength and vulnerability, justice and compassion, realism and idealism, material and spiritual.[22]

Church communities thus grasp Jesus as a corporate reality in ways that remain dependent upon grace.[23] Barrington-Ward was well aware that the Anglican Church, of which he was a part, was a mixed bag: "It is a vessel containing a strange fusion of what is richly good and nourishing combined with what is alas sinful and has a bitter aftertaste."[24] Only standing in grace can we see Christian communities growing in ways that nourish and show Christ.

Thus, for Barrington-Ward, we always come to "be still and know...[to] stand still, and see the salvation of the Lord."[25] We come silent and still before the cross and so encounter the grace of God by the Holy Spirit that brings forgiveness and draws us into community.

As should already be clear, this standing still in grace does not mean we remain the same. Rather, to stand in grace is to be transformed into the likeness of Christ so that we reflect more of God's grace in the totality of who we are. This is a "transfiguration in an extraordinary mingling of suffering and joy" that life in an imperfect world brings.[26]

Barrington-Ward encourages people to seek such places of stillness where we can stand and remain in the gracious presence of God. These places bring to the surface repressed negative "passions" that are then brought into the "healing fire of the Holy Spirit—grace itself, warming and illuminating the soul, stopping sinful thoughts and filling our fleshly being with light."[27] Standing in grace thus brings with it an overflow of forgiveness that transforms us to live with God and so become more Christlike through the work of the Holy Spirit (cf. 2 Cor. 3:18). Grace brings us to places of wonderful, overflowing affirmation, forgiveness, peace, and love. These are uncomfortable places that will change us if we choose, in faith, to remain there.

MOVING IN GRACE

It is inevitable, for Barrington-Ward, that as we are grasped by love, so we must move outward in mission; hence the title of his collected writings on mission, *Love Will Out*. Mission flows irrepressibly from grace and must be undertaken in the way of grace.

This is a resurrection movement expressed by Barrington-Ward to be a second form of exchange: that we enter into the death of the Son of God and so enter into His risen life. The stress on the risen life is seen as a movement of the Holy Spirit outward. This is an eschatological vision in which we "are being drawn into a journey *with* Christ towards the goal to which, through the Spirit, he is leading us all—into the new creation, the new life to come, and eternal presence through him, by the Spirit's power, in the triune God."[28]

The second exchange takes the personal and communal aspects of the first exchange and places them within the wider movement of God in the whole creation. For it is "as we become more and more aware of being loved and accepted, we find ourselves being drawn into the whole joy of creation and of the ultimate fulfilment of the creation."[29] We are longing for "that day when the kingdoms of this world are transformed at last into the kingdom of our God and his Christ."[30] The classic biblical passage here is Romans 8, which speaks of the work of the Holy Spirit between the "now" and the "not yet," where we experience both a taste of the joy to come and the struggles of the present. This is another "equipoise of grace" as love, suffering, and yearning come together in our experience of the Spirit.[31]

This movement of grace connects our personal story with God's purposes for the whole of the world and through history. At this point we might be tempted toward grand visions of God's plans for creation, as illustrated by the great evangelical and Pentecostal plans for world mission. Yet Barrington-Ward is ever aware of the need for grace in our approach. We need to ensure God's great purposes are not sought through means that use power unwisely or exclude others. Thus, he speaks imaginatively of

> a whole widespread movement of the Spirit flowing gradually through and beyond the Church of our time in so many areas of the world. It is a gently pervasive patterning of light and

shadow, of sound and quiet, throwing out its reflection on its surroundings. Suddenly you realise that it is there, changing the whole character of the scene like the swelling of flood-waters that make their appearance unobtrusively in the night and come with the morning.[32]

It must be remembered that this is offered within the context of Barrington-Ward's positive encounters with revivalist and Charismatic movements and so does not discount more dramatic workings of the Spirit. Rather, he seeks to sensitively integrate grace and power within approaches to Christian mission. Small, gentle touches of new creation become evident as God moves by the Spirit.[33] This view sees both mission and prayer as "participation in a central purpose, a sharing in a movement of love working through history."[34] This is a kind of "spirituality for mission" that combines the stillness of contemplative grace with the movement of intercessory grace.[35]

Moving in this kind of grace leads to testimony—shared stories of how grace transforms the lives of ordinary people. Evangelism is then seen as a "spontaneous communication" of a gracious way of living and praying that brings new Christian communities into being.[36] Missionaries carry with them the gospel seed that is then planted in new lives and cultures, giving rise to "new apprehensions of the Gospel arising from within the heart of changing religions and culture, fresh visions of 'God with us' in person, in Jesus Christ."[37]

This is a holistic, grace-and-life-based approach to translating the gospel.[38] The gospel must always be embodied rather than presented as a formula to be rigidly applied to others. There is always a positive level of "dissent" as a result of engagement with the gospel: the gracious gospel as embodied in those who come to Christ stands against the reality of life as it is often lived. Barrington-Ward represents a gracious but culture-critical approach to contextualization that seeks to reflect something of Jesus as "full of grace and truth" (John 1:14, NIV).

As should be evident, Barrington-Ward seeks an approach to mission based on the growth of communities of disciples. He saw this in the 1980s as a "new mode of mission," although it has now become mainstream in missional thinking.[39] Grace at work in individuals draws people together into small communities of disciples that are characterized by "a sensitive responsiveness to the Sender," an inward quality that best fits with a reliance on grace.

This stress on power through weakness and small community differs from some of the subsequent models of discipleship and is rooted in the way the cross and resurrection bring about a resolution to the fundamental problems of life. It also reflects Barrington-Ward's experience of coming to one of his ministry posts with high ideals and finding it very difficult to turn those ideals into reality. During that time, he says they "learned just how small was our capacity for sacrificial loving…we were tested and thrown back more deeply on grace, grace both in our mutual relationships and in being enabled to receive hints, touches, of the coming of God's kingdom."[40] Grace requires a movement in mission, but always one with a sense of weakness and dependence on the initiative of the triune God.

Small Christian communities of grace that move in mission by the Spirit should not move in isolation from one another. Rather, in Christ and at the cross all Christian communities are brought together. So also are all cultures and nationalities in ways that speak of the multiracial nature of the church and also of a wider hope for humanity. Barrington-Ward encouraged the practice of "interchange" in his work with the Church Mission Society, through which gifts were shared between mission communities and churches.[41] These required mutual repentance and forgiveness in order that the gospel might be communicated in a plural world.

Churches should encourage and support international missionary movements and mission across the differences within their own localities. This was what Barrington-Ward sought as bishop of Coventry within the diocese and through bringing in international mission teams to the diocese.[42] In attempting this, he sought to model something of God's gracious aims for the whole of humanity. Particularly as the world and each locality becomes more of a melting pot of cultures and ethnic groups, so there is a need to see how God is breaking and remaking humanity in the way of Christ.[43] In the discovery of a common humanity appreciated and yet transfigured by Christ through the Spirit, we see something of "God's goal for us of a just, loving, and sustainable society."[44] Ultimately, grace draws Christians together and moves them to participate in the transformation of the whole world.

INTEGRATING GRACE IN LIFE

We have been following Barrington-Ward's thoughts on grace in a way that reflects an Anglican integration of the Catholic and Reformed traditions. I have suggested that this is seen in both the stillness of grace and also the way grace ensures that we are still moving in an eschatological direction through mission. We next ask the natural Anglican question as to how this understanding is embodied in Christian life: What are the means of grace? What patterns of spirituality support this approach?

Barrington-Ward often speaks of Christian faith as a way of being that reflects the way of the cross, a way of brokenness and restoring. This suggests a certain imaginative approach to spirituality that becomes increasingly rooted in the practice of the Jesus Prayer. Barrington-Ward realizes that all of life is best seen within the initiative of God, as grace has greater precedence and reality in life. Thus, he can speak of how through "our very weakness, failure and sadness, our emptiness, the Spirit flows, the light breaks. We will learn to live solely from grace, until 'grace upon grace' surprises us."[45]

Grace is integrated into our lives as our imaginations and

practices are shaped around the way of the cross and resurrection. This is Barrington-Ward's third model of exchange, described as "mutual indwelling" in which there is a deeper integration of God's initiative and human response in all that life brings.

There is a "double rhythm" of life and prayer that finds expression in the practice of the Jesus Prayer. This is a rhythm of tenderness and severity in love, of celebration and suffering, of thanksgiving and pain, of affirming and yearning, of "now" and "not yet," and ultimately of the resurrection and the cross held together in grace.[46] It is an expression of the "breaking and remaking" that Barrington-Ward saw as essential to understanding his life in mission.[47] Mission in a world context brought him into contact with deep suffering and miraculous joy that forced him to struggle for a better way of prayer as an expression of his whole life in Christ.[48]

Barrington-Ward was introduced to the Jesus Prayer in a communal setting at a Russian Orthodox monastery in Essex. The practice is simply this: saying the prayer "Lord Jesus Christ, Son of God, have mercy on me, a sinner," pausing, and then repeating it until we are drawn into the presence of the triune God and experience all of life in that context. The prayer affirms that Jesus is Lord and Christ, the Son of God. Yet it also highlights the yearning for mercy that draws out the groanings and sighs of the world. For Barrington-Ward, it is a Romans 8–shaped prayer in which we enter a "passion of the Holy Spirit."[49] This moves us to intercession and mission as prayer empowers the practical and the personal empowers the social within grace that longs for transformation.

This prayerful, practical, personal, and social spirituality holds together the "still and still moving" movements of grace. Theologically, this is rooted in the doctrine of the incarnation and can at times lead to grace, peace, and even palpable light infusing the body of those praying.[50] This is an experience of both stillness and movement that is often, within the Orthodox tradition that Barrington-Ward draws on, explored in terms of *theosis*, "of being drawn, by the Spirit, into the perfect love of the most intimate union with the Holy Trinity, the triune God!"[51] This is the *hesychist* tradition that stresses both stillness in God and transformation in Christlikeness.[52]

This theosis is the ultimate fulfilment of 2 Corinthians 5:19, which Barrington-Ward emphasizes as the start of Christian life. It happens as the Jesus Prayer leads us into "the way down" that becomes also "the way up."[53] Here the pain and the joy come together somehow, with joy discovered through pain and loss, not by attempting to escape it. This is only possible as the Jesus Prayer enables people to grasp the essence of life as lived within the steady flow of the Holy Spirit. It is "like suddenly finding it possible to step into a boat which has already been moving, or even to dive into a stream which is already flowing in the very direction in which you wanted to go, and then being simply borne along by the current!"[54] This is Orthodox and yet also revivalist and Charismatic: the way of union with God; the way of agape revival; and the way of Holy Spirit transformation.

This approach to spirituality is personal, yet Barrington-Ward emphasizes that the Jesus Prayer can be practiced in community. He stresses that the practices of the wider church can be informed by and inform this practice.[55] Thus the Jesus Prayer is "seen, along with baptism and communion, as a way into union with God in Christ in the Spirit even in this life."[56]

Barrington-Ward concludes an article on the Anglican Church with a story of a Communion service among people of differing faiths and denominations in a country at war, noting how the "central action" of the person presiding "now seemed to affirm the reality of the infinite presence and power of God's love, released in the midst of our striving and pain in the most ordinary human and material form."[57] Here is the same double rhythm that is also linked to the incarnation as it applies to those gathered: "Glancing at the faces round us there was no doubt anywhere that this essential brokenness of the God-man on the cross undergirded and strengthened the hold of all of us upon faith and life and opened up for all a way through meaninglessness and death."[58]

The same is found when he turns to consider the wider vocation of the Anglican Church. At its best, Barrington-Ward sees Anglicanism as able to bring together the differences of culture, theology, and history to form a church in which no one form of Christian faith has long-term power over others. However, given its mixed history, most recently as allied to colonialism, he suggests that perhaps "the real significance of the Anglican church lies in this, that it is, of all denominations, the most obviously provisional, the most apt for death, or indeed, as I must then say, for life through death."[59] This is an integrated way of grace in the Holy Spirit that brings together stillness and movement, breaking and remaking, cross and resurrection, and the "now" and "not yet" as they apply to personal spirituality, community life, sacramental life, and denominational life.

Anglican Grace Amongst Pentecostals

I've chosen to explore the nature of grace as embodied in one Anglican leader whose approach fits with the more general pattern of Anglican theology. Barrington-Ward may seem unusual in his engagement with revivalist, Charismatic, and Orthodox movements alongside his Anglicanism, but it is common for Anglicans to engage beyond their tradition. I want now to consider how this approach to grace might engage with some of the issues and theology in the Pentecostal movement. This is natural, given the Charismatic experience of Barrington-Ward and the centrality of the Holy Spirit to his understanding of grace.

One of the perennial tensions is what I have called the "still and still moving" aspects of grace. Some Christians want to stress how we are to be still before the grace of God so that nothing is by works—that salvation is free and unmerited. For them, grace needs to be defined in terms of *our* inaction (stillness) and *God's* action (movement). For some, this is about resisting the Catholic tendencies that were rejected in the Reformation. This approach recognizes the sinfulness and brokenness that characterizes human life and the wonderful grace of God that comes by the Holy Spirit to us just as we are.

This is wonderful good news, yet it can leave us "still" as we are. In response, Barrington-Ward might say, "Yes, this is grace...but not all that grace involves." As I have framed his understanding, grace is about our stillness before the wonderful grace of God seen in Christ at the cross and experienced through the Holy Spirit, but it is also about a movement toward being more like Christ, an eschatological movement rooted in the cross *and resurrection*. The Spirit of resurrection keeps working to transform us in holiness. Given that Christ was raised to a transformed body by the Spirit, how can we stay the same if the same Spirit is at work in us?

Further, grace is also about being part of a community in which each person shapes the others. Furthermore, grace is a movement of mission in which the glorious hope of stillness and transformation is shared. God's grace is not limited and so cannot be held within any individual but must always spill out into a community and into the wider world; otherwise we are severely limiting grace. Finally, grace requires practices that enable us to receive further grace, practices that are personal, communal, and institutional.

The rich diversity of grace and the holistic working of the Holy Spirit need to be kept, explored, and experienced. Care needs to be taken when articulating this, and Barrington-Ward does not address directly the issue being raised here. Yet neither can his approach be dismissed as simply Catholic or uninterested in the cross. Rather, he is an example of how we might work forward to embrace and live more fully in the grace of the triune God.

The Christian life isn't easy, and we often struggle to experience the overflowing love of God. We can find ourselves frustrated with our lack of progress and personal change. We also see the church failing and wonder whether this is all we can hope for in this life. The church seems to present an ideal but leave people feeling guilty they can't live it. Such struggles often give rise to a question of whether we should stress a grace that moves us onward, as our experience might suggest God's grace hasn't been sufficient to bring the glorious life and church we were promised. Maybe we would be better off being still in grace and leaving any movement and change to God.

Such reasonable motivations perhaps lie behind why some people have joined the so-called hyper-grace movement affecting Pentecostalism today, particularly in the United States. It is a movement that stresses we can "experience the power to live above defeat" as Christians are liberated from the legalism of idealized "dos and don'ts" that leave us preoccupied with our failings.[60] It is a calling to be with Jesus and, through an intimate relationship with Him, find that we are effortlessly transformed, as we have the righteousness of Christ. It is not that such teachings always say there will be no change, but rather that we are still and God moves us to change.

Pentecostal critics of this approach to grace value some of the teachings but are concerned it leads to a lack of discernment, ultimately seeming happy not to confront sin or challenge people to live a Christlike life.[61] They suggest that what is needed is a more holistic biblical approach that doesn't try to force particular texts through the lens of hyper-grace belief.

The issues at stake here resonate with the Anglican approach if stillness were separated from movement. Yet the issue seems quite distant for many Anglicans, for whom holistic, rather than separated, approaches are more representative of the tradition. It would seem strange for Barrington-Ward to separate stillness from movement and not to consider how they might be integrated in practice in different ways.

Perhaps the Anglican approach can provide a constructive and world-embracing approach to grace. This is not to say evangelical Anglicans have not struggled with similar tensions. Indeed, they can be traced back to Paul's letter to the Romans, where his presentation of grace led some believers to go as far as to ask, "Shall we go on sinning so that grace may increase?" (Rom. 6:1, NIV). Paul's response is firm: "By no means! We are those who have died to sin; how can we live in it any longer?" (v. 2, NIV). During the 1980s the tension between faith and works led Anglican evangelicals to clarify their relationship in the Christian life.[62] Generally, they found ways to hold both together in encouraging discipleship: a disciplined approach to living in grace.[63]

The Anglican way explored above resonates less with the issues of hyper-grace than it does with Pentecostals seeking to understand grace in wider terms. In this regard, the work of Amos Yong is significant, alongside that of the Godly Love project.[64] This project is a multidisciplinary study of the way in which those who encounter godly love are moved to benevolent action on behalf of others. Rooted in a particular sociological approach, it suggests that for many their "deep, ongoing experiences of God's unconditional love" lead them to "serve the poor" in their community, encourage renewal/revival, and seek social justice.[65]

For Pentecostals, this can be a rediscovery of the great impact God's grace has had through their history in ways that have been forgotten. Yong retrieves from the historical tradition the reality that baptism in the Spirit has always been a baptism in love that empowers holiness, reconciles people from different races, and motivates them to pacifism. This is another way of expressing the stillness of grace that leads to a movement of action.

In ways that echo Barrington-Ward, Yong speaks of a "cosmology of love" evident in Romans 8 in which the Spirit works transformatively in all.[66] Here he gives more theological and biblical depth to the thinking of Barrington-Ward, although without the same level of mission and prayer engagement. This work is suggestive of ways forward that might bring a deeper Pentecostal-Anglican engagement and provide a different way into significant issues that arise in understanding God's grace at work.

REV. ANDY LORD, PhD, is an Anglican priest serving in the Diocese of Southwell and Nottingham in the UK. He has a doctorate in Pentecostal Ecclesiology from the University of Birmingham and is the author of *Transforming Renewal, Network Church*, and *Spirit-Shaped Mission*.

Chapter 11

LAW AND GRACE AS PARTNERS: AN EXAMINATION OF REFORMED THEOLOGY

Mark Jumper

J OHN CALVIN IS considered the founder of the Reformed theological tradition in that his landmark book, *Institutes of the
Christian Religion*,[1] codified that way of knowing and thinking.
However, Calvin would be the first to state his theology was not
new—that it was founded, more truly than other theologies, not
only on biblical truth but on the best, most reliable theologies of
the ancient church.[2]

Calvin's thought often depended explicitly on Augustine. In
fact, many consider his thought to be a continuation and fulfillment of Augustinian theology:

> It has been said [by B. B. Warfield] that the "the Reformation,
> inwardly considered, was just the ultimate triumph of
> Augustine's doctrine of grace over Augustine's doctrine
> of the church." The measure of dependence of Luther and
> Calvin upon Augustine cannot easily be stated, but cer-
> tainly both Reformers were frank to recognize their debt to
> him...Calvin may be said to stand at the culmination of the

later Augustinianism. He actually incorporates in his treatment of man and of salvation so many typical passages from Augustine that his doctrine seems here entirely continuous with that of his great African predecessor.[3]

Calvin even concluded his preface to the *Institutes* with a quote from Augustine: "I count myself one of the number of those who write as they learn and learn as they write."[4]

Calvin's conscious debt to the ancient church included his design of the *Institutes* to follow the organizing outline of the Apostles' Creed, the Ten Commandments, and the Lord's Prayer. He held the church to be the highest expression of God's kingdom and Christian grace. Speaking of the church, he said, "But the purpose is for us to know that, even though the devil moves every stone to destroy Christ's grace, and though God's enemies also rage with the same savage fury, it [Christ's grace] cannot be extinguished."[5]

GRACE FROM THE BEGINNING

So, how is grace understood in Reformed theology?

To begin, grace was at the crux of the Protestant Reformation, beginning with Luther's struggle to return the church's theology of grace to its rightful scriptural preeminence. *Sola gratia*, meaning "by grace alone," was one of the Five Solas of Reformation thought and teaching. It meant that absolutely nothing—particularly works—could be or should be added to grace as a condition of salvation by God.

Augustine had stated in *The City of God*:

> Now, therefore, let us walk in hope, and let us by the spirit mortify the deeds of the flesh, and so make progress from day to day. For "the Lord knoweth them that are His;"...but by grace, not by nature. For there is but one Son of God by nature, who in His compassion became Son of man for our sakes, that we, by nature sons of men, might by grace become through Him sons of God.[6]

It is fascinating to observe Augustine's juxtaposition of the Spirit-enabled work of mortifying the deeds of the flesh with the insistence that this work depends on grace, not nature. He founded this idea on the incarnational dual nature of Christ, who by grace makes us in our nature like Him. In other words, for Augustine, grace and works are colleagues, not competitors; they are friends, not enemies; they are familiar with each other, not estranged from each other; they work in mutuality, not independence.

But the Reformers' view of grace went to the foundation of Scripture itself. It may be said that God's creation of the world and then presentation of it to man to act as steward (Gen. 1:28) was an act of grace founded on love. Perhaps the greatest gift of God's grace was breathing His very own breath of life into man's nostrils, creating man in His—God's—very own image. God's further gifts of grace to man included the elements of land, sea, and the heavens; the flora, fauna, crops, and creatures, which brought both beauty and sustenance; the gift of work, in which man tended creation in active partnership with its operations; and the crowning gift of grace, male and female designed to complete each other.

Again we see that gifts of grace were intimately involved with works. The breath of life is a gift, but man must then breathe, sometimes to the point of panting—a work! Creation was a gift, yet people had to keep it properly. Food was a gift, but people had to seek it and gather it. Having relationships with animals, starting with naming them, was a gift, but people had to actively manage them. Work itself was a gift, as it gave man an intimate relationship with the sustenance that came from the hand of God. Even when man sinned, gifts of grace included protective clothing, the promise of a Seed who would bruise the serpent's head, and forbearance of the death penalty for the murderer Cain and a mark that protected him from human vengeance.

Calvin noted that God's grace includes restraints and boundaries on human behavior, even among those not saved.[7] Surely the example of the flaming sword at Eden's entrance (Gen. 3:24), preventing Adam's and Eve's reentry and thus saving them from expanding their sin by living forever from the fruit of the tree of life, exemplified the grace of a God who protects people by restraining them from even worse than they had devised.

Further examples of the human tendency to "break through" God's protective boundaries of grace may be seen at Babel, in Noah's time, and at Sinai:

> And the LORD said to Moses, "Go down and warn the people, lest they break through to the LORD to look and many of them perish. Also let the priests who come near to the LORD consecrate themselves, lest the LORD break out against them." And Moses said to the LORD, "The people cannot come up to Mount Sinai, for you yourself warned us, saying, 'Set limits around the mountain and consecrate it.'" And the LORD said to him, "Go down, and come up bringing Aaron with you. But do not let the priests and the people break through to come up to the LORD, lest he break out against them."
> —EXODUS 19:21–24, ESV

At this very time, when God's people would receive the blessing of God's law, it was doubly important that they observed God's protective boundaries for their own good.

Such a "breaking through" did indeed infamously occur later, though, when the people intermingled with the Midianites. It took radical action by Phinehas, spearing a couple in their chamber, to stop the perversity and the plague from God that killed thousands as a consequence of it (Num. 25:1–15). We will see later how this episode prefigures the antinomian tendencies in our own time and how conformity to God's laws can act as preventive grace, saving people from many troubles.

Humanity had therefore abundantly experienced God's grace from creation's start. That grace had always been partnered with activity, or with work. Even as humans fell into sin, God gave great grace by protecting them in several ways from sin's full fury.

We have seen thus far, then, that in Reformed theology, grace is often experienced through means. "Means of grace" include tangible ways God speaks to us and works with us. They include everything from the secret inner working of the Spirit to tangible tokens of God's presence, such as in the sacraments of baptism and the Lord's Supper. If grace is experienced by means, should it not also be expressed by means?

We have also seen the unity of the law and gospel, of works and grace. Grace and gospel have pride of first place, but they cannot properly operate without the presence of works and law. We have seen the continuity of God's grace from earliest times. Additionally, we need to remember that radical grace is necessary to overcome human sin, which human action can never even come close to addressing, let alone solving. Also, the proper response to grace is action that leads to dynamic holiness, good works, and mission. And lastly, Calvin often emphasized the rule of moderation[8] that does not take things too far, does not treat others too severely, and does not take one's self too seriously. That in itself may be admired as . . . graceful.

WORKS FLOW FROM GRACE

It was God's answer to sin that would fully demonstrate the primacy of His grace and the junior partnership of works. In other words, works partner with grace but cannot replace grace as God's first initiative. Any attempt to replace God's initiative of grace with our own initiative of works constitutes idolatry, if not blasphemy. God initiates with grace; humans respond, after grace, with works. These works spring from gratitude, but they also occur in partnership with God's works: "But Jesus answered them, 'My Father is working until now, and I am working'" (John 5:17, ESV).

How does God work His grace in our salvation from our fallen state? And how does this grace work in us, once we are saved? This is a major emphasis in Calvin's *Institutes*, taking up the entire third book, of four books total, and encompassing almost five hundred pages. The topic is fully examined from many angles.

Calvin begins his writings on grace with the Holy Spirit. For Calvin, salvation must begin with the secret work of the Spirit in a person's heart and life. Indeed, it is impossible for anyone to come to Christ without that work of the Spirit, drawing the person to Christ, as Calvin says: "By his secret watering the Spirit makes us fruitful to bring forth the buds of righteousness."[9] This agrees with John's Gospel, which says it is the Spirit who works faith in a person: "But to all who did receive him, who believed in his name, he gave the right to become children of God, who were born, not of blood nor of the will of the flesh nor of the will of man, but of God" (John 1:12–13, ESV). The grace of salvation is thus applied to a person through faith, which is itself a gift of grace through the Spirit.

So God graciously saves sinners through the Spirit's work. One classic passage describes not only this work of grace through faith but the work of partnership and response God expects as the supernatural result:

> For by grace you have been saved through faith. And this is not your own doing; it is the gift of God, not a result of works, so that no one may boast. For we are his workmanship, created in Christ Jesus for good works, which God prepared beforehand, that we should walk in them.
> —EPHESIANS 2:8–10, ESV

This makes clear the necessary connection between grace and works, first mediated by the inner presence in the person of the Holy Spirit. Those who have been saved have been saved for a purpose: to glorify God through works that build His kingdom on earth, as in heaven.

In further evidence of the partnership of grace and works, it is missed by many that the Ten Commandments were given to a people who had already been saved from slavery. The law was given to those already freed, in order to help them keep their freedom. That law was never meant to be seen as salvation's way. It was given as a gift to those already delivered, showing them how to stay on salvation's way. This eternal law had been glimpsed in prior times, such as the earlier prohibition of murder, but its purpose was never to save. Some see God's law as limiting, when in actuality, as a means of grace, it is freeing.

This principle of law's partnership with grace, right there at Sinai's pinnacle, where so many think that laws of condemnation were given, is so revolutionary and counter to our common thinking that it bears a full hearing from author R. Kent Hughes:

> We must understand that law and grace are not antithetical or the least bit opposed. In point of fact, the Law was *founded* on God's grace. Significantly, the preamble which introduced the Law in Exodus 20:2 was a reminder of God's grace: "I am the Lord your God, who brought you out of Egypt, out of the land of slavery." Israel was delivered from Egypt for no other reason than God's good pleasure (cf. Deuteronomy 7:7, 8). The Decalogue, the Ten Words that follow the preamble of grace, are the Magna Charta of spiritual freedom given to a divinely redeemed people. Thus the preamble not only underlined their freedom but also the amazing grace that lay behind their deliverance from slavery. And because of this grace, God's people were to live for Him in obedience to the Commandments, not with the idea of attaining salvation by works, but in thanksgiving for what God had done. There was no thought in God's giving the Ten Commandments of providing a way for Israel, or anyone else, to earn salvation. The controlling thought was grace. The Law was, indeed, founded upon grace.[10]

Or, to put it another way, grace does not flow from law; law flows from grace and should always reflect grace as its fount.

Calvin very much emphasized that not only does grace undergird the law but freedom fulfills the law. When people live in accordance with God's law, as made possible by God's Spirit, they will find freedom from their fallenness and make progress in life. Calvin's chapter on "Christian Freedom," written to address those already saved, gives significant space to this truth, with abundant biblical examples.[11] It is now quite clear that grace and law are partners, not enemies, and that grace by its very nature leads not to formless freedom but to fruitful freedom that expresses itself in works of grace, given in gratitude for God's greater gifts.

We can summarize the basic Reformed view using the Westminster Confession of Faith, that enduring touchstone of Reformed theology that still serves as the standard for several Reformed and Presbyterian groups. It says:

> The Law of God
>
> 6. Although true believers are not justified or condemned by the law as a covenant of works, the law is nevertheless very useful to them and to others. As a rule of life, it informs them of God's will and of their obligation to obey it.... The fact that the law encourages doing good and discourages doing evil does not mean that a person who does good and refrains from evil is under the law and not under grace.
>
> 7. None of these uses of the law is contrary to the grace of the gospel. They rather beautifully comply with it, because the Spirit of Christ subdues and enables the will of man to do voluntarily and cheerfully what the will of God, revealed in the law, requires to be done.[12]

EXTREMES THAT LEAD TO FOLLY

The problem of balancing grace and law, or faith and works, is one that has long eluded final resolution. People tend toward one end of the seesaw or the other, despite Calvin's prescription of moderation and balance. The labels we give each of these extremists are *legalists* and *antinomians* (meaning "against the law").

Eve was the first legalist. Answering the serpent's distorted quote of God's command, Eve replied, "But God said, 'You shall not eat of the fruit of the tree that is in the midst of the garden, *neither shall you touch it*, lest you die'" (Gen. 3:3, ESV, emphasis added). Eve reported words as God's that He had not said. God had, in fact, set the human task as caring for the garden, which could well have involved trimming that tree, which would have required touching it. By adding conditions to the divine command, Eve became a legalist. Her invented condition was then challenged by the serpent. Lesson learned: legalism is a poor crutch that begets failure.

At the other end of the spectrum, we find the Bible and history rife with antinomians who want to abandon God's rules and make up their own or have none. There is a certain attraction to making yourself king, or some sort of god, as you make up the rules yourself, crossing lines of presumption and perhaps blasphemy.

Today's hyper-grace movement appears to have crossed these lines. The movement seems easy enough to identify, though its followers may be slippery to engage. The implicit philosophic and moral relativisms fit in with the warp and woof of the prevailing zeitgeist. It is indeed seductive to fit in with the way of the world, shielded, you think, by some inoffensively religious or excitedly experiential overlay. These folks may either lay low and blend or publicly and even wildly exult in and attempt to practice their claimed freedom, even as it leads to their bondage.

The larger Reformed community has done worse than some of the Spirit-touched renewal groups moving toward antinomianism, though. It has seen significant slippage in its standards of orthodoxy, theology, and praxis.

For example, the mainline Presbyterian Church (USA) may be said to have embraced a formal antinomianism in several aspects. In its ordination standards, its view of Scripture has become subjective, affirming that it is "God's Word to you." Its confessional standards have become so broad as to become meaningless, referencing numerous documents, some notorious for their flirtation with orthodoxy, by which the ordinand vows to be "instructed and led," instead of subscribing to them.[13] It is common to hear in worship, "Listen *for* the Word of God," instead of "Listen *to* the Word of God," as if God's Word may or may not make an appearance when the words are read.

It is therefore of little surprise that this body supports abortion, has abandoned the biblical and historic societal commitment to sexual chastity, approves homosexual practice, and has jettisoned the biblical creation view of marriage as only between a man and a woman.[14] These profound violations of Christian standards stand as warnings to antinomians of whatever strand of the danger of an inevitable complete collapse not only of biblical fidelity and Christian orthodoxy but of any reliable understanding of the nature of truth itself. The Christian life too will fall far behind, bereft of the Spirit who had brought about its start.

Looking at both legalism and antinomianism, a recent book leads eminent pastor/theologian Tim Keller to observe:

> *The root of both legalism and antinomianism is the same.* My guess is that most readers will find this the best new insight for them, one that could even trigger a proverbial paradigm shift. It is a fatal pastoral mistake to think of legalism and antinomianism as complete opposites. Sinclair says that, rather, they are "nonidentical twins from the same womb." He traces both of them back to the "lie of Satan" in the garden of Eden, namely, that you can't trust the goodness of God or his commitment to our happiness and well-being and that, therefore, if we obey God fully, we'll miss out and be miserable.[15]

Keller, musing on this conundrum that has vexed the church for centuries, finally concludes:

> *The cure for both legalism and antinomianism is the gospel....*
> "There is only one genuine cure for legalism. It is the same medicine the gospel prescribes for antinomianism: understanding

and tasting union with Jesus Christ himself. This leads to a new love for and obedience to the law of God." Since the root of both errors is the same, the cure is the same—to lift up the essential goodness and love of God by recounting the gospel, thereby making obedience a joy. The remedy for both is a fuller, biblical, and profound understanding of grace and of the character of God.[16]

There is still much to understand of this gospel. It is, rightfully, an eternal task to do so. Yet we on earth can make a good start as we realize that God's law, at its truest and best, reflects the character and holiness of God. Law then brings grace, embodies grace, and ministers grace. Grace, in turn, surrounds the law, sources the law, and confirms the law. Its freedom flows from form. When that form is lost, chaos ensues, bringing bondage as its baggage.

A RENEWALIST SUMMARY

If union with Christ is the cure for both antinomianism and legalism, then the Holy Spirit is the key to that cure. We Reformed understand from the Bible that it is the Spirit who draws people to Christ and it is the Spirit who helps us in our weakness. J. Rodman Williams, theologian of Holy Spirit renewal, said this of dry theological thinking:

> Traditional categories—such as regeneration, sanctification, confirmation—do not suffice; hence we must turn in another direction. The turn we need to make, I am convinced, is toward an action of the Holy Spirit which fits no category, but *one that does make much of our traditional theology operational.* For what has happened, in part at least, is that a new dynamism has been unleashed that has vitalized various theological categories. Before this occurred we had not really experienced the Holy Spirit in such a way for this vitalization to come about....
>
> Let me be quite clear on this point. I am talking about the *making operational* of sanctification.... What is at stake

in this dynamic movement of the Spirit is the *release* of the sanctifying Spirit, the *breaking through* into the totality of the self; hence, to repeat, it is the making operational of sanctification.[17]

It is indeed, in my opinion, crucial in all our considerations that we experience the Spirit, feel the Spirit, speak in the Spirit, move in the Spirit, be guided by the Spirit, and be empowered by the Spirit to accomplish those tasks of grace that God gives each of us. Then shall we be properly equipped to discern the dilemmas of grace and law, and how to address them well.

We have seen that Reformed theology is, in essence, a theology of the Holy Spirit that emphasizes grace that leads to the loving living out of God's law. It remains for us to not just know and discuss these things but, being personally filled with the Holy Spirit, to live them daily in all of God's goodness and fullness.

MARK JUMPER, PHD, is Director of Chaplaincy and Military Affairs, and assistant professor at the Regent University School of Divinity in Virginia Beach, Virginia. A third-generation Presbyterian minister and pastor, he is a retired United States Navy chaplain with twenty-four years of service with the navy, marine corps, and coast guard. He has served in regional and national leadership with the Evangelical Presbyterian Church and national leadership with the Military Chaplains Association. His design and delivery of the Warrior Transition Program for post-combat marines brought an invitation for congressional testimony. He has been published in *Journal for Preachers*; *War and Religion: An Encyclopedia of Faith and Conflict*; and *Evangelical America: An Encyclopedia of Contemporary American Religious Culture*. His works in progress include *Chaplaincy Handbooks: A Biblical, Evangelical Resource* (as lead editor); and *Presbyterian Prophet: J. Rodman Williams, Theologian of Holy Spirit Renewal*.

Chapter 12

EVIDENCE OF GRACE IN THE OLD TESTAMENT

Mark E. Roberts

A TEXT FROM JOHN seems to contrast—even place in opposition—the law that came through Moses with the grace and truth that came through Jesus:

> And the Word became flesh and dwelt among us, and we have seen his glory, glory as of the only Son from the Father, full of grace and truth....For from his fullness we have all received, grace upon grace. For the law was given through Moses; grace and truth came through Jesus Christ.
>
> —JOHN 1:14, 16–17, ESV

This passage prompts us to ask, how does Old Testament law relate to New Testament grace? Many Bible readers, myself among them, have viewed this contrast in absolute, black-and-white terms. They have read and quoted this passage to be saying, "The law was given through Moses, *but* grace and truth came through Jesus Christ." Such a reading, however, adds a contrasting *but* that is absent in the Greek. Rather, the English Standard Version rightly joins the two clauses with a semicolon.

How should we relate these two clauses, then? Do Old

Testament law and New Testament grace and truth oppose, even exclude, each other? Do the Testaments strain against each other within the canon of Scripture, the Old Testament centered on graceless law and the New Testament focused on a grace to be found only within its pages?

This chapter answers these questions by showing how grace permeates the Old Testament and how the law, grace, and truth in John 1 are not at all in opposition.

THE GRACE OF STEADFAST LOVE AND FAITHFULNESS

The phrase "full of grace and truth" exemplifies the Old Testament roots of John's Gospel and expresses this point: grace did not begin with Jesus but flowed through God's covenants with His ancient people long before "the Word became flesh."

Bible scholars find that the phrase "full of grace and truth" corresponds to the Old Testament phrase "abounding in steadfast love and faithfulness," which appears, among several places, in Exodus 34:6 (ESV): "The LORD passed before him [Moses] and proclaimed, 'The LORD, the LORD, a God merciful and gracious, slow to anger, and abounding in steadfast love [ḥesed] and faithfulness ['emeth].'"[1]

Biblical scholar Lester J. Kuyper analyzes occurrences of ḥesed in the Old Testament and shows its central meaning to be that of loyalty and faithfulness, sometimes of protection and deliverance,[2] whether expressed within a family or among two or more persons associated in other ways.[3] Such covenant or family loyalty and faithfulness "is not an outburst of unlooked-for mercy, nor an arbitrary demonstration of favor."[4] This differentiates it from our popular definition of *grace* as "wholly unmerited favor."

Kuyper's analysis of 'emeth likewise yields a definition different from our popular notion of truth. We typically define *truth* as "that which is real, not false; or that which corresponds to reality." But a survey of Old Testament occurrences of 'emeth shows instead that its core notions are "faith, confidence, and stability."[5] For example, the judges Moses appointed were to be dependable (Exod. 18:21); Hananiah was appointed governor because he was dependable (Neh. 7:2); and Israel was to serve the Lord in faithfulness (Josh. 24:14; 1 Sam. 12:24).

The overlap in meaning between *ḥesed* and *'emeth* suggests that when they occur as a pair, they form a figure of speech called *hendiadys* (literally "one through two"), by which "the second term intends to confirm and enrich the first."[6] Thus the two may denote "reliable loyalty to an existing bond," a meaning that fits God's faithfulness to the covenant He made with Israel and to the reciprocal faithfulness God expected of her.

Yet this phrase does not seem to correspond closely to our popular notion of grace. Is there no closer correspondence between Old Testament expressions and our cherished Christian understanding of grace as wholly unmerited favor? There is. The Hebrew word *ḥen* appears in Genesis 6:8, where "Noah found grace *[ḥen]* in the eyes of the LORD" (KJV), and it appears some seventy other places. It expresses generous, unearned favor given by a superior to an inferior and is used for both human and divine interactions.[7] For example, Shechem sought *ḥen* from Jacob and Dinah's brothers in his bid to marry her (Gen. 34:11), and Jacob sought *ḥen* from Joseph when he requested that Joseph bury him in Canaan (Gen. 47:29).[8] But Jacob also asked Joseph "to perform *ḥesed* and *'emeth*...the faithful loyalty [expected]...within the Hebrew family,"[9] Kuyper says, and then continues:

> In this touching scene...*ḥen* is a gracious, unmerited favor...a superior bestows on an inferior; *ḥesed* is also an act of goodness, but one that can be expected since it takes place within...a covenant of intimate fellowship....Through *ḥesed* the covenant is maintained and the relationship...manifests vitality.[10]

Furthermore, the *ḥesed* and *'emeth* God expressed toward Israel He also expected from her in obedience to covenant law. Israel's refusal to obey prompted God's discipline (Hosea 4:1–2).

Such examples of Old Testament occurrences of *ḥen*, *ḥesed*, and *'emeth* demonstrate God's wholly gracious choosing of Israel, entering a covenant with her (corresponding to *ḥen*), and manifesting His covenant-sustaining "steadfast love and faithfulness" even and especially when she rebelled. When Israel refused to reciprocate His *ḥesed* and *'emeth*, He disciplined her and then restored her with His *ḥesed* and *'emeth*.[11]

This understanding should shape our understanding of John's description of the incarnate Word being "full of grace and truth."[12] It attests first to the deity of Jesus because it describes Him with the Greek equivalent of the same phrase used in the Old Testament to describe God as "abounding in steadfast love and faithfulness."[13] Second, it clarifies the contrast between law and grace and truth in John 1:17 to be a *comparative* contrast, not an oppositional contrast. Kuyper explains:

> The God full of grace and truth revealed through the law had now fully come in Jesus Christ, who was indeed full of grace and truth.... Even as in the Old Testament God's covenantal faithfulness was bestowed to Israel time upon time, so also within the first generation of Christian believers God's faithful redemptive grace [God's faithful loyalty to His covenant people] in Christ came time upon time.[14]

This analysis points to a continuity between God's covenantal steadfast love and faithfulness expressed through Moses and the Law,[15] on the one hand, and that which came much more abundantly through the Word made flesh, on the other.

THE GRACE OF CREATION

Before God expressed His choice of a people in history, His act of creation was itself gracious. Truly free, God submitted to no being or force outside Himself to express His glory by creating all that is. Biblical texts emphasize creation's expression of God's glory (Ps. 8; 19), which includes Christ Himself as the end (goal, or *telos*) of creation (John 1:3; Col. 1:16; Rev. 4:11), but Scripture and Christian theology have emphasized grace in redemption more than in (pre-Fall) creation, which is understandable.[16] But we must affirm that creation is itself a divine act of grace, even if we discern this truth by reflecting theologically, including reflecting on our common human experience more than by biblical exegesis. Who can doubt that God's free decision to create humanity in the divine image and for male-female companionship is anything but an act of grace?[17]

If not generous grace, what should one call God's creating the world He repeatedly called good and then fashioning the garden as humanity's satisfying home?[18] Psalm 65 details some of God's creational generosity:

> You visit the earth and water it; you greatly enrich it; the river of God is full of water; you provide their grain, for so you have prepared it. You water its furrows abundantly, settling its ridges, softening it with showers, and blessing its growth. You crown the year with your bounty; your wagon tracks overflow with abundance. The pastures of the wilderness overflow, the hills gird themselves with joy, the meadows clothe themselves with flocks, the valleys deck themselves with grain, they shout and sing together for joy.
>
> —vv. 9–13, ESV

Were God not our heavenly Father but our heavenly Cost-Cutter instead, we might have a minimalist creation, with just one or only a few kinds of plants and animals and foods. They might all be painted in monochrome grey, with no heart-stopping sunsets, sweet lilacs, cool lakes, toasty beaches, or feasts of fruit, fish, or fowl. Instead, our common experience testifies to creation's ever-surprising beauty that shouts of God's grace even through its details.

THE GRACE OF THE PATRIARCHAL COVENANTS

From the paradise of Genesis 1–2 into the ever-widening spiral of sin and its abuse of creation in Genesis 3–11, God met sin with judgment and a note of grace. He judged the evil of Noah's time with the Flood, but "Noah found favor [*ḥen*] in the eyes of the LORD" (Gen. 6:8, ESV). That favor saved Noah, his family, and the stock of animals that together would resume God's creation project after the Flood. Then God repeated His blessing from Genesis 1 in Genesis 8:21–9:17 with variations, including the establishment of a covenant with all of humanity and a promise never to destroy all life by a flood (Gen. 9:11). With this covenant, God demonstrated the simplest description of grace: humanity not only did *not* get what it deserved but got so much more and better than it deserved.

Does the judgement that came at Babel (Gen. 11) follow the pattern of bringing with it a corresponding grace? With the story of Babel, we recognize the world as we know it today. Sin was infecting creation but with the sophistication of a culture "using all its resources to establish a city that is the antithesis of what God intended when he created the world."[19] God confused the proud tower builders and dispersed them "over the face of all the earth" (Gen. 11:9, ESV). But they received no promise of a future redeemer or clothing for their shame, as Adam and Eve did (Gen. 3:15, 21). Nor did they receive a protective mark, as Cain did (Gen. 4:15), or a covenant, as Noah and all his descendants did (Gen. 8:21–9:17). Did God show no grace after the judgment of Babel?

He did. In Genesis 12, we find a new chapter in the history of salvation. God advanced His plan to redeem humanity with great grace through the making of important covenants. A simple acrostic helps us see that God came to the *aid* of His people by making lasting covenants with

Abraham

Israel

David.[20]

These most important of Old Testament covenants flow like tributaries into the great river of God's covenant through Jesus Christ.

Old Testament scholars define a *covenant* to be "a means of establishing a relationship (not naturally existing), which is sanctioned by an oath sworn in a ceremony of ratification."[21] God's covenant with Abraham, made in Genesis 12, resumed, or restarted, His redemption of humanity and of all of creation by focusing on one man and his family (Gen. 11:10–26). Grace abounded here, first through God's choosing of Abram, who was, at the time, a Mesopotamian pagan idolater. Grace then extended through God's calling Abram to move "to the land that I will show you" (Gen. 12:1, ESV) and through the giving of the covenant itself, which included the gifts of land, a great name, and becoming the source of a great nation and of blessing to all families of the earth (Gen. 12:2–3).[22] Genesis 22 amplifies God's promise to include almost infinite offspring, through whom He would bless all nations "because you have obeyed my voice" (v. 18, ESV). God gave great grace with one obligation: obedience.

THE GRACE OF THE COVENANT WITH ISRAEL

The central event of salvation in the Old Testament is the Exodus. It consisted of several events, including God's entering into a new covenant with the descendants of Abraham He miraculously rescued from Egypt. In what was surely a Mount Everest of Old Testament revelation, at Mount Sinai God gave Moses these words for the people of Israel:

> You yourselves have seen what I did to the Egyptians, and how I bore you on eagles' wings and brought you to myself. Now therefore, if you will indeed obey my voice and keep my covenant, you shall be my treasured possession among all peoples, for all the earth is mine; and you shall be to me a kingdom of priests and a holy nation.
>
> —EXODUS 19:4–6, ESV

Grace alone accounted for God's rescuing this people and choosing them to be His "treasured possession" and "a kingdom of priests and a holy nation." Lest they would think otherwise, they were later reminded:

> You are a people holy to the LORD your God. The LORD your God has chosen you to be a people for his treasured possession, out of all the peoples who are on the face of the earth. It was not because you were more in number than any other people that the LORD set his love on you and chose you, for you were the fewest of all peoples, but it is because the LORD loves you and is keeping the oath that he swore to your fathers.
> —DEUTERONOMY 7:6–8, ESV

God gave the Ten Commandments in Exodus 20 as part of the Sinai covenant, the first expression of the Law of Moses, which was complete in its 613 commandments. "Law" and "commandments" denote directives to be obeyed. But in the Books of Exodus and Deuteronomy, one cannot detect any tension or contradiction between God's gracious choosing and covenant love, on the one hand, and His expecting Israel to obey, on the other. Obedience was not the prerequisite for God's gracious deliverance of them from Egypt, nor for God's continuing *hesed*, or covenant love. God rescued the children of Israel on the strength of His oath to their fathers, and He made clear multiple times that the covenant stayed alive not because of Israel's exemplary obedience but because of His *hesed* and *'emeth* to the covenant.[23]

The law was not an instrument by which God saved them, so what was its purpose? Many Christians see Old Testament law as burdensome, oppressive, and opposed to grace and freedom. Yet the only defect the New Testament finds with the law is serious: it cannot empower people to keep it. But that objection does not object to law itself, as the apostle Paul explains:

> God has done what the law, weakened by the flesh, could not do. By sending his own Son in the likeness of sinful flesh

and for sin, he condemned sin in the flesh, in order that the righteous requirement of the law might be fulfilled in us, who walk not according to the flesh but according to the Spirit.

—ROMANS 8:3–4, ESV

While the law cannot empower people to satisfy it, the law nevertheless expresses God's "righteous requirement," a divine revelation that, by itself, is valuable.

THE GRACE OF THE COVENANT WITH DAVID

God entered a covenant with King David and his house to govern His people perpetually (2 Sam. 7:8–17; Psalm 89:3 uses the word *covenant* to refer to this event). God's choosing of David after rejecting King Saul was yet another expression of grace, as was the covenant's provision for any Davidic ruler who "commits iniquity": "I will discipline him with the rod of men...but my steadfast love [*ḥesed*] will not depart from him, as I took it from Saul...And your house and your kingdom shall be made sure forever before me. Your throne shall be established forever" (2 Sam. 7:14–16, ESV).[24] God's guarantee of this covenant trumped even the iniquity of a Davidic ruler. Obedience matters, is required, is important, but disobedience does not end such a covenant with the Lord. Such covenant faithfulness of God expresses divine grace.

THE GRACE OF THE TORAH

Grace accounts for all these covenants and for God's keeping of them whenever their recipients—whether Abraham, the children of Israel, or the house of David—failed to keep them. Of these, only the Sinai Covenant included developed law, the Law of Moses.[25]

Some New Testament passages speak of the law in ways that cause many Christians to regard it—and often the Old Testament as a whole—quite negatively. But the law does not oppose grace; it expresses grace instead, a grace that God did not cancel or withdraw even when He exiled His rebellious people in Babylon, in accord with the terms of the covenant.

God expresses His covenant loyalty tenderly to His chastened people:

> Comfort, comfort my people, says your God. Speak tenderly to Jerusalem, and cry to her that her warfare is ended, that her iniquity is pardoned, that she has received from the LORD's hand double for all her sins.
>
> —ISAIAH 40:1–2, ESV

We discern the grace of Moses's Law better when we recognize that "law" as we think of it today does not correspond to what the Mosaic Law was. The Hebrew word *Torah* serves our understanding much better. Not only does *Torah* refer to the traditional Five Books of Moses, but it also means more and other than "law." It means instruction and discipline, like that given by a parent.[26]

"Law" in the Old Testament included statutes, judgments, commandments, and precepts, but "Torah" encapsulates something even broader than that, including all manner of instruction that, with statutory law, aims for the flourishing of life, for *shalom*. This understanding of Torah and its law accounts for the joy ancient Hebrews had for receiving God's law as part of His special covenant with them. We see this joy expressed in Psalm 119, the longest psalm in the Bible and one that "celebrates the gift of God's Torah, or covenant instruction, as the perfect guide for life."[27] See, for example, these passages from that psalm that express gratitude for God's law. Nothing in them suggests the psalmist found God's Torah burdensome:

> Blessed are those whose way is blameless, who walk in the law of the LORD!
>
> —v. 1, ESV

> Let your steadfast love [*hesed*] come to me, O LORD, your salvation according to your promise; then shall I have an answer

for him who taunts me, for I trust in your word. And take not the word of truth utterly out of my mouth, for my hope is in your rules. I will keep your law [*torah*] continually, forever and ever, and I shall walk in a wide place, for I have sought your precepts. I will also speak of your testimonies before kings and shall not be put to shame, for I find my delight in your commandments, which I love. I will lift up my hands toward your commandments, which I love, and I will meditate on your statutes.

—vv. 41–48, ESV

Oh how I love your law! It is my meditation all the day. Your commandment makes me wiser than my enemies, for it is ever with me. I have more understanding than all my teachers, for your testimonies are my meditation. I understand more than the aged, for I keep your precepts. I hold back my feet from every evil way, in order to keep your word. I do not turn aside from your rules, for you have taught me. How sweet are your words to my taste, sweeter than honey to my mouth! Through your precepts I get understanding; therefore I hate every false way.

Your word is a lamp to my feet and a light to my path. I have sworn an oath and confirmed it, to keep your righteous rules.

—vv. 97–106, ESV

To these passages, many more could be added, but another way to receive the Torah as a nourishing gift and not as a slavish burden is to recognize how God expresses His grace toward needy humans through many of the statutes of Moses's Law. In his chapter titled "The Holy Scriptures," Don Brandeis, who was born Jewish and became a Christian evangelist, praises these qualities of God's law:[28]

The statutes and laws which God gave recognized the dignity of men and regarded human life as sacred. These laws were designed to protect and aid the poor and underprivileged.

1. What other book ever had laws requiring that the wages of the workman should be paid, not quarterly, monthly, or

weekly, but before sunset every night? (See Deuteronomy 24:15.)

2. ...forbade the taking of a pledge from a widow for her indebtedness, or required a pawned garment to be returned to a poor man at night? (See Deuteronomy 24:12, 13.)

3. ...had a law allowing the poor or the traveler to eat and fill their hands with fruit from any vineyard or orchard through which they passed...? (See Deuteronomy 23:24, 25.)

4. ...had a law forbidding men to curse the deaf, or put a stumblingblock in the path of the blind? (See Leviticus 19:14.)

5. ...had a law which gave every man an inheritance of land, and so secured it that even the king on his throne could not take it from him?...(See Leviticus 25:23, 25, 10, 13; also 1 Kings 21:1–3.)

6. ...had a law [commanding]...the husbandman to [leave]...the gleanings of his harvest [and]...the fallen grapes of his vineyard...for the poor and the stranger? (See Leviticus 19:9, 10.)

7. ...had a law which forbade the muzzling of the ox as he was treading out the corn, or which protected the birds upon their nests, and commanded men to show kindness to beasts in distress, even though they belonged to their enemies? (See Deuteronomy 25:4; 22:6, 7; Exodus 23:4, 5.)

8. ...had a law which required men to love their neighbors as themselves, forbade them to cherish grudges against them, and prohibited malice, tale-bearing, revenge? (See Leviticus 19:16, 18.)

This chapter closes with the testimony of Old Testament scholars William Sanford LaSor, David Allan Hubbard, and Frederic William Bush, who find grace expressed through God's redemptive covenants with Abraham, Israel, and David, including the Law of Moses. While many think that only under the new covenant are people saved by grace alone through faith, these scholars insist that:

Careful study of the Torah as well as the rest of the Old Testament shows that people are never saved by their own efforts—but only by the grace of God. Everyone deserves condemnation and death for having sinned. God is graciously willing to accept a person on the basis of faith, having provided the means for redemption. Paul understood the covenant with Abraham in this way and declared that it was not annulled by the law given to Moses (Gal. 3:6–18).[29]

Such is the grace of God expressed generously throughout the Old Testament. That grace saved patriarchs and the children of Israel and comes to us supremely in the God-man Jesus Christ. He expresses most fully God's *ḥesed* and *'emeth*, God's ultimate covenant loyalty—"full of grace and truth"—and saves all who trust Him.[30]

MARK E. ROBERTS, PhD, is Professor and Dean of Learning Resources at Oral Roberts University in Tulsa, Oklahoma.

Chapter 13

GRACE AND WORKS— A JOHANNINE PERSPECTIVE

John Christopher Thomas

THE BIBLICAL AND theological understanding of grace—and especially its relationship to works—has been a major concern for some in contemporary Pentecostal and Charismatic circles over the last several years. While there are many ways this issue could be approached, it should come as no surprise that I, as one trained in biblical studies, would want to actually read a specific portion of the biblical text as a way of gaining leverage on this at-times-controversial topic. As such, I propose examining the Johannine literature. In what follows I will not use my space to discuss behind-the-text issues that may or may not be significant for interpretation, but rather by means of a simple literary analysis I will attempt to hear this distinctive voice from what I call the Black Gospel Choir of Scripture.

THE DISTINCTIVE SOUND OF THE JOHANNINE VOICE(S)

The distinctiveness of the Johannine voice(s)[1] found within the New Testament is well known to those who have spent much time with this section of Scripture. The independent witness of the fourth Gospel includes the signs of turning water into wine (John 2), the giving of life to the nobleman's son (John 4), making whole the man at the pool (John 5), giving sight to the man born blind (John 9), the raising of Lazarus (John 11), and the miraculous catch of fish (John 21). In addition to the unique description of these signs, only John's Gospel tells of Jesus's encounter with Nicodemus (John 3), His encounter with the Samaritan woman (John 4), His extended discourses, and His washing the feet of His disciples (John 13), as well as unique details from the passion account. The Gospel's breathtaking prologue pushes the origin story of Jesus back to before the creation of the world with His identification as the Logos and His absolutely unrivaled place in redemption history. While any number of similar observations could be made about the uniqueness of the Johannine witness, perhaps enough has been said to prepare us for what the Johannine voice(s) has/have to say about this topic.

To set the stage, I will begin with a quick statistical overview. On the one hand, it sometimes comes as a bit of a shock to find that the Greek word translated "grace" (*charis*) occurs just four times in the Gospel According to John with all occurrences found in the prologue (1:14, 16, 17), a single time in 1–3 John (2 John 3), and twice in Revelation (1:4; 22:21). On the other hand, the Greek word translated "work" (*ergon*) occurs a staggering twenty-eight times in the Gospel,[2] five times in 1–3 John,[3] and twenty-one times in Revelation.[4] Other relevant vocabulary notwithstanding, such an emphasis indicates that the role of grace, while present in the Johannine literature, is perhaps understood somewhat differently amongst this/these voices than in some of the other New Testament voices. At the same time, owing to the frequency with which the term *work* occurs in the Johannine literature, it appears that a Johannine understanding of grace must be discerned in the light of its relationship to works. Simply dismissing works as irrelevant will not do, if one seeks to gain guidance from this distinctive New Testament voice(s). Thus, in what follows I will offer a survey and some reflection on the relationship between grace and works in each category or genre of the Johannine literature and conclude with some observations about the significance of the Johannine witness on this topic.[5]

THE GOSPEL ACCORDING TO JOHN

As is commonly known, the Gospel According to John begins with a prologue (1:1–18) that is distinctive from the rest of the Gospel narrative in both literary style and some vocabulary. It has often been called a hymn or poem, and some have even thought that it existed before the writing of the Gospel. In many ways it is like a musical overture, where themes and topics that will be of significance later in the narrative appear already at this point. At the same time, in some ways it is fair to say that the gospel story is given in miniature in these verses.

Having introduced the divine Logos, the prologue describes His role in creation and redemptive history—punctuated by mentions of John (the Baptist)—while John 1:14 focuses upon the incarnation of the Logos in flesh. It is at this point that the language of grace first occurs when it is noted, "And the Word became flesh and tabernacled among us, and we beheld his glory, glory as the unique Son of the Father, full of grace and truth."[6] The first thing to note is that here there is an extremely tight interplay between grace and the Logos. However one conceives of grace in this context, it is clear that grace is to be understood as Christologically conditioned, for the Logos is full of grace and truth. Further, the Johannine understanding of grace seems to be revealed in part by the way in which grace stands in close relationship to the divine "glory" of the Logos incarnate as beheld by those described in this verse. In other words, the glory beheld—reminiscent of the glory of God revealed in the tent of tabernacle—is intimately connected to that with which the Logos incarnate is full. This tight relationship implies that the grace and truth that fills the Logos incarnate shines forth in glorious fashion. What is not yet known by the readers is the fact that there is such a close association between the Logos and truth in the Gospel According to John, that truth is so Christologically conditioned that it is possible to speak of Jesus as the truth—an identification Jesus Himself later makes (14:6). If Jesus is the embodiment of truth, is He also to be understood as the embodiment of grace?

But this is not all there is to know about a Johannine understanding of grace, for as the prologue continues—after an interlude that speaks of John the Baptist's testimony—it is stated, "and out of his fullness we all have received, one grace after another" (John 1:16).[7] Though the Greek phrase that underlies our English translations (*charis anti charis*) can be translated literally as "grace against grace," it is perhaps better understood to mean something like "grace upon grace," or "one grace after another." Thus, a connecting link is established between the Logos incarnate and the believing readers, whereby the One who is full of grace dispenses or bestows it upon or to believers, one grace after another. So, just as Jesus will be the instrument through whom His disciples come to know and experience the truth, so He is the One who gives grace upon grace to His disciples. The fact that this phrase is best understood as "one grace after another" is borne out in John 1:17, "because the law through Moses was given, grace and truth through Jesus Christ came."[8] The law—which is never disparaged in the Gospel According to John—and Moses become witnesses to Jesus and as such are viewed as positive, not negative, entities. This interpretation is borne out in part by the fact that no negative conjunction connects these clauses. Rather, they seem to stand together side by side as examples of the gracious activity of the Logos, made available to all believers. Thus, it appears that grace in the fourth Gospel is a divine bestowal that must be received, accepted, and acted upon for it to be efficacious—analogously "whoever received him, he gave to them the authority to become children of God, to those who believe in his name" (John 1:12).[9]

As noted above, the occurrence of work(s) in the fourth Gospel is extensive. The first references to works (John 3:19, 20, 21) indicate that works reveal whether or not one loves the (salvific) light who has been identified as the Logos in John 1:5, 9. The works of those who love darkness more than light are those whose works are evil, who do not come to the light lest their works be shown as such. This is one reason Jesus later gives for the fact that He is hated by the world, for "I testify concerning it because its works are evil" (John 7:7).[10] Conversely, the one who does the truth comes to the light in order that it might be manifested that his works are worked in God (John 3:21). In other words, one's works reveal one's relationship to God or the devil. Consistent with this understanding of works is the fact that elsewhere in John, one's works also reveal one's origins, for one manifests the identity of one's parentage by whether one's works are consistent with that of one's "father," whether it be Abraham (John 8:39) or the devil (John 8:41, 44).

The word's next occurrence introduces another major aspect of the meaning of *work* in the fourth Gospel. In John 4:34 Jesus says, "My food is in order that I might do the will of the one who sent me and I might complete his work."[11] Sandwiched as it is between Jesus's conversation with the Samaritan woman and the mass conversion of the Samaritan villagers, it is clear that the will of the One who sent Him and the work that is to be completed is that all might be saved through Him. This work is accomplished, at least in part, by the kind of work through which the man at the pool in John 5 is made whole—the Greek word translated "whole" (*hygiēs*) occurring here conveying the holistic salvation the man experiences in both body and soul. Even greater works than this will the Father show the Son (John 5:20), including raising the dead and making alive (John 5:21). Such activity indicates something of the tight relationship between Jesus's life-giving work and the testimony of the Son by means of the works that the Father has given Him to do, to complete His work (John 5:36). The holistic nature of this work is underscored in a dialogue in John 6:28–29 where, after the feeding of the five thousand, some in the crowd ask, "What can we do in order that we might work the works of God?"[12] Jesus replies, "This is the work of God, in order that you might believe in the one that one sent."[13] Such belief, it should be noted, leads to eternal life and resurrection at the last day. This emphasis continues later in the Gospel (John 9:3).

The works that Jesus does should offer individuals an opportunity to believe because they testify of Jesus (John 14:10–12), but not all who see such works believe (John 7:3, 21; 10:25). In point of fact, some even want to stone Him owing to His works (John 10:32–33, 37–38). But those who refuse to believe are actually condemned for having seen the works while refusing to believe (John 15:24).

It should be noted that the disciples are not only invited to believe in Jesus and His works but are invited to participate in them while it is day (John 9:4), and the disciples are promised that they will be able to do even greater works than He (John 14:12)!

The last mention of the work to which Jesus is called occurs in John 17:4, where appropriately enough in Jesus's prayer to the Father He says, "I have glorified you upon the earth, having completed the work which you gave to me in order that I do."[14] Perhaps such completion language is a not-so-subtle anticipation of Jesus's cry on the cross, "It is completed"[15] (*teleō*) in 19:30.

FIRST THROUGH THIRD JOHN

As noted earlier, there is but a single occurrence of *grace* in 1–3 John, coming in the greeting found in 2 John 3: "Grace, mercy, and peace will be with us from God the Father and from Jesus Christ the Son of the Father, in truth and love."[16] One of the peculiarities of this greeting is the way in which the pronouncement of grace, mercy, and peace is less of a wish and more of a statement of fact.[17] These will be with the believers! The greeting is also distinctive in that the elder includes himself in the blessing.[18] In 2 John 3 the occurrence of *grace* would no doubt be Christologically conditioned owing to its meaning in the prologue of the Gospel, not unlike the way in which *peace* would be, which occurs six times in the fourth Gospel, all six within the Book of Glory (14:27; 16:33; 20:19, 21, 26). Thus, it would not be surprising for the readers to learn that such grace comes from the Father and Jesus Christ His Son.

While there is but a single occurrence of the word *grace* in 1–3 John, conversely there are several occurrences of the noun *work(s)* or its verbal form *to work* in 1–3 John. In the shortest book in the New Testament, 3 John, reference to words from the "work" family occurs three times. In 3 John 5 the elder commends Gaius saying that he is acting faithfully when he works on behalf of the brothers, especially since they are strangers to him! The specific kind of work envisioned is very much connected to the hospitality offered to any number of emissaries who have come from the elder— in a manner worthy of God. This kind of hard work—this missionary support—would include things like provisions during the missionaries' stay and appropriate supplies for the journey ahead (food, money, washing their clothes, etc.).[19] Significantly, such work is equated with acting faithfully, work for which Gaius is known and testified of by the brethren. The theme of work continues in 3 John 8, where the elder instructs that "we [Gaius and others] are obligated to receive such ones as these—who go out for no other reason than the name—in order that we might be coworkers in the truth."[20] Owing to the fact that truth is Christologically conditioned in the Johannine literature, it appears that the hard work of missionary support, which in 3 John is described as acting faithfully, results in being considered a coworker with Jesus and His mission! In the third reference to works, in 3 John 10, the elder promises to visit the church—which Diotrephes is dominating—to set things straight. Among the things that the elder intends to address are Diotrephes's "works," which appear to include his refusal to receive the elder's emissaries, his saying of evil words about the elder and those who stand with him, and the casting out of the church anyone who desires to receive the emissaries! Such an understanding of works on this occasion does not appear to be too far removed from the "evil works" found in the fourth Gospel, for "the one who does evil has not seen God" (3 John 11).[21]

The theme of works continues in 2 John, a short letter that appears to be a warning about the imminent arrival of deceivers who are making their way to the elect lady and her children. The threat of their arrival is so grave that in 2 John 8 the elder warns his readers, "You watch yourselves, in order that you do not lose that which you have worked for but receive a full reward."[22] The closest Johannine linguistic parallels to this verse come in John 6:27, where Jesus says, "You should not be working for the food that is subject to loss but for food that lasts for eternal life."[23] Just after, in 6:29, He instructs, "This is the work of God: Have faith in him whom he sent."[24] The implication of 2 John 8, in the light of John 6, is that the readers are in danger of losing the work of God (eternal life) if they follow the deceivers who deny "Jesus coming in the flesh" (2 John 7).[25] Rather they should receive a full reward, which here would appear to be synonymous with eternal life. The threat of those who go beyond the teaching of Christ—those who do not have God—is that the believers will be adversely affected. By contrast those who remain in this teaching have both the Father and the Son (2 John 9). The threat is so grave that the elder instructs his readers on how they are to respond to anyone who bears such false teaching, "Do not receive such a one into the house and do not extend the greeting of peace to him or her" (2 John 10).[26] The reason for such draconian instructions is made known in the next verse, "For the one who says to him or her greetings shares in their evil works" (2 John 11).[27] Just as in 3 John, while the believers' right actions could make them coworkers in the truth, so here individuals' identification with false teachers and deceivers makes them have fellowship with the evil works of these deceiving missionaries.

In addition to its place in the smallest New Testament documents, this theme is also found in 1 John on three occasions, all clustered together near the physical and perhaps theological center of the book. The first of these three occurrences is found in 1 John 3:8 near the end of a stretch of text filled with interpretive challenges with regard to the relationship between sin and the believer. After having made clear that "the one who does sin is of the devil, because the devil has sinned from the beginning," the writer reveals that this is the very reason that the Son of God was manifested, "in order that he might destroy the works of the devil."[28] Clearly, this strikes the same chord as 1 John 3:5, where Jesus's manifestation is "in order that he might destroy the sins, and sin is not in him."[29] For our purposes, it is important to note that the "works" in question reveal that one belongs to the devil and here are equated with sin. Reminiscent of the words of Jesus in the fourth Gospel, the writer makes clear here in 1 John that one's works—whether or not one practices sin—indicate/manifest whether one is to be identified as part of the children of God or children of the devil. "The one who does righteousness is of God, and the one who does not love his brother is not of God" (1 John 3:10).[30]

Closely related to the idea that one's works reveal one's nature, the next occurrence of the term *works* is found just four verses later in 1 John 3:12. In a passage devoted to the theme of love for one another that was introduced at the end of the previous passage, and possibly the literary center of 1 John,[31] the term appears in an explanation of why Cain slaughtered his brother—"because his works were evil and those of his brother were righteous."[32] Coming on the heels of the previous section and with the knowledge that Jesus is hated because He testifies that the works of certain individuals are evil, the significance of the identification of Cain's works as evil could hardly be missed. His evil works reveal what is in his heart that is manifested in the slaughter of his brother. Standing in contrast to the righteous works of his brother—which indicate that his brother is righteous—Cain's evil works reveal on which side of the divide he stands. They reveal that he does not love the brothers and consequently is not of God.

The final occurrence of "works" language in 1 John occurs just six verses later in the same section of the book devoted to loving one's brother. Holding up Jesus as the model of such love—who laid down His life concerning us—we are obligated to lay down our lives for the brothers. Specifically, if one has the world's goods and sees his brother having a need but shuts off his compassion, how is the love of God in such a one? Rather, the writer says, "Children, let us not love with word nor with tongue but in work and truth" (1 John 3:18). The implication is quite stark. If one does not love in work, the love of God does not reside in such a one, meaning that such a one is not of God!

REVELATION

As noted earlier, the word *grace* occurs just two times in the Book of Revelation, but both in significant locations.[33] It is found very near the beginning of the book, in the book's prologue (Rev. 1:4), and in the very last verse in the book's epilogue (Rev. 22:21). The hearers would know that in Johannine thought the blessing of "grace and peace" is no perfunctory formula, but these are terms of special significance for the community. The pronouncement of grace comes with the knowledge that the Logos is the One full of grace and that out of His fullness we have all received one grace after another (John 1:14, 16). Consequently, the hearers understand that the grace conveyed in this greeting ultimately comes from Jesus Christ (John 1:17). In the same way, the other element of the blessing is also Johanninely charged, owing to Jesus's use of the term. On three occasions in the fourth Gospel, Jesus Himself speaks peace to His disciples. First, in John 14:27 Jesus promises to give the disciples peace when they face the prospect of His departure. Later, after the resurrection, He speaks peace both to the disciples (John 20:19) and later to Thomas (John 20:26). This same peace is now spoken to the seven churches who may also share with the disciples in the fourth Gospel a "troubled" context. The final occurrence of the term *grace* is found in the book's very last verse, "May the grace of the Lord Jesus be upon all" (Rev. 22:21).[34] These final words are likely to be of significance for the hearers in several ways. First, they would no doubt be struck by the fact that this circular letter ends with a benediction, which is most unusual for an epistle. However, the meaning of such unusual concluding words of blessing would not be lost on the hearers, for their appearance would extend the context of worship in which they experience the book. Second, neither would the significance of the word *grace* be missed. For the hearers would well remember that the only other occurrence of the term in the entire book stands at its beginning and is also part of John's words (Rev. 1:4), indicating that despite the ominous contents of this book of prophecy, the entire book is enfolded by grace. Johannine hearers might discern even greater depth in the occurrence of the word here, for they would no doubt remember that it is the Word made flesh who is full of grace and truth, and that it is out of His fullness that we have all received one grace after another (John 1:14–16). Thus, owing to the fact that the Book of Revelation is a revelation of Jesus Christ, it is possible that the hearers would now appreciate the way in which its unfolding is indeed the revelation of one grace after another as Jesus Christ is more fully revealed than ever before, further underscoring the fact that this book, despite its ominous contents, is actually a means of grace! This extraordinary grace is pronounced upon all those in the community who heed its call to pneumatic discernment that manifests itself in prophetic faithful witness to a hostile world with the goal of the conversion of the nations—for indeed Jesus is coming quickly!

As was also noted above, the term *works* occurs often in Revelation and appears to be one of the book's major and vital themes.[35] Limitations of space prohibit the kind of fuller treatment of the passages in which the term occurs as has been offered for the fourth Gospel and 1–3 John. At this point a bit of summary will have to do.

The hearers are first introduced to the term *works* in Revelation 2:2. In this book the word can be used of good (Rev. 2:2, 5, 19, 26; 3:1, 8, 15), bad (Rev. 2:6), or incomplete (Rev. 3:2) works. There are works for which repentance should be, but is not always, offered (Rev. 2:22; 9:20; 16:11). Some works are an extension of one's witness beyond death (Rev. 14:13). Other works are the direct actions of God (Rev. 15:3). On several occasions, works are the basis of one's (future) judgment (Rev. 18:6; 20:12, 13) and/or one's reward (Rev. 2:23; 22:12). Clearly, the idea of works is an integrative one that includes one's activity or actions, which carry with them a sign-like quality that reveals something about one's relationship with God and/or Jesus. As in the other Johannine voices, so in Revelation, the term *works* is not a vulgar word to be avoided, as is sometimes the case in various English translations of, or commentaries upon, the text of Revelation, but is a term that must be embraced in order to appreciate fully this dimension of Revelation's meaning. Clearly, its prominent place and meaning within the book indicates that works cannot be dismissed as insignificant but rather play a crucial role in the life and ultimate salvation of the believer.

Thus, Revelation presents a very engaging dialectical understanding of the relationship between grace and works. On the one hand, the significant role of works in the theology of the book reveals their essential nature in its understanding of soteriology. On the other hand, all the references to works are enfolded by references to grace at the book's beginning and end. How should this dialectical presentation of salvation be understood by contemporary interpreters?

The description of the marriage supper of the Lamb in Revelation 19:7–8 may well point the way forward. With the words, "the marriage of the Lamb has come, and his bride has prepared herself" (Rev. 19:7),[36] the hearers would discern a transition from a focus on the rejoicing that accompanies God's judgment of destruction upon those who destroyed the earth to rejoicing over the rewards that He now gives to His faithful servants. Not only is the arrival of the marriage of the Lamb announced, but it is also noted that His bride (literally "woman") has prepared herself. The hearers are likely to understand these words within the context of ancient Jewish two-stage weddings, where after the betrothal, at which point the couple is legally married, the bride continues to live in the house of her father, where she prepares herself as she awaits her husband's arrival—at a date in the future—to take her to his house. It would be clear to the hearers that the bride of the Lamb is preparing herself for this extraordinary event, owing in part to the occurrence of "herself" as the object of her preparations. At the same time, the specific vocabulary used to describe this preparation would suggest a cooperative, if not reciprocal, activity between the bride of the Lamb and God, as this verb's five previous occurrences in Revelation and one future occurrence (8:6; 9:7, 15; 12:6; 16:12) always describe the direct activity and intervention of God! As God's other preparations have not been altered nor retarded, so the hearers would understand that the bride's preparations result in the plan of God being accomplished in her as well!

The suspicions of the hearers with regard to the reciprocal relationship between God and the bride are confirmed and clarified somewhat by the next words the hearers encounter, "and it was granted to her in order that she might be clothed with fine linen, bright and pure" (Rev. 19:8).[37] In fact, both aspects of their reciprocal relationship appear in these words. On the one hand, the occurrence of the verb *there was given* (*didōmi*) in the passive voice (a form that appears throughout Revelation) leaves the subject of the action unnamed, a grammatical form known as a divine passive, implying that God (or the Lamb) is the One who gives this garment of fine linen to the bride of the Lamb. On the other hand, the purpose of this gift is made clear by the verb *to be clothed* (*periballō*), the middle voice of which indicates that she is to clothe herself in this gift. Not only would the hearers be struck by the continued attention given to the reciprocal nature of the relationship shared by God and the bride of the Lamb, but they would also be struck by the description of the bride's attire itself. Its bright and pure characteristics would no doubt remind them of the bright and pure stones with which the seven angels that come from the temple of the tabernacle of witness in heaven with the seven plagues of God are clothed (Rev. 15:6), suggesting that the bride too is in a very close relationship with God. At the same time the bride's "fine linen, bright and pure" would stand in striking contrast to the fine linen of the great whore, for while the latter's attire is the result of idolatrous opulence, the attire of the former is the result of an intimate relationship with the Lamb, perhaps underscoring His bride's sexual innocence in contrast to the sexual exploits of the great whore!

The next words the hearers encounter serve to extend their discerning reflection about the relationship between God and the bride, as well as the contrast between her attire and that of the great whore, "for the fine linen is the righteous deeds of the saints" (Rev. 19:8).[38] Several aspects of these words would be of significance for the hearers. First, it would be obvious that the fine linen here described is the same fine linen that was divinely given to the bride, the same with which she clothed herself. Second, despite the fact that this linen is a divine gift, it is here identified as "the righteous deeds" (*dikaiōma*) of the saints. This word would appear to be conditioned for Johannine hearers by their earlier encounter with this very term once before in Revelation, where it has reference to the righteous deeds of God (15:4). There, His righteous deeds of judgment are also described as great and marvelous works, as well as righteous and true ways. This occurrence, along with the fact that the root from which the "righteous" family of words come has reference only to God in Revelation, indicates a close association between God and the saints. At the same time, this term would also be understood by the hearers in light of the fact that the activities of Babylon, that God has remembered, are described as "unrighteous deeds" (*adikēma*) (Rev. 18:5),[39] indicating that the contrast between the attire of the bride of the Lamb and the attire of the great whore has its basis in their diametrically opposed activities. Thus, the deeds that characterize the great whore are unrighteous, while the deeds that characterize God and the bride are righteous.

In addition to these philological and theological associations, it is difficult to imagine that the righteous deeds of the saints would be understood by Johannine hearers apart from the idea of works that has proven so important throughout Revelation. In this light the identity of the righteous deeds and the works of the saints could hardly be thought to be anything but coterminous. Specifically, such language is likely to bring to mind the activities of love, labor, patient endurance, keeping faith/keeping My (Jesus's) Word, faithful witness, service, moral purity, and discernment. For the hearers, the fact that the fine linen given to the bride is at the same time the righteous deeds of the saints would well capture something of the divine human cooperation essential to a proper understanding of salvation in Revelation. In point of fact, the twofold occurrence of the term *the righteous deeds* (*dikaiōma*) in the book captures this dialectic well indeed, for on the one hand it describes the righteous deeds of God carried out on behalf of the saints (Rev. 15:4), while on the other hand it describes the righteous deeds of the saints carried out on behalf of God. To put it still another way, their righteous deeds are consistent with His righteous deeds; their actions reflect the God who has given them salvation. Third, the identification of the fine linen with the righteous deeds of the saints confirms for the hearers that the bride of the Lamb is indeed identical to the saints.

It appears then that Revelation 19:7–8 is an example of the way in which the book itself holds this dialectical tension together.

CONCLUSIONS AND IMPLICATIONS—WHAT IS THE SPIRIT SAYING TO THE CHURCHES?

What then might we conclude about the relationship between grace and works in the Johannine voice(s) found within the pages of the New Testament?

First, the definition of *grace* in the Johannine literature appears to be quite distinctive. Rather than being understood as "unmerited favor," the term *grace* appears to be Christologically conditioned. Grace is very closely identified with the Logos incarnate, not unlike the way truth functions in the Johannine world. The Logos incarnate is full of grace, and it is out of His fullness that we all receive one grace after another. Such grace must be received with a faithful response to be effective. Though grace seldom appears in the Johannine literature, its occurrences are always in significant contexts.

Second, works have a robust place in the Johannine world. They are part of its very fabric, found in all genre of the Johannine voices. Works are not theologically superfluous but are deemed as absolutely essential to one's soteriological journey.

Third, works reveal something about one's origins or parentage. They indicate whether one is a child of God or of the devil, thus testifying to their organic nature. In the Johannine world, works are naturally generated owing to one's origins—on the same order as fruit is produced by a true vine.

Fourth, works also reveal something about one's relationship to God or the devil, light or darkness. As with origins, works reveal one's association with the salvific light of the world or the one who keeps the world in uncomprehending darkness. Specifically, believers are invited to participate in the work of God that Jesus does, but also are promised that they will do even greater works than He. Such an idea again underscores the organic nature of works as participation in the work of God/Jesus.

Fifth, works are intricately connected to salvation. It seems impossible to understand salvation without works in the Johannine world, for one's works testify as to whether or not one walks in fellowship with the light and fellow believers. If one does not love in work, one does not love.

Sixth, works have a testamentary value in the life of the believer. They are the fruit that testifies of the believer's relationship to God. The fact that the resurrected Jesus discerns the lives of the churches in Revelation on the basis of their works indicates the symbiotic relationship that exists between one's works and one's relationship to Jesus.

Seventh, works clearly function as the basis of divine judgment for good or bad. The Johannine world simply cannot conceive of a positive assessment of the life of an individual that does not manifest its faith in works.

Eighth, works appear to have a value beyond the grave. The works of the godly follow them even after death. Somehow the Spirit continues to honor and use the testimony of the works of believers.

Ninth, grace and works are held together in a dialectical tension. In the Johannine literature, this dialectic refuses to be split apart into a choice between grace and works, but insists on an organic understanding that an individual does not, even cannot, have one without the other.

Perhaps these reflections on grace and works in the Johannine literature can be of some service to the Pentecostal and Charismatic movement as it seeks to discern its way forward on this sometimes contentious issue.

JOHN CHRISTOPHER THOMAS, PhD, (University of Sheffield), is the Clarence J. Abbott Professor of Biblical Studies at the Pentecostal Theological Seminary in Cleveland, Tennessee, USA, and the Director of the Centre for Pentecostal and Charismatic Studies at Bangor University in Bangor, Wales, UK.

Chapter 14

GRACE AND SPIRIT BAPTISM

Scott T. Kelso

ERTAINLY THE SUBJECT of Spirit baptism has been thoroughly investigated, and I do not purport to bring any new revelation to the fore on this subject. Mountains of material have been produced over the last century of biblical scholarship relative to the subject of Spirit baptism. However, I want to share some new insights I have recently gained concerning the central work of the Holy Spirit in the new covenant.

As Christians we understand that Jesus is the key link in all of salvation history. He is the divine link between the Father and the Spirit. He remains the bridge between God and man. In the old covenant, this bridge functioned as the written Scripture (Torah), a "'guardian/instructor' (Gk. *Paidagogas*, lit., 'child-leader') to take us to Christ and faith."[1] (See Galatians 3:24–25.) "The written scripture could act only as a mirror—to show our dirty faces (our sin), but it didn't actually wash our faces!...By contrast, the New Covenant Spirit, that now indwells us, not only guides us as to the content of God's will but also motivates us to do it."[2]

All of this is of prime importance because the new covenant Spirit (Spirit baptism) is what Jesus came to inaugurate and ratify through His death and resurrection. (See Jeremiah 31:31

and Ezekiel 36:26.) This new covenant Spirit is the Holy Spirit Jesus promised (Acts 1:4), Joel foretold (Joel 2:28–29), and Peter confirmed through Isaiah (59:20–21) and declared on the Day of Pentecost (Acts 2:39). The Spirit would function as firstfruits, a guarantee, a deposit on our inheritance of all that is to come. (See Ephesians 1:14; 2 Corinthians 1:22; 5:5; and Acts 20:32.) Indeed, the Holy Spirit in us acts as a kind of "eminent domain" of His presence, informing all that we do and think.

In addition, in the big picture, Jesus's death and resurrection is His gift to the world, but the baptism in the Holy Spirit is His gift to the church. Father Peter Hocken, a Catholic priest and theologian, says the baptism in the Holy Spirit "is the foundational grace of the Pentecostal and charismatic movements as a whole."[3] Hocken goes on to say there is an objective character to the baptism in the Holy Spirit from which the *charisms* mentioned in 1 Corinthians 12:8–10 provide clear witness.[4] Because of this, the baptism in the Holy Spirit is more than a subjective state, and it is clear that it serves as a gift (grace) for the church at large.

WHAT IS THE BAPTISM IN THE HOLY SPIRIT?

Concerning the Gospels and the Book of Acts, it was the understanding of the New Testament writers, especially Luke, that the seminal work of Jesus following His ascension was the sending of the Holy Spirit upon the waiting church for empowerment and mission. (See Acts 1:8.) Without this critical stage in the *ordo salutis* (the sequence of salvation that ends up in heaven), the church would be relegated to a ministry of "remembrance" devoid of the power to confront the waiting world.

Luke tells us that Jesus gave specific instruction to the disciples: "And behold, I am sending the promise of my Father upon you. But stay in the city until you are clothed with power from on high" (Luke 24:49, ESV). According to James Dunn, author of *Baptism in the Holy Spirit*, "The coming of the Spirit in terms of an 'enclothing' is found both in the Old Testament and in early Christian thought."[5] As the 120 waited on the promise, the opportunity arrived on the Day of Pentecost, a national festival held in Jerusalem, for maximum effect. (See Acts 2:1–4.)

As with most seasons when God is "on the move" in the earth, there are those who are disinterested or not looking for the prophetic fulfillment of Scripture. One can see them in Acts 2:12, where the Jews "were amazed and perplexed, saying to one another, 'What does this mean?'" (ESV). However, there were also those on the right side of history, Peter among them, who said:

> Men of Judea and all who dwell in Jerusalem, let this be known to you, and give ear to my words. For these people are not drunk, as you suppose, since it is only the third hour of the day. But this is what was uttered through the prophet Joel: "And in the last days it shall be, God declares, that I will pour out my Spirit on all flesh, and your sons and your daughters shall prophesy, and your young men shall see visions, and your old men shall dream dreams."
>
> —Acts 2:14–17, ESV

A striking aspect for our purpose here is the response of the people once Peter unpacked this Old Testament verse. Acts 2:37 records: "Now when they heard this they were cut to the heart, and said to Peter and the rest of the apostles, 'Brothers, what shall we do?'" (ESV). Every good preacher deserves a solid response tethered to the message of the hour. Peter certainly received his. Furthermore, as Peter gave instruction to them in verse 38, "conversion-initiation"[6] took place and three thousand people were baptized in one day. Such would define a harvest in most anyone's book.

However, the point I wish to establish rests in verse 39: "For the promise is for you and for your children and for all who are far off, everyone whom the Lord our God calls to himself" (ESV). This is a direct promise from Isaiah 59:20–21, echoed by Ezekiel 18:30–31; 37:14; 39:29; and Jeremiah 31:33. These scriptures are pregnant with the prophetic hope of the new covenant Spirit Jesus promised. Even the apostle Paul sees this fulfilled in the new covenant Spirit. (See 2 Corinthians 3:2–3.) Professor Jon Ruthven makes clear from Scripture that the essence of the new covenant is the presence of the communicating, prophetic Spirit in our hearts.[7] (See, again, Isaiah 59:21 and Acts 2:39.)

MINISTRY UNDER THE ANOINTING OF THE BAPTISM IN THE HOLY SPIRIT

Following Pentecost, it was a whole new day for the people of God. They began to "hear" and "do" a kind of show-and-tell ministry that overturned the ancient world. (See Luke 24:19; Romans 15:18; and Hebrews 2:4.) As people were introduced to the Christian gospel, they encountered the faith in a kind of "multi-image" (video) platform as opposed to a single-image (one-dimensional/picture) platform. The presentation of the gospel was dynamic and alive with signs following. Consider the following scriptures, which offer an accurate overview of ministry-related activity under this new anointing.

- "The signs of a true apostle were performed among you with utmost patience, with signs and wonders and mighty works" (2 Cor. 12:12, ESV).

- "It was declared at first by the Lord, and it was attested to us by those who heard, while God also bore witness by signs and wonders and various miracles and by gifts of the Holy Spirit distributed according to his will" (Heb. 2:3–4, ESV).

- "Does he who supplies the Spirit to you and works miracles among you do so by works of the law, or by hearing with faith?" (Gal. 3:5, ESV).

- "And my speech and my message were not in plausible words of wisdom, but in demonstration of the Spirit and of power, so that your faith might not rest in the wisdom of men but in the power of God" (1 Cor. 2:4–5, ESV).

- "Because our gospel came to you not only in word, but also in power and in the Holy Spirit and with full conviction" (1 Thess. 1:5, ESV).

- "For I will not venture to speak of anything except what Christ has accomplished through me to bring the Gentiles to obedience—by word and deed, by the power of signs and wonders, by the power of the Spirit of God—so that from Jerusalem and all the way around to Illyricum I have fulfilled the ministry of the gospel of Christ" (Rom. 15:18–19, ESV).

- "And what is the immeasurable greatness of his power toward us who believe, according to the working of his great might" (Eph. 1:19, ESV).

- "For the kingdom of God does not consist in talk but in power" (1 Cor. 4:20, ESV).

- "For this is why the gospel was preached even to those who are dead, that though judged in the flesh the way people are, they might live in the spirit the way God does" (1 Pet. 4:6, ESV).

- "And behold, I am sending the promise of my Father upon you. But stay in the city until you are clothed with power from on high" (Luke 24:49, ESV).

Herein we are looking not only at what the Bible says but also what it emphasizes. How do we determine emphasis? By such things as repetition, space devoted, summary statements, and correlation of themes (e.g., spirit to prophecy, salvation to healing, and faith to miracle).[8] In addition, a review of the previous scriptures reminds the student of the New Testament that one cannot divorce the apostle Paul's theology from his experience. For example, two words that Paul uses side by side and at times interchangeably are Spirit (*pneuma*) and grace (*charis*). Since our theme is "Grace and Spirit Baptism," it is incumbent on us to detail these two words.

SPIRIT (*PNEUMA*) AND GRACE (*CHARIS*) BRIEFLY CONSIDERED

Professor James Dunn has written extensively on the themes of Jesus and the Spirit. With respect to these two words, *pneuma* and *charis*, a clear theme emerges from Paul's use of the terms in the New Testament. In his book *Jesus and the Spirit*, Dunn begins a section on Spirit and grace by saying, "Spirit (*pneuma*) for Paul is essentially an experiential concept: by that I mean a concept whose content and significance is determined to a decisive degree by his experience."[9] This is confirmed (through repetition and the amount of space devoted) by reading the following passages: Romans 5:5; 6:1; 8:9; 14; 1 Corinthians 1:4–9; 6:9–11; 12:13; 2 Corinthians 1:21; Galatians 3:1–5; 4:6; Colossians 2:11; 1 Thessalonians 1:5; and Titus 3:5–7.

Dunn continues: "For the moment it is enough that the experiential dimension of Paul's Spirit talk be recognized as a basic fact of his whole religion and theology."[10] We see in this that for Paul, the inner life of the Spirit of God supersedes all ritual and outward requirements of faith. (See Romans 2:8; 2 Corinthians 3; Galatians 4:6; Philippians 3:3; and Ephesians 1:7.) In fact, "the Spirit is that power which transforms a man from the inside out, so that metaphors of cleansing and consecration become matters of actual experience in daily living."[11] (See 1 Corinthians 6:9–11.) Since the Holy Spirit is a person, Paul's experience correlates with a "lived relationship" with the third person of the Trinity, an experience Jesus mirrored at His baptism.

Second, the word *grace* (*charis*) unfolds in two aspects. First, it unveils the salvation event, which is an act of "wholly unmerited generosity on God's part."[12] The cross is God's eschatological deed! And second, grace for Paul is the grace of conversion, establishing a living relationship with the living God. (See Romans 3:24; 5:15; 17:20; 1 Corinthians 1:4; 15:10; 2 Corinthians 6:1; Galatians 1:6, 15; 2:21; and Ephesians 2:5–8.) Again, for Paul, "grace is not something merely believed in but something experienced,"[13] resulting in a transforming power, "a continuing experience of a relationship with God sustained by divine power."[14] (See Romans 5:2 and Colossians 3:16.) In fact, the word *grace* literally means "generous charismatic empowerment."[15] This means, for instance, that even Paul's greetings and benedictions at the beginning and end of his letters are not just formality but the most sincere wish "that they may know ever afresh the gracious power of God existentially moving in and upon their lives."[16] In a real sense, these become "code words" respecting the "normative life in the Spirit in their respective Christian communities."[17] The "'grace' ('generous charismatic empowering') and 'peace' ('wholeness, health, balance, harmony') are ways of focusing on the Holy Spirit, which in our present era is the essential operating principle of the church and the Christian Life."[18]

In addition, the concept of "charisma" is an idea we owe almost entirely to Paul.[19] Being a distinctively Pauline word, "of the seventeen occurrences in the New Testament, only one comes from outside the Pauline corpus, and that from a typically Pauline passage (1 Peter 4:10)."[20] Dunn goes on to say: "Josephus does not use the word at all, and the only two occurrences in Philo are in reference to creation."[21] It is therefore significant that Paul's choice of this word betrays his own experience and understanding of how God relates to man in the work of the cross and resurrection.

In summary, we see a consistency of thought and experience even overlapping each other in the use of these words in Paul's letters. This is seen in Romans 1:11 (ESV), where Paul says, "For I long to see you, that I may impart to you some spiritual gift" (*pneumatikon* qualifies *charisma*),[22] "underlining Paul's conscious dependence on the Spirit and grace for any benefit he can bring to the believers at Rome."[23] All of this spiritual power is reinforced with the baptism in the Holy Spirit, placing the disciple in an ongoing, dependent, lived relationship with the third person of the Trinity.

THE TRANSFORMATION OF THE ANCIENT WORLD

With this spiritual dynamic in tow, the church grew exponentially not only in numbers but in power as well, passing on the faith effectively and consistently. (See Acts 2:41; 4:4, 7; 5:14; 6:7; 8:12; and 9:31.) By the beginning of the second century, it was obvious that Jesus was not coming back as soon as originally anticipated. Furthermore, frontiers were opening up to the east, the north, and the south. While the church was dutifully settling in the cities of Jerusalem, Antioch, and Alexandria, the mission emphasis of Acts 1:8 lay before them as the specter of virgin territory welcomed their witness.

With this growth, a Spirit-baptized constituency toppled the ancient world. Professor Ramsay MacMullen in his book *Christianizing the Roman Empire (A.D. 100–400)* gives a convincing historical case that Christianity displaced the competing religions of the day as well as the Roman stronghold itself. One must acknowledge that this was done essentially through the early church's moving in signs, wonders, and deliverance ministry. MacMullen says that within the first three centuries, the church "had successfully displaced or superseded the other religions of the empire's population."[24] An amazing feat, as he continues, "Among all the leisurely great developments...this one of the period A.D. 100–400 might fairly be given pride of place in the whole of Western history."[25] In other words, the establishment of

Christianity as the central faith of the ancient world gets first place in the pursuit of the living God.

By the end of the fourth century, a seven-thousand-mile oval church belt had been established in the Mediterranean from Rome in the north to Alexandria in the south. This was accomplished with no printing press, no church buildings, and no banks to loan money while crossing language, cultural, and ethnic barriers at every turn. The faith that was "once delivered to the saints" was getting serious traction. A Spirit-baptized church moving in the *charismata* (gifts of grace) released a spiritual persona that was in many cases irreducible in the ancient world. Hence, the greater works that Jesus promised in John 14:12 were being manifest.

In effect, Jesus Himself admitted that the church would eventually outshine His own ministry in a prophetic sense. Jesus's three-year ministry prior to Pentecost was but a sampling of all that was to come after Pentecost. Yes, Jesus spoke to large crowds, but many left unconvinced or unwilling to change. His upbraiding of the cities of Chorazin, Bethsaida, and Capernaum was because they did not respond to the "mighty works" He performed in their midst. (See Matthew 11:20–24.) Additionally, Jesus's lament over Jerusalem signifies their refusal to repent as well. He concluded: "Behold, your house is forsaken and desolate" (Matt. 23:38, RSV).

This is hardly the resonance of a successful ministry. Even at the end the crowds rejected Jesus and yelled, "Crucify Him!" After His resurrection, a group of five hundred was the largest crowd to see Him, and only one hundred twenty waited on the promised Holy Spirit prior to Pentecost. Yes, He touched some individuals and turned their worlds upside down, but He was crucified and buried under a brutal Roman regime on the back side of the world, having never traveled more than one hundred miles from His birthplace and leaving no written record of His own hand of His life and works. However, because Jesus said, "I go to the Father" (John 16:10, ESV), we the church would be destined for greater things. These greater things began at Pentecost with the baptism in the Holy Spirit. Following this event, the number of people who became eligible for a faith-fueled life by hearing the gospel message swelled exponentially, as previously mentioned, because all distinctions were erased. These were the "greater things" Jesus spoke of, as the Spirit of God, through the church, conquered the ancient world. As a result, even the apostles admitted, "So we have stopped evaluating others from a human point of view. At one time we thought of Christ merely from a human point of view. How differently we know him now!" (2 Cor. 5:16, NLT).

From a pastoral perspective, one question a leader may ask is, how broad is the current Pentecostal movement embracing the baptism in the Holy Spirit? We know for a fact the movement is no flash in the pan. For over one hundred years it has swept people of faith to a higher plane, resulting in the largest single segment of the body of Christ throughout the world, some six hundred million. For those who are not in this stream of the church, perhaps a second look would be in order.

Following a thorough analysis of the world Christian scene going into the twenty-first century, Alister McGrath in his book *The Future of Christianity* predicts only four segments of the body of Christ will flourish in the twenty-first century. They are the Roman Catholic Church, the Eastern Orthodox Church, evangelicalism, and those congregations tethered to the Pentecostal-Charismatic wing of the church.[26] Particularly with respect to the latter, Pentecostalism stresses a direct, immediate experience of God and avoids the rather dry and cerebral forms of Christianity many find unattractive and unintelligible.[27] "In addition," McGrath writes, "the movement uses a language and form of communication that enables it to bridge cultural gaps highly effectively."[28] And as theologian Harvey Cox has said, "With Pentecostalism, the marginalized and disadvantaged have found a second and relevant home."[29] Since the Global South—comprised of Africa, Central and Latin America, and most of Asia—is aflame with Spirit-filled Christianity and highly represented by the poor, this seems to be a good fit for the end-times church.

INTO THE TWENTY-FIRST CENTURY

The twentieth century was marked by an amazing outpouring of the Holy Spirit and God's grace. With it we witnessed the Azusa Street Revival; the healing revival led by William Branham, Oral Roberts, and others; the Latter Rain movement of 1948 that began through the ministry of George Hawtin at the Sharon Orphanage and School in North Battleford, Saskatchewan, Canada; the emergence of the Charismatic movement that began through Dennis Bennett's ministry in the Episcopal Church; the Catholic Charismatic Renewal that began at Duquesne University; the Third Wave movement that emerged under the leadership of John Wimber and the Vineyard Church; the Toronto Outpouring at the Airport Vineyard Church in Toronto under the leadership of John Arnott; and more. All of these movements had at their core the baptism in the Holy Spirit and the practical dissemination of the gifts (*charismata*) of the Spirit for the whole church. This is not to mention the whole area of Pentecostal-Charismatic worship, "drawing from the divine treasury things new and old: new in their expression, old in their inner life and significance."[30]

It has been said that the Charismatic Renewal movement in the United States was really the first nationwide revival in history. This is because the First and Second Great Awakenings had affected only the Protestant sector of the church, and not all of them. But the Charismatic Renewal touched the full range of Protestant churches as well as the Roman Catholic Church and the Eastern Orthodox Church. Henry Lederle says in his excellent book *Theology With Spirit*, "For the first time in Christian history, all the major branches of Christianity, albeit to differing extents, were influenced globally by the same religious awakening or renewal movement."[31]

Similarly, when speaking to the Charismatic Leaders Fellowship in 2012, Father Hocken said concerning the renewal that it "was a huge joy for Catholics and Protestants to find that for the first time they were part of the same tide of the Spirit and were able to experience a real communion in the Holy Spirit with each other. This outpouring of the Spirit was profoundly transforming and life-giving."[32] As Hocken has said, "Catholics and Protestants have received the same gift."[33]

A theological challenge (for some) is "the claim that the basic spiritual reality being called the baptism in the Spirit is fundamentally the same grace across all the different church groupings impacted by the charismatic movement."[34] Hocken concludes: "The church needs such movements to shake it up, to challenge all forms of immobility and stagnation, and to unleash fresh dynamism from the Spirit of God."[35] This ecumenical thrust has been and remains one of the big stories of the Renewal movement.

For those who can remember or were in attendance, the visible and organic unity of the body of Christ was on display for the entire world to see in New Orleans, Louisiana, at an ecumenical Spirit-filled conference at the Superdome in 1987. There were forty thousand people in attendance, twenty thousand of whom were Roman Catholic. Hocken said of this event: "The body of Christ in North America had been given a unity or a communion at the level of the Spirit which became a spring board for the task of achieving a unity at the level of the mind (articulated faith), leading to a level of embodied community."[36]

For the past twenty years I have been privileged to be a part of the Charismatic Leaders Fellowship (CLF), which is made up of top-tier leadership from the four streams of the faith: Catholic, Protestant, nondenominational, and Pentecostal. I currently serve as chairman of the group, succeeding our immediate past president,

Francis MacNutt. The group has benefited from scholars of the Renewal such as David du Plessis, Vinson Synan, Larry Christenson, Francis MacNutt, Everett "Terry" Fullam, and Kevin Ranaghan. In addition, we have had within our ranks such apostles as the late Ken Sumrall, Matteo Calisi, Randy Clark, William "Billy" Wilson, and Gerald Derstine.

The CLF was originally convened by Dennis Bennett in Seattle, Washington, in 1971 as the Charismatic Concerns Committee. The group was commissioned to first solve various problems attached to the burgeoning Charismatic Renewal, such as how to handle exorcisms (at the time it was not uncommon for there to be group exorcisms with little or no follow-up) and water baptism (as some disputed allowing infant baptism). Our group made it possible for Charismatic leaders from different traditions, who really didn't know one another, to meet, come to esteem one another, and build relationships that allowed trust to develop so they could address problems like the ones just mentioned. To facilitate such an important good, the meetings were by invitation only, and because the meetings were off the record, no recordings of any kind were permitted. In this, the participants were able to freely speak when controversial issues came up for discussion and prayer.

The group eventually moved to the La Salle Retreat Center in Glencoe, Missouri, and became known as the "Glencoe Group." Over the years the group became a catalyst for other important meetings like the North American Renewal Service Committee (NARSC), which sponsored large ecumenical gatherings in Kansas City, Missouri; New Orleans, Louisiana; St. Louis, Missouri; San Antonio, Texas; Indianapolis, Indiana; and Orlando, Florida. Through the 1980s and 1990s, thousands attended these gatherings as the group gave focus to the growing Charismatic Renewal movement.

The most famous of these ecumenical meetings was held in 1977 in Kansas City when forty-five thousand people gathered in

Arrowhead Stadium. Reflecting on this conference on the last night of the event, Father Michael Scanlan, a Catholic renewal leader, said: "There is going to be a new and more powerful ecumenical leadership in unity of Christian life than we have seen in the last five hundred years. And that's going to come from this conference, and it's going to be the most important fruit of the whole conference."[37] In addition, most of the mainline denominations birthed renewal movements in their respective streams in the wake of the Kansas City conference. The United Methodists' Charismatic conference, Aldersgate Renewal Ministries, is still going strong with several thousand in attendance each summer.

As the godparent of the Kansas City conference, the CLF has a unique place in the worldwide renewal movement. What Father Scanlan suggested has become evident in the work of the CLF and beyond. Currently, we are forming an effective mixture of the wisdom of age and experience accomplished by including early renewal leaders as well as a growing number of current and next-gen leaders from the United States and around the world. The Charismatic Leaders Fellowship has been and continues to be a powerful tool of the Holy Spirit for promoting unity, reconciliation, and evangelism to the world today.

Scholars, leaders, and next-gen voices converge at strategic cities around the world to give strategy for the final days' harvest. As we move into the future, the greatest convergence of Spirit-filled Christians in history will "set the table" for the coming of our Lord Jesus Christ. The future looks replete with opportunities for ecumenical courage as the Pentecostal-Charismatic streams within Christianity coalesce. As we move deeper into the "last days" mentality, the whole church must present the whole gospel to the whole world. Then perhaps Matthew 24:14 will finally be realized and "this gospel of the kingdom will be proclaimed throughout the whole world as a testimony to all nations, and then the end will come" (ESV).

Scott T. Kelso, DMin, spent thirty-eight years as pastor of Trinity Family Life Church in Pickerington, Ohio, before launching a full-time apostolic ministry of preaching, teaching, and writing. He is a past president of the Board of Directors for Aldersgate Renewal Ministries, a Charismatic movement within the United Methodist Church, and is currently on its advisory council.

Chapter 15

GLOSSOLALIA AND GROANING: A MANIFESTATION OF GOD'S GRACE

Mark R. Hall

I N THE BOOK of Romans, Paul emphasizes the cost and the value of grace and the need for believers to eschew evil and embrace the good. The apostle desires to share "some spiritual gift" (Rom. 1:11, NASB) and to see the indwelling Spirit intercede in the life of the believer with "groanings too deep for words" (Rom. 8:26, NASB), which many scholars assert is a reference to glossolalia. In this chapter, we will explore evidence for and against this interpretation and ultimately connect grace to the gift of glossolalia as a manifestation of the good.

THE CONTEXT

In the Book of Romans, Paul begins the epistle by expressing his desire to impart some spiritual gift to the believers in Rome (Rom. 1:11).[1] The two Greek words for "spiritual gift" used here primarily occur in Paul's writings—one of them twenty-four of twenty-six times (of which fifteen are found in 1 Corinthians) and the other sixteen of seventeen times (with 1 Peter 4:10 being the non-Pauline reference).[2]

In this verse, Paul longs to be used of the Spirit to convey a grace-gift, a "gracious bestowment," or "*Spirit* gifting."[3] The Roman context emphasizes "the gifts of God" or "a gift from God" (Rom. 5:15–16; 6:23; 11:29), especially as seen in Romans 12:6, where Paul describes the gifts as differing according to the grace given to each believer. Therefore, grace is connected with the gifts.[4] In fact, the Greek can be translated "the gift of grace" (Rom. 5:15–16),[5] or "free gift" or "gracious gift." Moreover, this freely given grace is ever-increasing, reigning over sin and death (Rom. 5:20–21).

In 1 Corinthians 12:4, the apostle emphasizes the varieties of the gifts, also translated "various," "diversities," "different kinds," and "different." *Gifts* here in the Greek is also derived from the word for *grace*. These gifts are distributed to believers by the same Spirit according to His will (1 Cor. 12:11) for the "common good" (1 Cor. 12:7, NASB). Paul declares that this grace-gift will establish or strengthen Christians (Rom. 1:11)[6] as they stand in God's grace (Rom. 5:2).[7]

The grace the apostle Paul discusses in Romans is demanding, not cheap. Even though believers are undergirded by this grace, Paul expects them to live according to the dictates of Jesus Christ and avoid sin: "What shall we say then? Are we to continue in sin so that grace may increase? May it never be! How shall we who died to sin still live in it?" (Rom. 6:1–2, NASB).

Later in that same chapter, Paul asks another question about grace: "What then? Shall we sin because we are not under law but under grace? May it never be!" (Rom. 6:15, NASB). The Greek translated here for "May it never be!" is used "in a prohibitive sense … to express a negative wish or a warning."[8] Primarily found in Paul's letters,[9] the clause is "an emotionally charged and highly negative response" to a question the apostle asks.[10] To make grace an excuse to sin is reprehensible to Paul.

According to the apostle, believers, benefited by a grace that leads to righteousness (Rom. 5:20–21), must be inhabited by the Holy Spirit (Rom. 8:9) in order to live free from the law of sin and death (Rom. 8:2) and avoid being a slave to the flesh (Rom. 8:5–8, 15). Jesus came as a human being and became a sin offering (Rom. 8:3). The Spirit raised Him from the dead, and that same indwelling Spirit causes the "children of God" (Rom. 8:16, NASB) to "cry out 'Abba! Father!'" because they are adopted sons and daughters (Rom. 8:15, NASB).

This intense longing, described later in the same chapter as groaning, is experienced by three actors: creation (8:22), believers (8:23), and the Holy Spirit (8:26). Gordon Fee makes this insightful observation about the relationship of the groaning of the believer and the Holy Spirit: "Paul intends that the Spirit indeed does the praying/crying through our own 'spirits,' using our mouths, but in one instance the emphasis is on the Spirit, while in the other it is on our participation."[11]

IS IT GLOSSOLALIA?

In particular, Romans 8:26 provides insight into how the Holy Spirit "helps our weakness," especially in prayer, "for we do not know how to pray as we should, but the Spirit Himself intercedes for us with groanings too deep for words" (NASB). Pentecostals and others often cite this passage as support of the occurrence of glossolalia in the New Testament.[12] The Greek for "groanings too deep for words" is translated "sighs too deep for words" in the lexicon.[13] It has been translated variously: "groanings too deep for words," "groanings which cannot be uttered," "sighs too deep for words," "wordless groans," "inexpressible groanings," and "groanings that cannot be expressed in words."

The word translated "unexpressed" or "wordless"[14] occurs only one time in the Greek New Testament text. Because of this, it remains an ambiguous term. As John Bertone expresses the problem, "Romans 8:26 is notorious for its ambiguity; much of the difficulty revolves around the uncertainty in the meaning of the word."[15] There are three possible ways to understand this word, according to Fee: "inexpressible," meaning "that for which there are no words"; "silent," meaning "not vocalized at all"; or "inarticulate," meaning "sounds that are not recognizable as known words."[16]

The interpretation of this verse has been much debated by scholars. Even such a noted Pentecostal scholar as Gordon Fee has actually changed his understanding of Romans 8:26. He explains, "One does a lot of soul-searching before concluding that a text refers to something different from what the majority of scholars believe, especially so, when it also means changing one's own position."[17] Although not dogmatic and with "Pentecostalism well in hand," Fee concludes that "this interpretation [groanings = glossolalia] moves in the right direction."[18] Even James D. G. Dunn, who is certainly not a Pentecostal scholar, allows for Fee's understanding of the verse.[19]

To help address this question, we find important connections between Romans 8:26 and 1 Corinthians 14:4, 5, and 14 and the depiction of "private glossolalic speech," according to John Bertone. These passages "speak of the Spirit's work as benefitting the individual," that it is an act of prayer, and that "it is potentially the prerogative of all believers to pray by the Spirit in this fashion."[20] These connections help set the foundation for a study of this verse in Romans.

Scholars are not unanimous in their belief that this verse refers to speaking in tongues. Adolf Schlatter clearly denies this assertion by pointing out that (1) the inability of the believer to pray is something that every believer faces, as opposed to tongues, where only certain believers manifest this gift; (2) glossolalia is a gift of praise and a singing of divine mysteries, not groaning; and (3) tongues are not "unspeakable," for some are able to interpret them, but in Romans 8:26 the groaning is without words and is intercessory.[21]

Keith Warrington argues against tongues being the groaning described in the passage for several reasons, asserting that the Spirit inspires tongues but not necessarily what is spoken; that the Spirit is more involved with the prayer than in tongues-speech; that those not gifted in this kind of prayer would be excluded; that the word translated "wordless" would not allow for actual speech; that the prayer of the Spirit is limited if it occurs only when the person speaks in tongues; that Paul just wants to identify this practice, not necessarily explain it; and that Paul is using this entire section as a metaphor to teach that the Spirit intercedes for those who are believers.[22] Leon Morris asserts that the groaning is not likely a reference to glossolalia, and "there seems little reason to hold such a view."[23]

Of course, each of the assertions can be easily refuted from a Pentecostal perspective. First of all, the Pentecostal would assert that all believers may speak in tongues after they receive the baptism of the Holy Spirit, citing the examples of the outpouring of the Spirit in the Book of Acts, where everyone who received the Spirit spoke in tongues (Acts 2:4; 10:46; 19:6). They would concede that the gift of tongues is given only to certain individuals in the church for public demonstration, as the Spirit wills, according to Paul (1 Cor. 12:10, 28; 14:5).

Second, there is nothing to indicate that glossolalia cannot have some element of groaning even if it is a gift of praise, for the whole experience may be intense and emotional. And finally, it is true that tongues can be interpreted, but Paul indicates that glossolalia can be spoken and not interpreted if the individual is speaking to himself and to God (1 Cor. 14:27–28). In this case, the words are unspeakable. This should not be a surprising discovery. The Book of Acts gives no indication that all tongues are interpreted.

C. H. Dodd interprets the "groanings too deep for words" by saying, "Inarticulate aspiration is the deepest form of prayer, and it is itself the work of the Spirit within."[24] He provides further definition: "An inarticulate aspiration is itself the work of the divine in us, and though we ourselves may not be conscious of its meaning, God knows what it means and answers the prayer."[25]

John Murray agrees with Dodd. He believes these groanings "are not expressed in articulate speech; they are not requests or petitions or supplications which are formulated in intelligible utterance.... They... transcend articulated formulation."[26] C. K. Barrett allows for the possibility of tongues but asserts that "it seems on the whole more probable that the point is that communion between Spirit (-filled worshipper) and God is immediate and needs no spoken word."[27]

Of particular note is Ernst Käsemann's position on the verse. Citing Dodd and Schlatter as well as other modern commentators, he says that they define the phrase as "wordless sighs" and points out that the phrase actually means "ecstatic cries." Käsemann clearly rejects the idea that Paul is "dealing with the problem and technique of prayer" and maintains that "it makes good sense, however, if what is at issue is the praying in tongues of 1 Corinthians 14:15."[28]

Käsemann poses the question as to why Paul used the Greek phrase "ecstatic cries" rather than "praying in the Spirit," if he had 1 Corinthians 14:15 in mind. He finds the answer in 2 Corinthians 12:4, where a man in Christ (probably Paul) was caught up into the third heaven to hear "inexpressible words" (NASB), which in the Greek does not mean "wordless" but "inexpressible in earthly language." Paul heard the language of angels and was unable to speak it.

Käsemann argues that the reason the Corinthians valued tongues above all other gifts was because they believed it was the speech of angels (1 Cor. 13:1) and thus demonstrated that they were taking part in the numinous. For Paul, glossolalia has a different function in worship, because heavenly speech indicates a moving of the Spirit and highlights the weakness of the worshippers, not their advanced spirituality. The Holy Spirit must intercede in their prayers if they are to pray in a manner that is pleasing to God.[29]

Käsemann poignantly describes the agency of the Spirit in the believer through the manifestation of glossolalic utterance:

> In tongues at worship there sounds forth in a singular way, and in such a manner that we do not ourselves comprehend the concern of the Spirit who drives us to prayer, the cry for eschatological freedom in which Christians represent the whole of afflicted creation. In this the Spirit manifests himself as the intercessor of the community before God and he takes it up into his intercession.[30]

He asserts that this Holy Spirit–inspired prayer reflects the desire for all of creation to experience liberty:

> By its ecstatic cries prayer is made for the whole of enslaved and oppressed creation. The intercession of the exalted Christ takes place at the right hand of God. The Spirit, however, is the earthly presence of the exalted Lord and does his work, intercession included, in the sphere and through the ministry of the community.[31]

He continues:

> If this intercession is regarded as possible only in the heavenly world…, the point is missed that the reference here is to the intercession of the Spirit and that this coincides with the cries of those who speak in tongues. This makes sense, however, if it is the earthly reflection of what the heavenly High Priest does before the throne of God.[32]

Thus, according to Käsemann, in Romans 8:26, Paul is showing how the community of believers are allowed to participate in the intercession of the High Priest of the faith, Jesus Christ, through Spirit-driven prayer.

Käsemann has been roundly criticized by scholars for this position. C. E. B. Cranfield adamantly rejects Käsemann's contention that Paul is not referring to Christian prayer. He writes, "We take Paul's meaning to be that all praying of Christian men, in so far as it is *their* praying, remains under the sign of this not-knowing, of real ignorance, weakness and poverty, and that even in their prayers they live only by God's justification of sinners."[33] Cranfield also points out that the Greek cannot refer to glossolalia since glossolalia contains mostly praise, and Paul is discussing here in Romans the presentation of needs and desires to God. Cranfield believes Paul would not conceive of the speaking in tongues of Christians as the groanings of the Spirit. He argues that the indication is that these groanings are unperceived by Christians; they are unspoken. There is no utterance needed since the Holy Spirit does not have to speak to communicate with God.[34]

A. J. M. Wedderburn also rejects Käsemann's interpretation of Romans 8:26 and asserts:

> It seems far more natural to take the phrase of a sighing that cannot find expression in any language or words, a form of wordless communication comparable perhaps to that which may pass between two people very much in love, who find their feelings to be too deep to express in words.[35]

Wedderburn believes Pentecostals may claim this verse as support for the public and private practice of glossolalia if they accept two restrictions: (1) they would have to concede they do not speak in a real language unknown to them but see the manifestation as a wordless dialogue between themselves and God at a deeper level not allowed by their weakness, and (2) they must believe there may be different kinds of "unspeakable groans," such as those expressed in anger or disgust or those made during intense emotion. He sums up rather weakly: "To one tied up in himself and unable to break out of himself, the release involved in surrendering himself to sheer God-ward babblings may indeed be seen, at least sometimes, as a gracious intervention of God's Spirit and a divine answer to his particular need."[36]

Others agree with Käsemann that the phrase "groanings too deep for words" refers to glossolalia, but they would not accept this as a reference to the public manifestation of tongues. Instead they would argue for the private manifestation of the Spirit. W. J. Hollenweger cites Romans 8:26 as the verse used by the Pentecostals to support "personal speaking in tongues, which can be described as a nonintellectual prayer and praise too deep for words."[37]

Oscar Cullmann, in his discussion of Paul and salvation history, mentions that the tension in the eschatological work of the Holy Spirit between the "already" and the "not yet" is expressed in Romans 8. Cullmann sees the groaning of the Spirit as the expression of the "not yet" aspect of the Spirit. He writes, "When the Spirit seeks to push through the limits of our imperfect organs which share in the...[flesh], the result is the 'unspeakable' groans that witness to our waiting for the freedom from all corruptibility." As the Spirit attempts to speak "through us in his own language, the result is speaking in tongues, which is at the same time the future, angelic language (1 Cor. 13:1), and yet represents a groaning because of the 'not yet.'"[38] As Bertone observes, "The Spirit's glossolalic groanings that are unintelligible to humans are perfectly intelligible to God."[39]

Käsemann indeed presents some excellent insight into these verses, enabling the reader to understand Paul's meaning. His evidence that this experience is glossolalic utterance is convincing and seems to be the most accurate way to interpret the Scripture. However, the passage could definitely refer to the prayer language of the individual believer as well as the corporate congregation assembled together praying in tongues. In contrast to Cranfield, nothing in Scripture indicates that glossolalia cannot include presenting needs and requests before the Lord as well as showing forth praises to God. Therefore, according to Käsemann, the agency of the Holy Spirit is manifested in the soul of the believer through the utterance of glossolalia in prayer.

Käsemann also indicates that, if the meaning of Romans 8:26 is that the Holy Spirit intercedes through the believer with these inarticulate or inexpressible groanings that are glossolalia, then the phrases "pray at all times in the Spirit" (Eph. 6:18, NASB) and "praying in the Holy Spirit" (Jude 20, NASB) are also likely references to that experience.[40] In these verses, the apostles demonstrate the importance of the Holy Spirit as an active partner in prayer. If this does refer to glossolalia, and the evidence seems to support this assertion, then the significance of that grace-gift cannot be underestimated. If believers are to follow the admonition of Paul and Jude concerning praying in the Spirit, then it is important they experience this phenomenon in their lives.[41]

The groaning Paul describes in Romans 8:26 has given rise to the assertion that Jesus spoke in tongues. The Greek words used in Mark 7:34 (NASB) ("deep sigh") and in Mark 8:12 ("sighing deeply") have been linked with the inarticulate groans of Romans 8:26. As demonstrated above, this verse could very well refer to glossolalia, but that is because the description of the groans as "unutterable, inarticulate, too deep for words" is attributed to the action of the Spirit, not because of the Greek word used here. It is important to note that Mark 7:34 occurs in a healing situation and that in the culture of the time, the word spoken that produces a miracle can be unintelligible sounds or an unfamiliar language. In this case, the word in Greek demonstrates intense emotion, not necessarily ecstatic utterance. Besides, the word Jesus spoke for the healing of the deaf man, "Be opened!," was spoken in Aramaic, a language familiar to Jesus.[42]

A GREAT GOOD

If Paul is discussing a manifestation of the charisma of speaking with tongues when he describes the "groanings too deep for words" (Rom. 8:26, NASB) and that same Spirit "searches what the mind of the Spirit is, because He intercedes for the saints according to the will of God" (Rom. 8:27, NASB), then everything moves together for the common good, as mentioned in 1 Corinthians 12:7. With confidence and assurance, the believer can "know that God causes all things to work together for good to those who love God, to those who are called according to His purpose" (Rom. 8:28, NASB).

Practicing this grace-gift, believers are led by the Spirit as sons and daughters of God participating in the good, following His calling, fulfilling His purpose. As Gordon Fee observes, "God purposes our good, which takes the form of our being 'conformed' into the image of his Son—this is what we have been predestined for—which in turn concludes with our finally being glorified with him."[43] Douglas Moo views the good as God's "fixed and eternal purpose to bring all things touching our lives to a triumphant conclusion."[44] This good is the manifestation of Holy Spirit intercession.

John Bertone asserts, "There is a sense of assurance that God will bring the divine plan to its intended goal through the experience of the Spirit praying through the believer."[45] This good is God's grace in action.

Gordon Fee exclaims, "Here is the wonder of grace that leads Paul to the final rhetoric of vv. 31–39—that God should do all of this (vv. 1–30) for us, sinners all, who once walked in the ways of the flesh that led to death, but now by the Spirit know the love of God in Christ from which nothing can separate us. The Pentecostal in me is wont to say, 'Hallelujah!'"[46] This good leads to eternal joy.

MARK R. HALL, PhD, is Professor of English and Dean of the College of Arts and Cultural Studies at Oral Roberts University in Tulsa, Oklahoma. Along with his studies in English, he has completed three additional master's degrees in Biblical Literature, Theological and Historical Studies, and Biblical Literature (Advanced Languages). He continues to write articles on biblical topics as well as C. S. Lewis and the Inklings.

Chapter 16

GOING BEYOND THE DEBATE ON GRACE: LEARNING FROM A SOUTH ASIAN TRADITION

Brainerd Prince[1]

W
HAT, EXACTLY, IS the debate of grace? As both the hyper-grace movement and the Pentecostal-Charismatic movement believe in grace, I would argue that the debate concerns how grace is mediated in our everyday lives. But we need to narrow this down even further to understand what kind of mediation of grace is sparking this debate.

Theologically speaking, if we were to state that grace is at work in both justification and in sanctification, then we find that the debate has primarily to do with the mediation of grace for sanctification as opposed to justification, as there appears to be consensus between the two groups regarding the role of grace in justification. It is with relation to sanctification that the differences arise.

While the Pentecostal-Charismatic movement believes God's grace is mediated even as the believer follows the laws of God and thus the works commanded by God, the hyper-grace movement argues that man needs to do nothing toward sanctification, so much so that even if he disobeys the commands of God, the

210

abundance of God's grace is freely mediated to him. For the former, grace is mediated through works. For the latter, grace is mediated without works. This difference can be stated as a debate between *grace mediated by law* versus *grace mediated without law*.

TWO VIEWS OF SANCTIFICATION

This debate on the role of grace in sanctification can be traced all the way back to the apostle Paul, through whom the Christian tradition received the idea of a perfect grace. This idea has inspired Christian theologians to "purify" the notion of grace, which has resulted in a Christian tradition that speaks of grace as

> "pure grace" or "sheer gift"; salvation is sola gratia (by grace alone). The grace of God is free, sovereign, totally gratuitous, indiscriminate, unconditional, unconditioned, uncontingent, unmerited, unstinting, and a whole set of other "un"-adjectives.[2]

Barclay traces the perfection of grace throughout the ages, first identifying one strand of thought that says God's love and mercy, as revealed in Jesus, makes Him a supremely good God who could do nothing but love and give, a God who was not capable of judging or condemning. Augustine then "perfected the incongruity of grace, the utter mismatch between the favour of God and the fittingness or worth of the human recipient."[3] Barclay further traces interpretations to the Reformation, where Luther shared Augustine's notion of God giving not to the deserving but to the utterly unworthy and unfit and where Calvin developed Augustine's thought through his inquiry into the function of grace in the process of sanctification. For Calvin, it was a "double grace," the grace of sanctification and justification.[4]

The efforts to perfect Paul's theology of grace continued with Barth's emphasis on grace as the "absolutely free and unconditioned act of God."[5] This was part of his insistence on the "'infinite qualitative difference' between humans and God, time and eternity; if God acts in grace towards us it is never because of our condition but always despite it."[6] Bultmann calls grace a pure gift, as opposed to the idea that one can achieve or procure it for ourselves.[7]

Barclay, thus drawing from the various interpretations of Paul's theology of grace and their efforts at its perfection, concludes, "'Pure grace' in this reading means without demand and without recompense, a unilateral transaction completely free of the circular motion which was everywhere associated with gift in antiquity."[8]

Notwithstanding the original purpose of Paul's theology of grace, which was missional in motive and offered in the context of Gentiles not having to fulfill the circumcision requirements and other requirements of the Mosaic Law, we are left with an understanding of perfect grace whose giver gives freely and generously to whomever He wills without finding fault and who requires no returns. This historical narrative has been the foundation for the development of the doctrine of *positional sanctification*, which is the hallmark of the hyper-grace movement.

What, then, is the origin of the doctrine of sanctification by works? It begins with Wesleyan Methodism, which proclaims the idea of *entire sanctification*. Wesley described this in his book *A Plain Account of Christian Perfection*, discussing purity of intention and the need to dedicate every part of one's life to God.[9] Pentecostalism arose out of the holiness movement and continued the holiness movement's stress on living by a moral code for sanctification. It particularly spread in the western and southern United States. Thus, one could say that grace mediated through works, in other words known as *progressive sanctification*,[10] began with Wesleyan Methodism and has become the hallmark of the Pentecostal-Charismatic movement.

The two main theories of positional sanctification and progressive sanctification have led to different understandings of the mediation of grace and the means of attaining it. Positional sanctification, which calls the believer holy in the sight of God on the basis of his new position, does not necessitate any work or a specific moral code. It is a change in position caused by God in which one moves from an unclean state to a sanctified, holy one. This view, held by the hyper-grace movement, takes a low view of works, as works are not required for the change in status. One need not work to be worthy of attaining grace.

On the other hand, the holiness movement, following a progressive understanding of sanctification, looks at character change almost as a prerequisite for receiving grace, thus requiring the following of moral codes and the doing of works. It is these different visions of sanctification that has brought about this debate on the mediation of grace between the holiness movement and the hyper-grace movement.

LIMITATION OF "GRACE AS GIFT" RESPONSE

Within contemporary Christian theology, John Milbank's "grace as gift" idea can be seen as a response to the critique of positional sanctification, which considers grace a gift-giving practice.[11] Billings states, "For Milbank, a purified gift is a gift that replicates itself in cycles of gratitude and obligation: gift-exchange involves 'delay' and 'non-identical repetition' of the gift in gratitude, thus extending obligation as a new gift is given. Milbank believes that Christian theology can point the way to these purified gift-exchanges."[12] Within the discourse on sanctification, this would imply that the giving of grace and the fulfilling of the obligation to receive grace are satisfied. The obligation part—that we do something in return upon receiving a gift—satisfies the holiness group. And the brilliance of the Milbank model, through the notions of delay and nonidentical repetition, also creates a scenario where the hyper-grace movement cannot accuse it of being grace by law. Thus,

Milbank's "grace as gift" model creates a mutual exchange between God and the believer that repeats in a cyclical manner.

However, a critique of this model comes from Jacques Derrida, for whom the very idea of a gift is annihilated by this form of mutuality. For Derrida, for a gift to completely be a gift, it must necessarily interrupt the economy of exchange. Thus, a gift that incurs obligation ceases to be a free gift.[13] For him, a gift is a gift only when it requires and expects nothing in return.[14]

While this Derridian position echoes the stand of the hyper-grace movement, which views grace as a gift of God without any requirement of human obligation attached to it, it fails to satisfy the requirements of the holiness group, which does ask for some response from the believer. Thus, we could say that the "grace as gift" model in the end does not resolve the standoff between these two positions.

WE NEED AN OUTSIDE VOICE

Thus it appears the debate has reached an impasse. Alasdair MacIntyre refers to these unresolved issues as an "epistemological crisis" within traditions, one in which it ceases to make progress.[15] However, MacIntyre also argues that when a tradition faces an internal impasse, the only way it can renew itself and overcome its impasse is to borrow from another tradition through dialogue.[16] He writes:

> When they [the tradition facing the epistemological crisis] have understood the beliefs of the alien tradition, they may find themselves compelled to recognize that within this other tradition it is possible to construct from the concepts and theories peculiar to it what they were unable to provide from their own conceptual and theoretical resources.[17]

This, then, would require us to engage the discourse on grace and sanctification with another tradition of grace that could potentially offer us insights that allow us to move our internal discourse past its limitations. I propose bringing the discourse on grace within the theistic Vaishnava tradition.

This move to learn from another tradition, particularly the Vaishnava tradition, might at first blush sound slightly unnerving. However, in Amos Yong we find a Christian theologian who echoes the key tenets of MacIntyre's model and explores their application for Christian theology. Yong claims that emergent churches already participate in these forms of inter-tradition engagement, in that they "emphasize genuine dialogue, encourage visiting other sacred sites and even participating in their liturgies, and insist on learning about the lives and religious commitments of others."[18] Yong argues that "these activities are informed by the conviction that there is much to be learned from other cultures, even to the point of being evangelized by those of other faiths in ways that transform Christian self-understandings."[19]

It is in such "transformed Christian self-understandings" of grace and sanctification that we are deeply interested, and I claim there is, indeed, much to be learned from the Vaishnava tradition's understanding of grace and hope. With that as our foundation, let us continue.

HOW THE THEISTIC VAISHNAVA TRADITION HELPS US

Within the Indian tradition of Vaishnava, both sanctification and grace are understood primarily in a relational context. In this model, the relationship between a teacher and student is given as a model for the mediation of grace.

Kiyokazu Okita presents this model by relying heavily on Madhva's (a prominent Indian thinker) articulation of the role of the guru, and more particularly on the role of the guru's grace.[20] According to Okita, the student's ultimate pursuit is to understand or obtain *Brahman*, which is ultimate reality.[21] Toward that end, the guru becomes significant and inevitable because knowledge leads to the most excellent state if it is obtained from a guru.[22] As we shall see, the role of the guru and his role in the mediation of grace of the supreme being is necessary to obtain Brahman. The veneration of the guru lies in the conviction that he is a link in a long chain of transcendental beginnings, a mediator able to bring his disciple and god together, or a medium through whom god is willing to reveal himself.[23]

I want to share three insights from this model. First, the grace of god is mediated through a guru. In other words, grace is mediated only in the relationship between the guru and his student. It is important to note that the disciple, who must make an effort to please his guru, initiates this relationship.

Why must the student please the guru? Because he realizes the guru's grace, or instruction, leads to attaining Brahman, and this grace comes to him only in the context of a personal relationship.[24] The disciple expresses his desire to "stay" and learn with the guru, because "a teacher does not teach unless and until he is approached by the student."[25] The central observation here is that the guru gives instruction to the student only after a personal relationship is established between them, one that is initiated by the student.

Second, we might ask, what is grace in this relationship? The guru, filled with the mercy and power of god, teaches spiritual practices to his student. The main task of the guru in the Hindu tradition is to teach and impart the grace of the supreme being. The guru is responsible for not only the intellectual development of the student but the uplifting of the disciple's life and well-being in all aspects.[26]

In the light of this, let us learn how grace is imparted in this tradition. We see this in what follows:

> In Hindu mysticism as far as it expressed itself in Hindu literature the true guru separates matter from spirit for the sake of his disciple's spiritual upliftment; he is to sharpen his intellect, removing all the rust and dirt of passions and

desires. There are two views about this process: the disciple may either attempt by a process of self-purification to perfect himself, or await his guru's grace: in a single moment he can reach the goal of his endeavour (i.e. the door of liberation) by the grace of his spiritual teacher. In the third place, the guru takes away all the defects and deficiencies of his disciple's mind, enlarging his receptivity and making him worthy and capable.[27]

There seems an implicit message in these lines that seems to say that the disciple realizes the vanity for an attempt at self-purification and thus "awaits his guru's grace." The impartation of grace by the guru "takes away all the defects and deficiencies...enlarging his receptivity and making him worthy and capable." We might then ask, worthy and capable for what? To put it simply, the disciple becomes fit and equipped to practice the instructions that are bestowed on him.

This teaching of spiritual practice—which in our Christian language would be called "works"—is the impartation of grace. Thus, while the instruction is understood as the impartation of grace, the practice is the actual work done for the reception of grace.

The debate between *grace with works* and *grace without works* is transcended here, in that it is only in the work of the spiritual practice that the grace is received. We could use the phrase *grace in work* to denote this model. In other words, the working out of the spiritual practice is nothing but the very act of the reception of grace. There are not two processes, but one.

Third, the student has to please the teacher in order to acquire grace. To do this, the student leaves his family and lives with his teacher. He serves the teacher with the view to please him, so that the teacher will bestow his favor or grace and teach him the spiritual practices and give him its knowledge.

It is pertinent to note that without the guru's favor, one's spiritual practices do not bear fruit.[28] Pleasing the guru and evoking his grace comes through a personal relationship *through service*. In the Vaishnava tradition, one guru asks his disciple to tend to his cows. The disciple later becomes a guru himself, and another disciple comes to live with him as a student. He requires the student to tend his household fire for twelve years.[29] In both instances, the students carry out the responsibilities given by the gurus who instruct them.

In this *grace in work* model, the student has to do a kind of double work—one to please the teacher and another to receive his grace. There is an intrinsic relationship between grace and work that is not causal but rather complementary in this relational model. It entails service toward the guru to invoke his grace. Furthermore, the student must invoke the grace so that his spiritual practices and understanding of the truth bear fruit and are complete. It may be added that in developing a relationship with the guru and in obtaining his grace, the student also develops a relationship with the supreme being and attains his grace, because the guru is a direct manifestation of Brahman.[30]

TOWARD A RELATIONAL MODEL OF SANCTIFICATION

I would like to argue that one way to go beyond the deadlock between the holiness movement and the hyper-grace movement is to unpack the conceptual requirements of a relational approach to sanctification, as informed by the Vaishnava tradition.

In the language of Martin Buber, there is an "I-You" relationship between God and the believer. In this relational context, we find both the flow of God's grace and the sanctification of the believer. It requires for God to open Himself voluntarily to enable a relationship between the "I" (the believer) and the eternal "You." Indeed, the very possibility of the relationship is due to the grace of God, which enables the seeker to know Him.[31]

Okita's guru-student relationship can be read as the relationship between God and the believer in Christian theology. Here, grace as charismata will indeed be none other than the spiritual practices or spiritual gifts given by God. Its being given and received is constrained by the relationship the believer shares with God, even as she understands her role in the larger community in which she is placed and where her charismata finds meaning.

The believer's relationship with God is always rooted in the context of her relationship with the larger community of God. It is here that grace as charismata comes to its full, which enables the community to do a range of activities in Christ for a mutual building up of the body. In this community, Rudolf Sohm argues that God has placed Charismatic rulers as teachers, like the Indian guru.[32] David Smith, summarizing Sohm, states that "teachers convey a truth they have not invented, and they lead without being elected."[33]

Thus, the relational model is not completely alien to Christian theology, and this could be one way we find to go beyond the conflict between the holiness movement and hyper-grace movement. Here, grace is the impartation of spiritual gifts and practices (charismata) cherished by the holiness movement in the context of a community. However, it is only made possible through the disciple's ecstatic love in action toward God, as promoted by the hyper-grace movement.

Taking Sohm's argument out of context and placing Charismatic teachers as the Hindu equivalent of gurus for the purpose of this paper would be a misrepresentation of the dynamics of the relational model in the way I would like to argue. However, taking the teachers as mediators of Christian instruction in the believer's efforts to develop and dwell in a personal relationship with God may serve better as a starting point.

Having said that, the mechanics of how the guru imparts knowledge and instruction to the student on behalf of the supreme being can be explained in Christian terminology as the Son, Jesus, revealing the Father through His life and teachings. Thus, the act of giving and receiving grace within the dynamics of the student-teacher relationship between the disciple and the guru can also be understood within Christian theology as a relationship between a believer and Jesus, who is the whole and complete representation of God, the Father.

Of course, to try to force an interpretation of the Vaishnava tradition into a Christian Trinitarian understanding is one way of appropriating its insights. However, because a Christian theology of grace anchors itself in the person of Jesus Christ, and as the understanding of grace in the hyper-grace movement is the gift of God through the Christ event,[34] it might help to see the Hindu disciple-guru model as a parallel to the Christian believer–Jesus model.

In what follows, we try to relate the three insights gleaned from the theistic Vaishnava tradition to the Christian relational model of sanctification.

The first insight

Just as grace is mediated through the guru in the Hindu tradition, we have Charismatic teachers placed among us or above us to impart grace in the form of instruction and teachings. The source of grace remains God, who is ultimately the One the student or disciple tries to please.

We noticed that in the guru-student model, the latter makes the effort to please his teacher and takes the initiative for developing the relationship with the guru because he realizes grace will come to him only through the guru's favor. It shows a sense of helplessness on the part of the disciple. This correlates with the Christian idea of the incongruity of grace. The believer's utter hopelessness leads him to realize that only in God can he find grace and thus he must take the initiative to approach God to receive the gifts of forgiveness and salvation. The believer must take the effort to be in a personal relationship with God, because God reveals Himself as a person.[35] Thus to receive His grace, we have to meet and relate to

God in the context of a relationship. It is here that His grace flows and here that sanctification functions.

The second insight

In the second insight we see that the guru's impartation of grace coincides with the performing of the spiritual practices by his students. The goal of these instructions is surely that the disciple may understand and follow. Daley sheds light on "a new relationship" that humans develop from their side, even as they live as a new creation: "'To live for God, to live from God' is to be nourished by his life and to see by his light, is to experience the reality of grace directly in our human lives."[36] Thus, apart from the realization that grace is mediated only within a relationship with God, God places teachers with *charismata* over us to teach us. In doing so, He imparts His grace to us continuously.

In this, the acts of imparting and receiving grace coincide, in that in the very acting or working out of the charismata, grace is manifested. It is also in the very act of receiving grace that we see the cleansing act of being made worthy and capable of serving God, doing so according to the understanding that stems from the appropriation of the received grace.

The third insight

Finally comes the idea that the student has to please his teacher in order to receive his grace and that the student faithfully caries out the responsibilities given by the guru. This further states that his grace comes through extending a personal relationship through service.

To appropriate this for the relational model, I affirm again that the believer's reception of charismata finds meaning in the larger community of believers, where she works her grace out by serving her fellow beings, thus participating in mutual edification and sanctification of the body of Christ. The gift of grace, or charismata, can be seen as spiritual gifts that are bestowed on the believers in various forms, which "both qualify and call individual Christians to the range of activities in Christ."[37]

Understanding the reception of grace in this sense enables us to embrace the idea of works as advocated by the holiness movement because these gifts are "worked out" by the very act of exercising them in relationship with others in the Christian community. In this way, the believer serves God, reciprocating His gift of grace as she uses her charismata toward mutual edification of the body of Christ.

RESPONDING TO THE TWO VIEWS

The positional stand on sanctification, which holds a rather passive view of the reception of grace, maintains a once-for-all bestowal of grace that makes a believer's "position" permanent and unchangeable with regard to sanctification. Such is the view of the hyper-grace movement, as has already been seen.

The relational model we are advocating compels us to insert an added step before arriving at a positional view of the reception of grace. It suggests the need for the believer to take the initiative to enter into a relationship with God after she realizes her sheer unworthiness. This does not cloud the incongruity of grace—that it is given despite the believer's complete undeserved condition. Yet while it is given freely to anyone, it is bestowed in the context of a relationship, and this relationship is one that is initiated by the believer.

Further, the believer's position is always understood within the relationship that he has with God. Thus, we once again reflect on the understanding that it is within the context of the "new relationship" we have with God that we as "new creations" can live *for* and *from* God, by the grace that we receive from Him.[38] Thus, grace remains readily available to the believer in abundance. Yet this grace refers not only to the gift of forgiveness and justification but also as gifts of teachings that ought to guide the life and practice of the believer. This satisfies the positional sanctification view because a relationship indeed places us in a position where God freely and voluntarily bestows His grace on the believers *in the context of the personal and vital relationship between them*, and He does so because He is pleased to do so.

Second, the idea of progressive sanctification, as the holiness movement understands it, is an adherence to a set of moral standards that must be kept for the ongoing sanctification process to continue. Here again the relational model puts the understanding of works, or performance, in context. Works are not implemented as the means to attain grace but rather to manifest the presence of grace in a believer's life as she seeks to find meaning for her charismata in the larger Christian community. Thus, the spiritual gifts and practices of a believer flow naturally out of the personal relationship and because of grace that God bestows on her.

Also, the impartation of spiritual practices in the relationship itself is seen as the impartation of grace. This may lean closer to Milbank's idea of a mutual gift-giving practice, where the gift of grace is reciprocated in the act of the believer manifesting her charismata. This makes the reciprocal gift not necessarily an obligation back to God but one offered in community life—in a sense, a continuance of the received grace through its giving out, a way of paying forward grace rather than paying back.

Classical Pentecostals hold that believers are set apart from the world. In this view, association with the world is considered a constraint on the process of sanctification. This idea requires believers to dedicate themselves to strict morality and to lead holy lives evidenced in "conduct, dress and speech."[39] To satisfy this requirement, we look at the Hindu model that holds the need for the student to live with the teacher as an effort to please his teacher who bestows grace to him. A Christian understanding of being in a relationship with God indeed requires the disciple to say no to the world and to live a distinct, separate life that will eventually lead to his entire sanctification.

BRAINERD PRINCE, PHD, works with various institutions around the world as an academic research consultant, designing and implementing research tracks for their programs. He is currently a visiting research tutor at the Oxford Centre for Mission Studies and a research fellow at the Oxford Centre for Hindu Studies, a recognized independent center of Oxford University. He is the author of *The Integral Philosophy of Aurobindo: Hermeneutics and the Study of Religion.*

Chapter 17

BEWARE OF COUNTERFEIT GRACE

Joseph Prince

WE LIVE IN exciting times. Our Lord Jesus is truly restoring the gospel of grace that was first given to the apostle Paul. Over the last decade, I have had the great privilege of reading a constant stream of praise reports and testimonies sent to our ministry office from precious people set free from all kinds of addictions, including smoking, drugs, alcohol, and especially pornography.

Beyond being unshackled by the heavy yoke of guilt and condemnation, real lives, real marriages, and real families are being transformed, and these people are living for the glory of Jesus through the power of His amazing grace. Grace is not a movement, teaching, or subject to be studied. It is all about a person. His name is Jesus. What one believes about our Lord and Savior, Jesus Christ, and what He has done at the cross makes all the difference.

REIGNING OVER SIN THROUGH GRACE

To understand the grace of God, it is essential we understand the difference between the old covenant of law and the new covenant of grace. John 1:17 tells us, "For the law was given through Moses, but grace and truth came through Jesus Christ" (NKJV). The law was given through a servant; grace and truth came through the Son. The law talks about what man ought to be; grace reveals who God is. The letter kills, but the Spirit gives life (see 2 Corinthians 3:6). Under the law, God demands righteousness from sinfully bankrupt man. But under grace, God provides righteousness as a gift. All who believe in Jesus and acknowledge Him as their Lord and Savior are under the new covenant of grace.

Yet many believers today still live in confusion. They get law and grace all mixed up by holding to some aspects of the law and some aspects of grace in their Christian walk. As such, they continue in defeat rather than reigning over the power of sin through the abundance of grace and the gift of righteousness. Romans 5:17 tells us clearly that "those who receive abundance of grace and of the gift of righteousness will reign in life" (NKJV). When we reign in life, we reign over sin, addictions, and all forms of evil.

Thankfully, our Lord Jesus is restoring the purity of the gospel of grace today, and many are finding freedom from long-term addictions and other bondages. They share with great joy how the Lord has supernaturally delivered them from decades of substance abuse and sexual addictions, frequent panic attacks, and even long-term clinical depression. Others write in brimming with thanksgiving because He has restored their marriages and their relationships with their estranged children and has healed their bodies when doctors had given them no hope. One common denominator took these precious people from defeat to victory, from breakdowns to breakthroughs: they all had an encounter with our Lord Jesus and caught a revelation of His amazing grace.

DISTORTIONS TO THE
RESTORATION OF GOD'S TRUTH

Nonetheless, it is important we realize that as with any restoration of God's truths in church history, there are distortions today to the restoration of the truth of grace. There are many controversies, inaccuracies, and counterfeits to the genuine work of grace that God is doing in His church and in people's lives. It is unfortunate that a small number misrepresent the truth of God's amazing grace, using "grace" as an excuse for living a licentious lifestyle that is in clear violation of God's Word. It is essential that we do not draw our conclusions about God's grace based on the few who abuse it but instead study God's Word for ourselves to understand what the original, unadulterated gospel of grace truly is.

Our responsibility as ministers entrusted with the gospel is not to back away from the truth of God's grace but to heed the advice that the apostle Paul gave Timothy. He instructed his young protégé to "be strong in the grace that is in Christ Jesus" and to "study to shew thyself approved unto God, a workman that needeth not to be ashamed, rightly dividing the word of truth" (2 Tim. 2:1, 15, KJV).

For this reason, I would like to address here some of the key inaccurate and counterfeit grace teachings that have grown prevalent and led some astray. These counterfeit and pseudo-grace teachings have also turned off some pastors and ministers to the gospel of grace. This is most unfortunate, and my prayer is that pastors and church leaders all around the world will receive for themselves an accurate revelation and understanding of the good news that is changing lives and drawing precious people into an intimate relationship with our Savior. I pray that as God-appointed shepherds over our flocks, we do not make judgments based on incomplete sound bites and hearsay but will thoroughly examine what each grace preacher actually teaches and carefully check it against Scripture.

IS GRACE A LICENSE TO SIN?

Because of the abuses and inaccurate representations of the teaching of true grace, I have heard many warn others, "Watch out for that dangerous grace teaching. It gives people a license to sin."

If you hear of any "grace" teaching that tells you it is all right to sin, to live without any regard for the Lord, and that there are no consequences to sin, my advice to you is to flee from that teaching. You have just been exposed to counterfeit grace. Genuine grace teaches that believers in Christ are called to live holy, blameless, and above reproach. It teaches that sin always produces destructive consequences, and that it is only through the power of the gospel of Jesus Christ that one can be set free from the dominion of sin. Study Titus 2:11–15 (NKJV):

> For the grace of God that brings salvation has appeared to all men, teaching us that, denying ungodliness and worldly lusts, we should live soberly, righteously, and godly in the present age, looking for the blessed hope and glorious appearing of our great God and Savior Jesus Christ, who gave Himself for us, that He might redeem us from every lawless deed and purify for Himself His own special people, zealous for good works.
>
> Speak these things, exhort, and rebuke with all authority. Let no one despise you.

The Word of God states in no uncertain terms that the grace of God teaches us to deny ungodliness and live godly lives. Therefore, watch out for counterfeit grace teachings that contradict Scripture.

So how do we know if someone is truly living under the grace of God? We look at his life. If someone is leaving his wife for his secretary and tells you he is under "grace," tell this person that he is not under grace but under deception! Go by the authority of God's Word, not what this man says. Romans 6:14 states, "For sin shall not have dominion over you, for you are not under law but under grace" (NKJV). If this person were truly living under grace, he would not be dominated by such a sin. And no one living in sin can legitimately use grace as an excuse to sin, because it is antithetical to God's holy Scriptures. Genuine grace is not a license to sin; it is the power to live above the dominion of sin. Genuine grace doesn't compromise God's holy standards and condone sin; it is the answer that gives people power to live glorious lives, zealous for good works.

There will always be a small number of people who abuse grace, stir controversy with counterfeit grace teachings, and live in ways that do not glorify the Lord. But what should our response be? Should we shy away from preaching and teaching the true grace of God because of the controversies and abuses? Certainly not. I exhort you today, with the words of Titus, to "speak these things, exhort, and rebuke with all authority. Let no one despise you."

In other words, don't back away from preaching the grace of God. In fact, we should be doubling down on our preaching of the genuine gospel that teaches all to "[deny] ungodliness and worldly lusts" and to "live soberly, righteously, and godly in the present age." The more genuine grace is preached, the more counterfeit grace teachings will be stamped out.

People may use the word *grace* freely, calling themselves "grace preachers" with "grace ministries" or "grace churches." But we need to be discerning. Just because they use the word *grace* doesn't mean they are accurately or truly representing the gospel of grace. Test everything! Be sure that their position against sin is clear, as sin is destructive and brings with it a whole host of damaging consequences.

TRUE GRACE DOESN'T DISREGARD THE MORALS OF THE TEN COMMANDMENTS

Inaccurate explanations of the Ten Commandments abound in counterfeit grace teachings. Be clear that true grace teaches that the Ten Commandments are holy, just, and good. True grace teaching upholds the moral excellencies, values, and virtues espoused by the Ten Commandments. The Ten Commandments are so perfect in their standard and so unbending in their holy requirements that Galatians 3:11 states that no man can be justified by the law in the sight of God. Justification before God can only come by faith in Christ.

The Ten Commandments are glorious. The problem has never been the Ten Commandments or God's perfect law. The problem has always been imperfect man's inability to keep God's perfect law. Based on the terms of the Mosaic covenant, if you kept God's law, you were blessed. But if you didn't, you were cursed and condemned with a death sentence hanging over your head.

The fact is that under the old covenant, no man could keep the law perfectly. That is why soon after the law was given, God made a provision of animal sacrifices so that man's curse, condemnation, and death sentence could be transferred to the sacrificial bull or lamb. This is a picture of Jesus at the cross! When John the Baptist saw the Lord Jesus on the banks of the Jordan River, he said, "Behold! The Lamb of God who takes away the sin of the world!" (John 1:29, NKJV). So even in the law we see that man's only hope to be right with God once and for all is Christ. True grace teaching esteems the moral excellencies of the law, but it also makes clear to us that no man can be justified by keeping the Ten Commandments. This is so that we see our need for Christ.

TRUE GRACE CAUSES YOU TO MORE THAN FULFILL THE LAW

In the fifteen hundred years that God's people lived under the law, not a single man, apart from our Lord Jesus, could obey the Ten Commandments perfectly and be justified. Listen carefully to what I am about to say. Under grace, when we experience the love of our Lord Jesus, we will end up fulfilling the law! Under true grace, we will end up being holy. Grace produces true holiness! As the apostle Paul boldly proclaimed, "Love does no harm to a neighbor; therefore love is the fulfillment of the law" (Rom. 13:10, NKJV).

When the love of Jesus is in us, we can't help but fulfill the law. When our hearts are overflowing with God's grace and loving-kindness, we lose the desire to commit adultery, to murder, to bear false witness, or to covet. We will have the power to love our neighbors as ourselves. Where does this power come from? From our being firmly rooted and established in the grace of God. We have the power to love, because He first loved us (1 John 4:19)!

The fact is that when God's people are under grace, not only do they fulfill the letter of the law, but they also exceed it or go the extra mile. The law commands us not to commit adultery, and there are people who can fulfill just the letter of the law and not commit adultery outwardly. However, inwardly, they have no love for their spouses. Grace changes all that. Grace doesn't just deal with the surface; it goes deeper and teaches a man to love his wife as Christ loved the church.

In the same way, the law can command us not to covet, but it has no ability to make us cheerful givers. Again, God's grace goes beyond the superficial to inwardly transform our covetous hearts into hearts that are loving, compassionate, and generous. Remember the story of Zacchaeus in Luke 19? Not a single commandment was given. Yet when the love and grace of our Lord Jesus touched his heart, the once-covetous and corrupt tax collector wanted to give half of his wealth to the poor and repay fourfold every person he had stolen from. The love of money died when the love of Jesus came.

In contrast, the rich young ruler in Luke 18 came to our Lord Jesus boasting that he had kept all the commandments. This young man was probably expecting Jesus to compliment him on his law keeping and was feeling really confident of himself. But notice what Jesus said to him. Instead of complimenting him, Jesus said, "You still lack one thing" (Luke 18:22, NKJV).

You see, every time we boast in our ability to be justified by the law, our Lord will point out an area in which we are lacking. He told the young man to sell all that he had, give it to the poor, and follow Him. Jesus was giving him the very first commandment—"You shall have no other gods before Me [not even money]"—and look at what happened. The young ruler walked away sorrowful. He was not even able to give away one dollar!

I believe the Holy Spirit placed these two stories side by side in Luke 18 and 19 to show us what boasting in the law produces and what the power of the Lord's unconditional grace produces in people's lives.

GROW FROM GLORY TO GLORY

God's grace is not against God's perfect and glorious law of the Ten Commandments. In fact, the apostle Paul says, "For I delight in the law of God according to the inward man" (Rom. 7:22, NKJV). However, he goes on to say, "But I see another law in my members, warring against the law of my mind, and bringing me into captivity to the law of sin which is in my members" (v. 23, NKJV). Can you see? The law of God is holy, just, and good, but it has no power to make you holy, just, and good. Hear what Paul says earlier in the chapter:

> Well then, am I suggesting that the law of God is sinful? Of course not! In fact, it was the law that showed me my sin. I would never have known that coveting is wrong if the law had not said, "You must not covet." But sin used this command to arouse all kinds of covetous desires within me! If there were no law, sin would not have that power.... The law itself is holy, and its commands are holy and right and good.... Sin used what was good to bring about my condemnation to death.... So the trouble is not with the law, for it is spiritual and good. The trouble is with me, for I am all too human, a slave to sin.
>
> —ROMANS 7:7–8, 12–14, NLT

We learn from Paul that when we combine God's perfect law with the flesh, the result is not holiness. It is, as Paul described, a life dominated by sin, condemnation, and death. In man's flesh dwells no good thing, and as long as we are in these mortal bodies, the sin in our flesh will continue to be stirred.

But praise be to our Lord Jesus Christ, this doesn't have to end in misery and hopelessness! Because of what Jesus has accomplished on the cross, we can have the veil of the law removed, so that we can behold Jesus face-to-face and be gloriously transformed:

> So if the old way, which has been replaced, was glorious, how much more glorious is the new, which remains forever!...But the people's minds were hardened, and to this day whenever the old covenant is being read, the same veil covers their minds so they cannot understand the truth. And this veil can be removed only by believing in Christ....So all of us who have had that veil removed can see and reflect the glory of the Lord. And the Lord—who is the Spirit—makes us more and more like him as we are changed into his glorious image.
>
> —2 Corinthians 3:11, 14, 18, NLT

It is clear from God's Word that the law stirs up our sinful nature, whereas grace produces true holiness. Holiness is all about becoming more and more like Jesus, and it comes about when the veil of the law is removed. When the veil is removed, we see our beautiful Savior face-to-face, and His glorious grace transforms us from glory to glory. The glorious gospel of grace always produces glorious lives. As we behold Jesus, we will grow from glory to glory and shine as a testament of the Lord's goodness and moral excellencies.

GRACE DOES NOT MEAN AUTOMATIC SALVATION FOR ALL

When our Lord Jesus died at Calvary, He took on all of humanity's sins with one sacrifice of Himself at the cross. He took the judgment, punishment, and condemnation for every sin upon Himself. That's the value of the one Man, Jesus. He is an over-payment for all our sins.

Now, does this mean everyone is automatically forgiven and saved?

Of course not! While everyone's sin was paid for at Calvary, every individual needs to make a personal decision to receive for-giveness of all his sins by receiving Jesus as his personal Lord and Savior. Any so-called "grace" teaching that teaches otherwise is counterfeit grace teaching. There is no other way to be saved except through Jesus and His shed blood. Look at what God's Word says:

> If you confess with your mouth the Lord Jesus and believe in your heart that God has raised Him from the dead, you will be saved. For with the heart one believes unto righteousness, and with the mouth confession is made unto salvation. For the Scripture says, "Whoever believes on Him will not be put to shame." For there is no distinction between Jew and Greek, for the same Lord over all is rich to all who call upon Him. For "whoever calls on the name of the LORD shall be saved."
> —ROMANS 10:9–13, NKJV

There is no ambivalence in Scripture as to how a person becomes a born-again believer in Christ. To be saved, you have to confess with your mouth that Jesus is your Lord and believe in your heart that God raised Him from the dead.

Therefore, if any "grace" teacher tells you that you don't need to receive Jesus as your Lord and Savior in order to be saved because there are "other ways," he or she is being scripturally inaccurate. Jesus is the only way. There is no salvation without Jesus. There is no forgiveness without the cleansing blood of Jesus. There is no assurance that all our sins have been forgiven without the resurrec-tion of Jesus. Salvation is found in Jesus and Jesus alone!

I am also aware there are counterfeit grace preachers who teach that everyone, even Satan and his fallen angels, will one day, in the ages to come, be saved. Because of this belief, they also teach that hell isn't a real place of everlasting punishment. These people take an extreme position on God's love to the exclusion of His righteousness and judgment, refusing to believe what the Scriptures clearly teach about eternal torment in hell for the unsaved. This is not the gospel of grace.

ARE ONLY OUR PAST SINS FORGIVEN?

Coming back to forgiveness of sins, the real gospel tells us that the moment we invite Jesus into our hearts and confess Him as our Lord and Savior, all our sins—past, present, and future—are forgiven. To understand the total forgiveness of sins, we have to understand the value of the person who sacrificed Himself on the cross for us. Jesus alone, because He was the sinless Son of God, could pay for every sin of every man who would ever live with just a one-time sacrifice of Himself.

But there are teachings that suggest that when we receive Jesus, only our past sins are forgiven—that our future sins are forgiven as we confess them and ask God for forgiveness. This simply contradicts the Scriptures, as we shall see.

Ephesians 1:7 states, "In Him we have redemption through His blood, the forgiveness of sins, according to the riches of His grace" (NKJV). In the original Greek text, the verb for "have" is in the present tense, which indicates durative action, meaning we are continually having forgiveness of sins, including every sin we will ever commit.[1]

First John 2:12 says, "I write to you, little children, because your sins are forgiven you for His name's sake." The Greek perfect tense is used here for "are forgiven," meaning this forgiveness is a definite action completed in the past, with the effect continuing into the present.[2] This means that God's forgiveness avails for us in our present and continues into our future.

Let me give you another clear scripture that states that all our sins, including our future sins, have been forgiven:

> You were dead because of your sins and because your sinful nature was not yet cut away. Then God made you alive with Christ, for he forgave all our sins. He canceled the record of the charges against us and took it away by nailing it to the cross.
> —COLOSSIANS 2:13–14, NLT

Jesus forgave all our sins. The word "all" in the above Scripture is the Greek word *pas*, meaning "every kind or variety…the totality of the persons or things referred to."[3] It refers to "all, any, every, the whole."[4] So "all" means all. God's forgiveness of our sins covers every sin—past, present, and future! When we received the Lord Jesus as our Savior, we received the total and complete forgiveness of all our sins.

Our role as ministers of God is to impart to our people the confident assurance of their salvation and forgiveness that is found in Christ. It is not to teach a mixed message that deposits insecurity and uncertainty in their hearts, leaving them wondering if they are truly forgiven and if the work of their Savior at the cross is complete. Assurance of salvation and total forgiveness of sins form the foundation of the good news we preach.

I submit to you that this revelation of the good news of God's forgiveness doesn't lead one to live wantonly. Jesus Himself said that those who are forgiven much will love Him much (Luke 7:47). It is those who are forgiven little—actually, these creatures do not exist because all of us have been forgiven much, so I should say it is those who *think* they have been forgiven little—who will love Him only a little.

My prayer is that everyone who hears us preach the true gospel of grace will hear just how complete God's forgiveness is toward those who would receive His Son, Jesus Christ. It will surely lead them to fall deeper in love with Jesus and produce a life of praise, honor, and glory unto Him.

True Grace Teaches Progressive Sanctification

Now, I understand there are ministers who are genuinely worried that when the truth of the gospel is told like that, people will take advantage of their total forgiveness in Christ and lead godless lives. They are worried that such teaching places no emphasis on sanctification or the desire to live holy, God-glorifying lives. This is a misconception, because true grace does teach progressive sanctification.

Let me state clearly that while a believer has been justified and made righteous by the blood of Jesus, it is also true that sanctification is ongoing in his growth as a Christian. This is why the author of the Book of Hebrews says that we are "being sanctified" even though we have been "perfected forever" by Christ's one act of obedience at the cross (Heb. 10:14, NKJV).

As believers, we cannot become more righteous, but we can become more sanctified or holy in terms of how we live our lives. Justification by faith happened instantaneously. The moment we received Jesus, we were forgiven, cleansed, perfected in righteousness, and saved. We were also sanctified in Christ (Heb. 10:10). However, it is important to understand that the revelation and outworking of our sanctification in Christ is progressive. This means that the more we grow in our relationship with the Lord Jesus, the more holy we will become in every area of our lives.

The Word of God proclaims that "all Scripture is given by inspiration of God, and is profitable for doctrine, for reproof, for correction, for instruction in righteousness" (2 Tim. 3:16, NKJV). So be wary of any counterfeit grace teaching that says behavior, discipline, correction, and right living are not important. The revelation of forgiveness does not detract from, nor is it at the expense of, right living. Instead, it is the fuel that makes right living happen.

Merriam-Webster's dictionary describes sanctification as "the state of growing in divine grace as a result of Christian commitment after baptism or conversion."[5] You see, it is all about growing in grace. We should encourage our people today to establish themselves in the gospel of grace. Paul told Timothy to "be strong in the grace that is in Christ Jesus" (2 Tim. 2:1, NKJV). Peter encouraged believers to build a strong foundation with these closing words in his last epistle: "Grow in the grace and knowledge of our Lord and Savior Jesus Christ" (2 Pet. 3:18, NKJV).

True grace always produces true holiness. The more one grows in grace—the more one is washed again and again by the water of the Word of God's grace—the more one grows in sanctification and holiness. When our people experience the true grace of our Lord Jesus, the allure and passing pleasures of sin fade in the light of His glory and grace. And they begin to live victorious over the power of sin.

LET'S NOT BE ASHAMED OF THE GOSPEL

My prayer is that these words help pastors, ministers, and leaders in the church begin a journey of discerning the differences between genuine grace and counterfeit grace. Many of the thoughts shared here are taken from and covered more extensively in my book *Grace Revolution*.[6] I implore you, as a sibling in Christ, to not back away from the gospel of grace because of hearsay, counterfeit teachings, controversies, or a small minority who abuse and misrepresent the gospel by the way they live.

The gospel of grace is the answer. Grace lifts a person who is struggling with sin out of a life of defeat. Grace produces not an outward form of holiness that is transient but an enduring holiness that is birthed from a transformation that begins in a person's heart when he encounters Jesus.

This is what happened to Neil from the United Kingdom, who

wrote to my ministry about how the Lord set him free from a forty-year struggle with a sexual addiction:

> While reading a book by Pastor Prince, I was delivered from a forty-year addiction to pornography. In the past, I had tried to break free from this addiction by my own power and in my own strength, but failed every time.
>
> Throughout that time, the devil used this addiction to heap fear, guilt, and condemnation on me. This fear and shame kept me from asking for help from the pastors of the various churches I attended over the forty-year period. I had even held leadership positions in some of these places.
>
> As I read the book, I got a fresh revelation of who I am in Christ—I am the righteousness of God in Christ Jesus—and how there is no condemnation for those who are in Christ Jesus. It was through this fresh revelation that the grip of this addiction was broken off my life forever.
>
> I now wear a ring to remind myself that I am righteous. Every time the devil tries to tempt me to view pornography, I just have to look at the ring to remind myself that I am the righteousness of God in Christ, and the temptation loses any hold on me.[7]

This is the power of the gospel! Precious lives like Neil's are being touched, changed, and transformed by the love of our Lord Jesus. Our part as ministers entrusted with the gospel is not to back away from the truth but to study the Word of God diligently, to rightly divide His Word, and to boldly proclaim His truth with absolute clarity and love.

We must not be ashamed of the gospel. It is without doubt, as the apostle Paul proclaimed, "the power of God to salvation for everyone who believes.... For in it the righteousness of God is revealed from faith to faith; as it is written, 'The just shall live by faith'" (Rom. 1:16–17, NKJV). The gospel is not about our self-righteousness but the righteousness of God given as a gift to those who put their faith in our Lord Jesus.

Perhaps we are not winning souls to the degree that we should be because we have presented a gospel of Christ plus works, albeit unintentionally in many cases. Good works are the evidence of salvation, but they are definitely not the condition for salvation.

It is when we know that we are saved by grace through faith that moral excellence results. It does not happen the other way around. I know the only reason testimonies of precious lives being set free from sin, addictions, and all kinds of bondages flood our ministry office every week is that the gospel of Jesus Christ is being preached. May we all be accurate carriers of the true gospel of grace that changes lives!

JOSEPH PRINCE is a highly sought-after conference speaker and the senior pastor of New Creation Church in Singapore, which has a congregation of more than thirty thousand attendees. He separately heads Joseph Prince Ministries, one of the fastest-growing television broadcast ministries in the world today, reaching millions with the gospel of grace.

NOTES

Introduction
From Graceless Law to Lawless Grace

1. This article was written in the early 1980s, long before the advent of the modern grace movement.

Chapter 1
Jack Hayford, the Security of the Believer, and the Need for Pentecostal Pastor-Theologians

1. For an accessible discussion of varying views on the subject of eternal security, see J. Matthew Pinson, ed., *Four Views on Eternal Security* (Grand Rapids, MI: Zondervan, 2002). For a helpful volume on Arminian theology, see Roger E. Olson, *Arminian Theology: Myths and Realities* (Downers Grove, IL: InterVarsity Press, 2006).

2. I make no apologies for my advocacy of the life and ministry of Jack Hayford. Hayford's story is remarkably unstained by scandal or any serious breach of integrity. This is despite his remarkable recognition and success.

3. For an excellent example of his handling of the Shepherding Movement, see Jack W. Hayford, "Conciliation Without Compromise," *Logos Journal* (November/December 1975): 26–32.

4. Although Hayford has, on many occasions, expressed his opinions regarding controversial theological and pastoral issues, the hyper-grace teaching is not one of them. In a recent phone interview, he expressed some concerns but felt he was not well enough informed on the hyper-grace teaching to offer an opinion publicly at this point. Jack W. Hayford, telephone interview with the author, May 4, 2016.

5. Resource Catalog 1972-2000, Van Nuys, CA: SoundWord Tape Ministry/Church on the Way.

6. Jack Hayford, *The Sin of Suicide* (Van Nuys, CA: SoundWord Tape Ministry, 1984), audiocassette. An abridged transcript is available at http://www.jackhayford.org/assets/files/TheSinOfSuicideby JackHayford.pdf (accessed September 14, 2017).

7. Hayford, *The Sin of Suicide.*

8. Hayford, *The Sin of Suicide.*

9. Jack W. Hayford, *The Church on the Way: Learning to Live in the Promise of Biblical Congregational Life* (Lincoln, VA: Chosen Books, 1982), 56.

10. Hayford, *The Church on the Way*, 56.

11. Hayford, *The Church on the Way*, 57–58.

12. Hayford is not a Calvinist. Regularly in sessions at his School of Pastoral Nurture, Hayford presented his contrasting version of the TULIP acronym denoting the five points of classic High Calvinism. Jack W. Hayford, Class Handout: "TULIP According to Hayford," School of Pastoral Nurture, The King's University, Southlake, TX.

13. Jack W. Hayford, "Transcript of Consultation II," 2000, School of Pastoral Nurture, The King's University, 6.

14. Hayford, *The Sin of Suicide*.

15. Hayford, *The Sin of Suicide*.

16. Hayford, *The Sin of Suicide*.

17. Hayford, *The Sin of Suicide*.

18. Hayford, telephone interview with the author, May 4, 2016.

19. Such issues included situational ethics and euthanasia.

20. Kevin J. Vanhoozer and Owen Strachan, *The Pastor as Public Theologian: Reclaiming a Lost Vision* (Grand Rapids, MI: Baker Academic, 2015).

21. Vanhoozer and Strachan, *The Pastor as Public Theologian*, 1.

22. Vanhoozer and Strachan, *The Pastor as Public Theologian*, 1–2.

23. Vanhoozer and Strachan, *The Pastor as Public Theologian*, 1.

24. Vanhoozer and Strachan, *The Pastor as Public Theologian*, 2.

25. Vanhoozer and Strachan, *The Pastor as Public Theologian*, 16.

26. Vanhoozer and Strachan, *The Pastor as Public Theologian*, 16.

27. Gerald Hiestand, "The Pastor as Wider Theologian, or What's Wrong with Theology Today," *First Things*, January 3, 2011, https://www.firstthings.com/web-exclusives/2011/01/the-pastor-as-wider-theologian-or-whats-wrong-with-theology-today.

28. Hiestand, "The Pastor as Wider Theologian, or What's Wrong with Theology Today," italics in original.

29. Hiestand, "The Pastor as Wider Theologian, or What's Wrong with Theology Today."

30. Hiestand, "The Pastor as Wider Theologian, or What's Wrong with Theology Today."

31. Hiestand, "The Pastor as Wider Theologian, or What's Wrong with Theology Today."

32. Hiestand, "The Pastor as Wider Theologian, or What's Wrong with Theology Today."

33. Vanhoozer and Strachan, *The Pastor as Public Theologian*, 1–10.

34. Vanhoozer and Strachan, *The Pastor as Public Theologian*, 7.

35. Douglas Jacobsen, *Thinking in the Spirit: Theologies of the Early Pentecostal Movement* (Bloomington, IN: Indiana University Press, 2003), xi.

36. James K. A. Smith, "Thinking in Tongues," *First Things* (April 2008): 28, https://www.firstthings.com/article/2008/04/003-thinking-in -tongues.

37. Pentecostals have always valued pastors as their primary theological voices. Accordingly, the sermon takes on great significance in shaping faith communities and their biblical/theological self-understanding. In addition, Pentecostals acknowledge experience as a contributor to theological formation and tend to be less philosophically or academically oriented in their preaching.

38. The Foursquare Church has not required any formal theological training in order to qualify for ministerial credentials. This practice is presently under review.

39. See Roger E. Olson, *The Mosaic of Christian Belief: Twenty Centuries of Unity and Diversity*, 2nd ed. (Downers Grove, IL: InterVarsity Press, 2016).

Chapter 2
Are All Our Sins—Past, Present, and Future—Already Forgiven in Jesus?

1. See Michael L. Brown, *Hyper-Grace* (Lake Mary, FL: Charisma House, 2014), 39–50.

2. This chapter was previously published in Michael L. Brown, *The Grace Controversy* (Lake Mary, FL: Charisma House, 2016). Used with permission.

Chapter 3
The Hyper-Grace Gospel

1. It is also referred to as "modern grace" and "extreme grace" theology.

2. Clark Whitten, *Pure Grace: The Life Changing Power of Uncontaminated Grace* (Shippensburg, PA: Destiny Image, 2012), 26.

3. Whitten, *Pure Grace*, 26.

4. Whitten, *Pure Grace*, 27.

5. Steve McVey, *The Secret of Grace* (Eugene, OR: Harvest House, 2014), 75.

6. John Crowder, *Mystical Union* (Santa Cruz, CA: Sons of Thunder, 2010), 17.

7. Brown, *Hyper-Grace*, 14.

8. Steve McVey, *Grace Walk* (Eugene, OR: Harvest House, 1995), 110.

9. McVey, *Grace Walk*, 113. Taken at face value, it appears that McVey is an antinomian and is recommending that approach to others.

Having read several of his books, however, I know his abhorrence of performance-based Christianity and his belief in a life lived in union with and focused on Christ.

10. "About the Ministry: How the Grace Revolution Began," Joseph Prince Ministries, accessed December 5, 2017, https://www .josephprince.org/about/the-ministry; see also https://web.archive.org /web/20100615055511if_/http://josephprince.org/About_The _Ministry.html?active=about.

11. "Clark Whitten," Trinity Fellowship, accessed April 9, 2016, http:// www.justasyouare.com/default.aspx?tabid=380.

12. Grace Walk Ministries, "About Us," accessed November 6, 2017, http://www.gracewalk.org/our-team/.

13. "Paul Ellis," Amazon.com, Inc., accessed November 6, 2017, https:// www.amazon.com/Paul-Ellis/e/B003DAOP32/ref=dp_byline_cont _book_1.

14. For example, Clark Whitten in his book *Pure Grace* says this of his objectors: "The rock-throwing legalists who fill modern Christian churches and spawn the pharisaical preachers they listen to each Sunday seem to be more dimwitted than the Pharisees of Jesus' day. They, at least, walked away without saying a word...which is more than can be said of the mean-spirited Pharisees of our day" (121).

15. Rob Rufus, *Living in the Grace of God* (Milton Keynes, UK: Authentic Media, 2007), 14.

16. Andre Van der Merwe, *GRACE, The Forbidden Gospel* (Bloomington, IN: WestBow, 2011), 28.

17. Andrew Wommack, *Grace, the Power of the Gospel: It's Not What You Do, But What Jesus Did* (Tulsa, OK: Harrison House, 2007), 213, https://books.google.com/books?id=Ttrg4UawmUQC&pg.

18. Andrew Farley, *The Naked Gospel* (Grand Rapids, MI: Zondervan, 2000), 69. It is with much grudging reluctance that Whitten grants that "The Law expresses a wise way to live and order one's life and is valuable as a resource for decision making" (*Pure Grace*, 121).

19. Farley, *The Naked Gospel*, 61.

20. Farley, *The Naked Gospel*, 84.

21. Andrew Farley, *Relaxing with God* (Grand Rapids, MI: Baker Books, 2014), 127.

22. Farley, *The Naked Gospel*, 86.

23. Ryan Rufus, *Extra Virgin Grace: The Fig Tree vs. the Olive Tree* (n.p.: New Nature Publications, 2011), 93–4.

24. Joseph A. Fitzmyer, "Romans," *The Anchor Bible* (New York: Doubleday, 1993), 584. See also Colin G. Kruse, "Paul's Letter to the Romans," *The Pillar New Testament Commentary* (Grand Rapids, MI: Eerdmans, 2012), 402–5.

25. Kruse, "Paul's Letter to the Romans," 405.

26. D. A. Carson, "Matthew," in *The Expositor's Bible Commentary*, vol. 8, gen. ed. Frank Gaebelein, (Grand Rapids, MI: Zondervan, 1984), 142.

27. Carson, "Matthew," 143.

28. George E. Ladd, *Theology of the New Testament*, 3rd ed. (Grand Rapids, MI: Eerdmans, 1993), 553–4.

29. D. Martyn Lloyd-Jones, *Studies in the Sermon on the Mount*, reprinted (Grand Rapids, MI: Eerdmans, 2000), 196.

30. Andre Rabe, *Metanoia*, Clarity Book 1 (n.p.: Andre Rabe Publishing, 2011), Kindle.

31. Joseph Prince, *Destined to Reign: The Secret to Effortless Success, Wholeness and Victorious Living* (Tulsa, OK: Harrison House, 2010), 107. Extreme grace teachers dismiss John's clear statement regarding the universal reality of sin in believers and the promise of God's forgiveness upon one's repentance (1 John 1:8–9), (wrongly) claiming that the apostle had Gnostics, not true believers, in mind.

32. Whitten, *Pure Grace*, 166.

33. Hyper-grace advocates do believe there is a place for confession, repentance, and forgiveness—but not in the traditional sense. Such actions are in response to what God has already done, not dismissal from the consequence of infraction.

34. Paul Ellis, *The Hyper-Grace Gospel* (Birkenhead, New Zealand: KingsPress, 2014), 26.

35. Ellis, *The Hyper-Grace Gospel*, 28.

36. Steve McVey, *Beyond an Angry God* (Eugene, OR: Harvest House, 2014), 67.

37. Ellis, *The Hyper-Grace Gospel*, 31.

38. Merrill C. Tenney, "The Gospel of John," in *The Expositor's Bible Commentary*, vol. 9, gen. ed. Frank Gaebelein (Grand Rapids, MI: Zondervan, 1981), 184.

39. Leon Morris, "The Gospel According to John," in *The New International Commentary on the New Testament* (Grand Rapids, MI: Eerdmans, 1971), 815.

40. Crowder, *Mystical Union*, 36–37.

41. Cleon L. Rogers Jr. and Cleon L. Rogers III, *The New Linguistic and Exegetical Key to the Greek New Testament* (Grand Rapids, MI: Zondervan, 1998), 539.

42. Brown, *Hyper-Grace*, 102.

43. Albert Barnes, *Barnes' Notes on the New Testament*, reprint, (Grand Rapids, MI: Kregel, 1982), 1305.

44. McVey, *The Secret of Grace*, 17.

45. McVey, *Beyond an Angry God*, 94.

46. Farley, *Relaxing with God*, 79.

47. Whitten, *Pure Grace*, 117.

48. Brown, *Hyper-Grace*, 15.

49. Dietrich Bonhoeffer, *The Cost of Discipleship*, trans. R. H. Fuller (New York: Macmillan, 1963), 45.

50. Bonhoeffer, *The Cost of Discipleship*, 46–47.

51. Bonhoeffer, *The Cost of Discipleship*, 47–48.

52. Thomas Oden, *The Transforming Power of Grace* (Nashville, TN: Abingdon, 1993), 164, 165.

Chapter 4
John Wesley's Fuller Understanding of Grace

1. John Wesley, "The Sermons of John Wesley—Sermon 43: The Scripture Way of Salvation," Wesley Center Online, accessed December 5, 2017, http://wesley.nnu.edu/john-wesley/the-sermons-of-john-wesley-1872-edition/sermon-43-the-scripture-way-of-salvation/.

2. John Wesley, *Explanatory Notes on the New Testament* (London: Epworth Press, 1950), 1 John 4:8.

3. John Wesley, "God's Love to Fallen Man," ¶I.1. *The Works of John Wesley* [Bicentennial Edition] (Nashville: Abingdon Press, 1975) 2:423.

4. Charles Wesley, "O Love Divine, What Hast Thou Done," *The United Methodist Hymnal* #287, 1742, accessed December 6, 2017, https://hymnary.org/text/o_love_divine_what_hast_thou_done.

5. John Wesley, "A Farther Appeal to Men of Reason and Religion," Part I, ¶I.3. *Works* [Bicentennial] 11:106.

6. John Wesley, "The Scripture Way of Salvation," ¶I.1. *Works* [Bicentennial] 2:155.

7. Wesley, "The Scripture Way of Salvation," 155.

8. John Wesley, "A Blow at the Root; Or, Christ Stabbed in the House of His Friends," ¶1. *The Works of John Wesley, M. A.* [Jackson Edition] (1872) X:364.

9. John Wesley, "Letter to Mr. Walter Churchey, of Brecon" (February 21, 1771), *Works* [Jackson] XII:432.

10. Albert C. Outler, ed., *John Wesley* (New York: Oxford University Press, 1964), 287.

11. See John Wesley, "Original Sin," *Works* [Bicentennial] 2:172–85; "Heaviness Through Manifold Temptations," *Works* [Bicentennial] 2:222–35; and "On Patience," *Works* [Bicentennial] 3:170–9.

12. John Wesley, "The Witness of Our Own Spirit," ¶15. *Works* [Bicentennial] 1:309.

13. John Wesley, "On Conscience," ¶I.5. *Works* [Bicentennial] 3:482.

14. John Wesley, "The General Spread of the Gospel," ¶9. *Works* [Bicentennial] 2:488–9.

15. Wesley, "The General Spread of the Gospel," 488–9.

16. Wesley, "The General Spread of the Gospel," 488–9.

17. John Wesley, "On Working Out Our Own Salvation," ¶III.3. *Works* [Bicentennial] 3:206.

18. Wesley, "On Working Out Our Own Salvation," ¶III.7. *Works* [Bicentennial] 3:208.

19. John Wesley, "An Earnest Appeal to Men of Reason and Religion," ¶9. *Works* [Bicentennial] 11:47–8.

20. John Wesley, *Journal* (November 25, 1739). *Works* [Bicentennial] 19:123.

21. Wesley, "An Earnest Appeal to Men of Reason and Religion," ¶2. *Works* [Bicentennial] 11:45.

22. John Wesley, "On the Wedding Garment," ¶19. *Works* [Bicentennial] 4;148.

23. John Wesley, "The Law Established by Faith I," ¶II.6–7. *Works* [Bicentennial] 2:27–29.

24. John Wesley, "The Law Established by Faith II," ¶II.1. *Works* [Bicentennial] 2:38.

25. Wesley, "The Law Established by Faith II," ¶II.3. *Works* [Bicentennial] 2:39.

26. Wesley, "The Law Established by Faith II," ¶II.2.

27. John Wesley, "Justification by Faith," ¶II.4. *Works* [Bicentennial] I;188.

Chapter 5
The Grace Revolution and Person-Centered Therapy:
A Comparative Analysis from a Pastoral Care Perspective

1. Pastor Joseph Prince of New Creation Church in Singapore is the major proponent of "Grace Revolution," known also as hyper-grace.

Some of his followers accept the term *hyper-grace* to describe their theology while others consider it derogatory and prefer *amazing grace*, *abundant grace*, or *grace message* (Jeremy White, "Why I Am Hyper-Grace: Answering Five Common Objections," *Surrendered Image* (blog), August 21, 2014, https://www.facebook.com/notes/leopoldo -b-solis/why-i-am-hyper-grace-answering-five-common-objections-by -jeremy-white/813869541964943/?refid=17; Michael Reyes, "'Hyper-Grace' Is True!" *Loved by God, Loving Others* (blog), February 19, 2013, http://love-god-love-others.blogspot.com/2013/02/hyper-grace -is-true.html). One teacher calls his critics the "hyper holiness" side (Jeff Turner, "Jeff Turner Speaks on Hyper Grace Horror Stories," posted in Chris Welch, *080808 On, Now, To the 3rd Level* (blog), March 4, 2013, http://www.thethirdlevel.info/2013/03/jeff-turner -speaks-on-hyper-grace.html).

2. Name withheld, in communication with the author, November 26, 2014.
3. Joseph C. Hough Jr. and John B. Cobb Jr., *Christian Identity and Theological Education* (Chicago: Scholars Press, 1985), 5–6.
4. H. Richard Niebuhr, *The Purpose of the Church and Its Ministry* (New York: Harper & Row, 1956), 51.
5. William A. Clebsch and Charles R. Jaekle, *Pastoral Care in Historical Perspective* (New York: Jason Aronson, 1975), 32–66.
6. Clebsch and Jaekle, *Pastoral Care in Historical Perspective*, 32–66.
7. Howard Clinebell, *Basic Types of Pastoral Care and Counseling: Resources for the Ministry of Healing and Growth* (Nashville, TN: Abingdon Press, 1984), 43.
8. Carl R. Rogers, *On Becoming a Person: A Therapist's View of Psychotherapy* (Boston: Houghton Mifflin Company, 1995), 8.
9. Rogers, *On Becoming a Person*, 23–24.
10. Ralph W. Lundin, "Rogers, Carl Ransom (1902–1987)," *Corsini Encyclopedia of Psychology*, 4th ed., vol. 4, ed. Irving B. Wiener and W. Edward Craighead (Hoboken, NJ: John Wiley and Sons, 2010), 1474.
11. Lundin, "Rogers, Carl Ransom," 1474.
12. Carl R. Rogers, "The Basic Conditions of the Facilitative Therapeutic Relationship," in *The Handbook of Person-Centered Psychotherapy and Counselling*, ed. M. Cooper et al. (New York: Palgrave Macmillan, 2007), 1, as quoted in Tracy A. Knight, "Client-Centered Therapy," *Corsini Encyclopedia of Psychology*, vol. 1, ed. Irving B. Weiner and W. Edward Craighead, 4th edition (Hoboken, NJ: John Wiley & Sons, 2010), 324.

13. Knight, "Client-Centered Therapy," 324.
14. Carl R. Rogers, *A Way of Being* (Boston: Houghton Mifflin, 1980), 124–126, as quoted in Knight, "Client-Centered Therapy," 324.
15. C. R. Rogers, "A Theory of Therapy, Personality, and Interpersonal Relationships as Developed in the Client-Centered Framework," in *Psychology: A Study of Science*, vol. 3, ed. S. Koch (New York: McGraw Hill, 1959), 210, as quoted in Knight, "Client-Centered Therapy," 325.
16. Rogers, *On Becoming a Person*, 282.
17. Maureen O'Hara, "Carl Rogers: Scientist and Mystic," *Journal of Humanistic Psychology* 35, no. 4 (Fall 1995): 45, SAGE. (Author is referencing Carl Rogers's and others' research, but the article is unclear in citing which body of work holds this material.)
18. Clinebell, *Basic Types of Pastoral Care and Counseling*, 9, 17.
19. C. R. Ridley, "Client-Centered Therapy," *Dictionary of Pastoral Care and Counseling*, ed. Rodney J. Hunter (Nashville, TN: Abingdon Press, 2005), 176.
20. Ridley, "Client-Centered Therapy," 176.
21. Rowena Fong, "Starting Over: Helping Immigrants and Refugees," in *The Church Leader's Counseling Resource Book: A Guide to Mental Health and Social Problems*, ed. Cynthia Franklin and Rowena Fong (Oxford: Oxford University Press, 2011), 318.
22. LeRoy Aden, "On Carl Rogers' Becoming," *Theology Today* 36, no. 4 (January 1980): 557, ATLA Religion Database, http://journals.sagepub.com/doi/abs/10.1177/004057368003600410.
23. Aden, "On Carl Rogers' Becoming," 558.
24. Aden, "On Carl Rogers' Becoming," 558.
25. Michael L. Brown, "A Compromised Gospel Produces Compromised Fruit," *Ministry Today*, March 12, 2013, http://ministrytodaymag.com/news/main/19922-the-fruit-of-a-compromised-gospel.
26. Michael L. Brown, "Dr. Paul Ellis Underscores the Errors of Hyper-Grace," *ASKDrBrown* (blog), January 28, 2015, https://askdrbrown.org/dr-paul-ellis-underscores-the-errors-of-hyper-grace/; Michael Brown, "Confronting the Error of Hyper-Grace," Charisma News, February 18, 2013, http://www.charismanews.com/opinion/38297-confronting-the-error-of-hyper-grace.
27. Whitten, *Pure Grace*, 29, as quoted in Brown, *Hyper-Grace*, 8.
28. Crowder, *Mystical Union*, 94, as quoted in Brown, *Hyper-Grace*, 9.

29. Michael Brown, "Is a New Grace Reformation Taking Place Today?" *The Christian Post*, January 1, 2014, http://www.christianpost.com /news/is-a-new-grace-reformation-taking-place-today-111853/.

30. Andrew Farley, "What I'm Really Saying!" *Patheos* (blog), June 6, 2013, http://www.patheos.com/blogs/andrewfarley/2013/06/what-im -really-saying/.

31. Colin Dye, "Should We Confess Our Sins?," Colin Dye, January 4, 2012, http://www.colindye.com/2012/01/04/should-we-confess-our -sins/.

32. Dye, "Should We Confess Our Sins?"

33. Dye, "Should We Confess Our Sins?"

34. White, "Why I Am Hyper-Grace."

35. White, "Why I Am Hyper-Grace."

36. White, "Why I Am Hyper-Grace."

37. White, "Why I Am Hyper-Grace"; see also Jason Dollar, "What the Hyper-Grace Movement Gets Wrong," Glory Focus, November 26, 2016, http://gloryfocus.com/2016/11/26/what-the-hyper-grace -movement-gets-wrong/.

38. White, "Why I Am Hyper-Grace."

39. Whitten, *Pure Grace*.

40. Clark Whitten, "Team Grace Message for May 29, 2013," *Pure Grace Online*, May 29, 2013, http://puregraceonline.com/team-grace -message-for-may-29-2013/.

41. D. R. Silva, "That Time Grace Gave Me a License to Sin," *Saints-notsinners* (blog), August 19, 2015, http://saintsnotsinners.org/license -to-sin/.

42. Silva, "That Time Grace Gave Me a License to Sin."

43. Ryan Rufus, "Totally Forgiven! Totally United! Totally Filled!," Grace and Glory Conference 2011, Manila, Philippines, April 25–26, 2011, as quoted in Dan Bowan, "Ryan Rufus—Glory and Grace Conference—Philippines," *Ryan Rufus* (blog), June 8, 2011, http:// ryanrufus.blogspot.com/2011/06/ryan-rufus-glory-and-grace -conference.html.

44. Rufus, "Totally Forgiven! Totally United! Totally Filled!"

45. Rufus, "Totally Forgiven! Totally United! Totally Filled!"

46. Rufus, "Totally Forgiven! Totally United! Totally Filled!"

47. Rufus, "Totally Forgiven! Totally United! Totally Filled!"

48. Simon Yap, "Grieving the Holy Spirit," *His Grace Is Enough* (blog), November 15, 2012, https://hischarisisenough.wordpress.com /2012/11/15/grieving-the-holy-spirit/.

49. Simon Yap, "What Is the Sin That Easily Entangle Us? Hebrews 12:1," *His Grace Is Enough* (blog), May 5, 2011, https://hischarisis enough.wordpress.com/2011/05/05/what-is-the-sin-that-easily -entangle-us-hebrews-121/.

50. Reyes, "'Hyper-Grace' is True!"

51. Bill Snell, "Grace Is Neither 'Hyper', Nor 'Dangerous,'" *Grace Church Orlando* (blog), accessed October 28, 2015, http://www.graceorlando .com/grace-is-neither-hyper-nor-dangerous/, as quoted in "Questions about Grace—by Grace Church Orlando," *Under the Waterfall* (blog), November 6, 2012, http://underthewaterfallofgrace.blogspot.com /2012/11/questions-about-grace-by-grace-church.html.

52. Joseph Mattera, "Is Joseph Prince's Radical Grace Teaching Biblical?," Charisma News, September 11, 2013, http://www.charismanews .com/opinion/40943-is-joseph-prince-s-radical-grace-teaching-biblical.

53. Mattera, "Is Joseph Prince's Radical Grace Teaching Biblical?"

54. Mattera, "Is Joseph Prince's Radical Grace Teaching Biblical?"

55. David Kowalski, "A Brief Overview of the Teachings of Joseph Prince," Apologetics Index, June 29, 2013, http://www.apologetics index.org/3115-joseph-prince.

56. Kowalski, "A Brief Overview of the Teachings of Joseph Prince."

57. Kowalski, "A Brief Overview of the Teachings of Joseph Prince."

58. Kowalski, "A Brief Overview of the Teachings of Joseph Prince."

59. David Kowalski, "The Modern 'Grace Message'—Revolution or Rebellion," Apologetics Index, December 3, 2014, http://www .apologeticsindex.org/4981-antinomianism.

60. Andrew Wilson, "The 'Grace Revolution,' Hyper-Grace, and the Humility of Orthodoxy," *Think* (blog), January 2, 2013, http://think theology.co.uk/blog/article/the_grace_revolution.

Chapter 6
Reformed Theology and Grace in Newfrontiers Churches

1. "The History of Newfrontiers," New Frontiers International Trust Limited, accessed November 7, 2017, https://newfrontierstogether .org/about-us/our-history/; "Planting Churches," Newfrontiers USA, accessed November 7, 2017, http://newfrontiersusa.org.

2. W. K. Kay, "Martyn Lloyd-Jones's Influence on Pentecostalism and Neo-Pentecostalism in the UK," *Journal of Pentecostal Theology*, 22, no. 2 (2013): 275–294, https://doi.org/10.1163/17455251-02202011; Andrew Atherstone, David Ceri Jones, and W. K. Kay, "Lloyd-Jones and the Charismatic Controversy," in *Engaging with Martyn*

Lloyd-Jones, ed. Andrew Atherstone and David Ceri Jones (Nottingham, UK: Apollos, 2011), 114–155.

3. My brother-in-law, a Newfrontiers minister, bought a property that had been inadequately examined by a surveyor; thousands of pounds' worth of extra work was required before the property was habitable. He spoke to the surveyor, explained that he had the right to mount a prosecution for professional negligence, but then said that he wished to show the grace of God to the man so that he would understand how God treated sinners. No prosecution was mounted and my brother-in-law bore the loss himself.

4. Terry Virgo, *Restoration in the Church* (Eastbourne, UK: Kingsway, 1985), 134.

5. Terry Virgo, *Does the Future Have a Church?* (Eastbourne, UK: Kingsway, 2003), 56.

6. Terry Virgo, *God's Lavish Grace* (Oxford: Monarch, 2004) 75.

7. Virgo, *God's Lavish Grace*, 98.

8. Virgo, *God's Lavish Grace*, 113.

9. Virgo, *God's Lavish Grace*, 113.

10. Virgo, *God's Lavish Grace*, 115.

11. Virgo, *God's Lavish Grace*, 135.

12. Virgo, *God's Lavish Grace*, 138.

13. Virgo, *God's Lavish Grace*, 141.

14. Virgo, *God's Lavish Grace*, 154.

15. Virgo, *God's Lavish Grace*, 160.

16. Virgo, *God's Lavish Grace*, 169.

17. Virgo, *God's Lavish Grace*, 173.

18. Virgo, *God's Lavish Grace*, 175.

19. Virgo, *God's Lavish Grace*, 179.

20. Virgo, *God's Lavish Grace*, 180.

21. Virgo, *God's Lavish Grace*, 181.

Chapter 7
A Spirit of Unity and Grace:
Learning from the Assemblies of God Ireland

1. Donald Grey Barnhouse, *Expositions of Bible Doctrines Taking the Epistle to the Romans as a Point of Departure*, vol. 1 (Grand Rapids, MI: Wm. B. Eerdmans, 1952), 72.

2. Charles R. Swindoll, *The Grace Awakening* (Nashville, TN: Thomas Nelson, 2003), 139.

3. *Profile 7: Religion, Ethnicity and Irish Travellers* (Dublin, Ireland: Central Statistics Office, October 2012).

4. Other studies in the Irish context that focus in part on the Pentecostal community are as follows: David Carnduff, *Ireland's Lost Heritage* (Ireland: IPBC, 2003); Robert Dunlop, ed., *Evangelicals in Ireland: An Introduction* (Dublin: Columba Press, 2004); James Robinson, *Pentecostal Origins: Early Pentecostalism in the Context of the British Isles* (Milton Keynes, UK: Paternoster Press, 2005); Abel Ugba, *Shades of Belonging: African Pentecostals in Twenty-First Century Ireland* (Trenton, NJ: Africa World Press, 2009).

5. Sean Mullarkey, *Connect*, June 2015, https://www.scribd.com /document/284748741/AGI-Draft.

6. Sean Mullarkey, "Opening Remarks," (speech, The Power of Connection conference, Dublin, Ireland, December 2015).

7. Mullarkey, "Opening Remarks."

8. Emil Brunner, *The Misunderstanding of the Church* (London: Lutterworth, 1953), 10–11, cited in Veli-Matti Kärkkäinen, "The Church as the Fellowship of Persons," *Pentecostal Studies*, 6, no. 1 (2007): 1–15.

9. Ron Rolheiser, "The Relationship between Unity and Diversity," *The Irish Catholic*, April 16, 2015, http://irishcatholic.com/the -relationship-between-unity-and-diversity/.

10. Pope Francis, "Seek the Unity Which Is the Work of the Holy Spirit," Vatican Radio, October 31, 2014, http://en.radiovaticana.va /news/2014/10/31/pope_seek_the_unity_which_is_the_work_of_the _holy_spirit/1109856.

11. Pope Francis, "Seek the Unity Which Is the Work of the Holy Spirit."

12. Mel Robeck, "Homily," Diocese of Sacramento, January 23, 2013, https://www.scd.org/sites/default/files/2017-06/Homily-Mel-Robeck -Week-of-Prayer-for-Christian-Unity.pdf.

13. Swindoll, *The Grace Awakening*, 143–5.

14. Corneille Nkurunziza, "Pentecostal Spirituality: A Disregarded Cornerstone for the Contextualization of African Theologies," *Journal of Theology for Southern Africa* 145 (March 2013): 59–74.

15. Ugba, *Shades of Belonging*, 126.

16. Livingstone Thompson, "Pentecostal Migrants—A Challenge to the Churches," *Search* 33, no. 3 (2010): 185–93.

17. Jean Vanier, *Community and Growth*, rev. ed. (New York: Paulist Press, 1989), 266, cited in Christine D. Pohl, "Hospitality, a Practice and a Way of Life," *Vision* (Spring 2002): 38–9.

18. Vanier, *Community and Growth*, 267, cited in Pohl, "Hospitality, a Practice and a Way of Life."

19. See Daryl Balia and Kirsteen Kim, eds., *Edinburgh 2010, Volume II, Witnessing to Christ Today* (Oxford: Regnum Books International, 2010), http://www.edinburgh2010.org/fileadmin/files/edinburgh2010/files/Study_Process/reports/E2010%20II-whole-final.pdf.

20. Irish Inter-Church Committee, "Irish Churches' Affirmations on Migration, Diversity and Interculturalism," 6, accessed November 2, 2017, https://www.embraceni.org/wp-content/uploads/2010/09/IRISH%20CHURCHES.pdf.

Chapter 8
Grace, Sanctification, and Italian Pentecostalism

1. Carmine Napolitano, "The Development of Pentecostalism in Italy," *European Pentecostalism*, ed. William K. Kay and Anne E. Dyer (Boston: Brill, 2011), 189–204.

2. Vinson Synan, *The Holiness-Pentecostal Tradition: Charismatic Movements in the Twentieth Century* (Grand Rapids, MI: W.B. Eerdmans, 1997), 149–52.

3. Jean-Daniel Plüss, "Pentecostal Theology and Protestant Europe," in *European Pentecostalism*, ed. William K. Kay and Anne E. Dyer (Boston: Brill, 2011), 301.

4. Plüss, "Pentecostal Theology and Protestant Europe," 301–2.

5. Paolo Mauriello, "La Formazione Teologica in Ambito Pentecostale" (Theological education in Pentecostal circles), *Odos*, no. 0 (2011): 85–97.

6. Roberto Bracco, "Il Cristianesimo" (Christianity), *Risveglio Pentecostale*, no. 6 (1948): 11–12. The translation in English of all the citations in Italian is mine.

7. L. Tomasello, "Della Grazia" (About grace), *Risveglio Pentecostale*, no. 9 (1949): 7–9.

8. Samuel L. Brengle, "La Santificazione nel Pensiero di S. L. Brengle" (Sanctification in the thought of S. L. Brengle), *Risveglio Pentecostale*, no. 9 (1949): 3–4.

9. G. Steinberger, "La Santificazione Pratica" (Practical sanctification), *Risveglio Pentecostale*, no. 1 (1950): 11–12.

10. "Relazione del IV Convegno Regionale di Puglia e Lucania" (Report of the Conference of the Churches of Puglia and Lucania), *Risveglio Pentecostale*, no. 3 (1953): 13–14.

11. "Un Felice Esperimento" (A happy experiment), *Risveglio Pentecostale*, no. 9 (1953): 10–11.

12. "Un Felice Esperimento," 11.
13. Roberto Bracco, "Salvati per Grazia?" (Saved by grace?), *Risveglio Pentecosale*, no. 7–8 (1954): 3–4.
14. Roberto Bracco, "In Lotta con il Mondo" (Fighting against the world), *Risveglio Pentecostale*, no. 9 (1954): 3–4.
15. Roberto Bracco, "Capelli Tinti" (Dyed hair), *Risveglio Pentecostale*, no. 8 (1968): 6–7. It is interesting to see that in 1968 the subject of women's makeup and permed and dyed hair was still very strong in some Pentecostal churches.
16. Stefano Alla, "I Zaccardiani: una Componente del Movimento Pentecostale Italiano" (The Zaccardiani: an element of the Italian Pentecostal Movement), (BA dissertation, Facoltà Pentecostale di Scienze Religiose, 2014).
17. Silvano Lilli, interview by author, March 25, 2016.
18. Lirio Porrello, interview by author, March 19, 2016.
19. Giancarlo Rinaldi, "John Wesley: la Perfezione Cristiana" (John Wesley: Christian Perfection), *Quaderni di Ecumene*, no. 6 (1989): 22.
20. Stephen B. Bevans and Roger P. Schroeder, *Teologia per la Missione Oggi. Costanti nel Contesto* (Theology for the mission today. Constant in the context) (Brescia, Italy: Queriniana, 2010), 537–9.
21. John H. Taylor, *Lo Spirito Mediatore. Lo Spirito Santo e la Missione Cristiana* (The Spirit Mediator. The Holy Spirit and the Christian mission) (Brescia, Italy: Queriniana, 1975), 197–8.

Chapter 9
Manifestations of Grace:
A Latin American Witness

1. J. I. Packer, *Knowing God* (Downers Grove, IL: IVP Books, 1973), 226.
2. Paul Enns, *Moody Handbook of Theology* (Chicago: Moody Publishers, 2014), 196.
3. See for example, Randy L. Maddox, *Responsible Grace: John Wesley's Practical Theology* (Nashville, TN: Kingswood Books, 1994), 48–9.
4. See the classic work of Charles H. Spurgeon, *Grace: God's Unmerited Favor* (New Kensington, PA: Whitaker House, 1996), 65–71.
5. Packer, *Knowing God*, 228–31.
6. Andrew H. Trotter Jr., *Baker's Evangelical Dictionary of Biblical Theology*, s.v. "Grace," ed. Walter A. Elwell (Grand Rapids, MI: Baker Books, 1996), https://www.biblestudytools.com/dictionary/grace/.
7. Trotter Jr., *Baker's Evangelical Dictionary of Biblical Theology*, s.v. "Grace."

8. See, for example, Justo L. González and Ondina E. González, *Christianity in Latin America: A History* (New York: Cambridge University Press), 80–6.

9. See Jorge Alberto Zavala Salgado, "The Evolution of the Human Right to Religious Freedom of the Indigenous People of Latin America," in *The Reshaping of Mission in Latin America*, ed. Miguel Álvarez (Oxford: Regnum Books International, 2015), 282–91.

10. Ronald M. Schneider, *Latin American Political History: Patterns and Personalities* (Boulder, CO: Westview Press, 2007), 274–5.

11. Some of the first Protestant missionaries that arrived in Latin America were Anglicans. See the historical account described by Pedro Julio Triana Fernández, "We Found Identity Through Our Diversity: A Historical Account of the Anglican Episcopal Church of Brazil," in Álvarez, *The Reshaping of Mission in Latin America*, 206–18.

12. Gustavo Gutiérrez, *Las Casas: In Search of the Poor of Jesus Christ* (Eugene, OR: Wipf and Stock, 2003), 21–6.

13. Leslie Bethell, *The Independence of Latin America* (New York: Cambridge University Press, 1987), 5–15.

14. Bethell, *The Independence of Latin America*, 12.

15. Hans-Jürgen Prien, *Christianity in Latin America*, trans. Stephen Buckwalter (Leiden, Netherlands: Brill, 2013), 271–84.

16. See González and González, *Christianity in Latin America*, 41–57.

17. Prien, *Christianity in Latin America*, 374–87.

18. Paul A. Gilje and Howard B. Rock, eds., *Keepers of the Revolution: New Yorkers at Work in the Early Revolution* (Ithaca, NY: Cornell University Press, 1992), 70–2.

19. See Patrick W. Carey, *Catholics in America: A History* (Westport, CT: Praeger, 2004), 1–6.

20. John A. Mackay, *The Other Spanish Christ* (Eugene, OR: Wipf and Stock Publishers, 1933), 42–4.

21. Mauricio Beuchot, "Bartolomé de Las Casas, el Humanismo Indígena y los Derechos Humanos," *Anuario Mexicano de la Historia del Derecho* 6, no. 1 (1994): 37–48.

22. Lewis Hanke, "Free Speech in Sixteenth-Century Spanish America," *The Hispanic American Historical Review* 26, no. 2 (May 1946): 135–49, https://doi.org/10.2307/2508321.

23. Gustavo Gutiérrez, *A Theology of Liberation* (Maryknoll, NY: Orbis Books, 1973), 49–51.

24. Jonathan Fox, Lynn Stephen, and Gaspar Rivera, "Indigenous Rights and Self-Determination in Mexico," *Cultural Survival Quarterly* 23, no. 1 (March 1999): 23–64.

25. Andrea Gagliarducci, "Fr Gustavo Gutiérrez: The Poor Are the Starting Point of Liberation Theology," Catholic News Agency, May 8, 2015, http://www.catholicnewsagency.com/news/fr-gustavo-gutierrez -the-poor-are-the-starting-point-of-liberation-theology-90963.

26. Virginia Garrard-Burnett and David Stoll, eds., *Rethinking Protestantism in Latin America* (Philadelphia: Temple University Press, 1993), 3–4.

27. See Valdir Steuernagel, "A Latin-American Evangelical Perspective on the Cape Town Congress," in *The Lausanne Movement: A Range of Perspectives*, ed. Lars Dahle, Margunn Serigstad Dahle, and Knud Jørgensen (Oxford: Regnum Books International, 2014), 304–9.

28. Samuel Escobar, *Changing Tides: Latin America and World Mission Today* (Maryknoll, NY: Orbis Books, 2002), 23–32.

29. Chris Sugden, "Mission as Transformation—Its Journey Among Evangelicals Since Lausanne 1," in *Holistic Mission: God's Plan for God's People*, ed. Brian Woolnough and Wonsuk Ma (Eugene, OR: Wipf and Stock, 2010), 31–5.

30. Miguel Álvarez, "Latin American Mission, Then and Now," in *The Reshaping of Mission in Latin America*, 1–5.

31. Calixto Salvatierra Moreno, "Catholic and Pentecostal Convergence on Practical Theology and Mission," in *The Reshaping of Mission in Latin America*, 65.

32. A good reading on this topic is the work of Amos Yong, *In the Days of Caesar: Pentecostalism and Political Theology* (Grand Rapids, MI: Eerdmans, 2010), 238–51. The author engages a thorough discussion on the role of Pentecostal empowerment in the incarnational and redemptive mission of God over civilian freedom.

33. Timothy Sims, *In Defense of the Word of Faith: An Apologetic Response to Encourage Charismatic Believers* (Bloomington, IN: AuthorHouse, 2008), 10–13.

34. Jeff Brumley, "New Study Documents Shifts in Latin American Religious Affiliation," Baptist News Global, January 25, 2016, https:// baptistnews.com/article/catholic-decline-in-latin-america-a-lure-for -joyful-churches-baptists-say/#.WgMfOmhSwdU.

35. Bernardo Campos, "Neo-Pentecostal Paradigms in Latin American Mission: Megatrends in the Theologies of Mission and Missionary

Practices Among Neo-Pentecostals in Peru," in *The Reshaping of Mission in Latin America*, 193–205.

36. Campos, "Neo-Pentecostal Paradigms in Latin American Mission," 197–9.

37. One of them seems to be the leading pastor of a megachurch in Guatemala City, Cash Luna. See Irma Yolanda Maribel Cano Ramos, "Análisis Crítico del Discurso del Pastor Carlos Cash Luna, Titulado: 'Lo Mío es Tuyo,'" (dissertation, Universidad de San Carlos de Guatemala, 2014).

38. Joseph Mattera, "8 Signs of 'Hypergrace' Churches," Charisma News, June 28, 2013, http://www.charismanews.com/opinion/40060-eight-signs-of-hyper-grace-churches.

39. See for example, Eliezer Valentín-Castañón, "Teología de Dominio," *P. Arieu Theologies Web* (blog), August 27, 2009, https://lasteologias.wordpress.com/2009/08/27.

40. See Campos, "Neo-Pentecostal Paradigms in Latin American Mission," 199–204.

41. C. Rene Padilla, "An Ecclesiology for Integral Mission," in *The Local Church; Agent of Transformation: An Ecclesiology for Integral Mission*, ed. Tetsunao Yamamori and C. Rene Padilla (Buenos Aires, Argentina: Ediciones Kairos, 2004), 76.

42. Juan Luis Segundo, *Liberation of Theology* (Maryknoll, NY: Orbis Books, 1976), 69–75.

43. Padilla, "An Ecclesiology for Integral Mission," 68–70.

44. R. Andrew Chesnut, *Competitive Spirits: Latin America New Religious Economy* (Oxford: Oxford University Press, 2003), 132–35.

45. Todd Hartch, *The Rebirth of Latin American Christianity* (Oxford: Oxford University Press, 2014), 59–62.

46. Carlos F. Cardoza-Orlandi and Justo L. González, *To All Nations from All Nations: A History of the Christian Missionary Movement* (Nashville, TN: Abingdon Press, 2013), 389.

47. Enrique Pinedo, "Mission and the Children of Latin America: A Historical Perspective from the Latin American Congress of Evangelization—CLADE," in *The Reshaping of Latin American Mission*, 103–16.

48. See Bernardo Campos, *De la Reforma Protestante a la Pentecostalidad de la Iglesia: Debate Sobre el Pentecostalismo en América Latina* (Quito, Ecuador: Ediciones CLAI, 1997), 90–106.

49. Bernardo Campos, "El Influjo de las Huacas: La Espiritualidad Pentecostal en el Perú," in *Protestantismo y Cultura en América Latina:*

Aportes y Proyecciones, ed. Tomás Gutiérrez (Quito, Ecuador: CLAI, 1994), 18.

50. Campos, *De la Reforma Protestante a la Pentecostalidad de la Iglesia*, 90–1.

Chapter 10
Still and Still Moving:
Grace in the Anglican Tradition

1. "East Coker" in T. S. Eliot, *Four Quartets* (London: Faber, 2000), quoted in Simon Barrington-Ward, *The Jesus Prayer* (Oxford: Bible Reading Fellowship, 1996), 76.

2. Stephen Sykes, John Booty, and Jonathan Knight, eds., *The Study of Anglicanism* (London: SPCK, 1998), xii.

3. See "History," Archbishops' Council, accessed June 8, 2016, http://www.churchofengland.org/more/media-centre/church-england-glance/history-church-england. Many within the Church of England prefer not to capitalize *Catholic* and *Reformed* when referring to the influence of those traditions on Anglicanism. They prefer to define *catholic* and *reformed* as influences that have roots in the Roman Catholic and Reformed traditions but that Anglicans have creatively engaged in conversation with other traditions.

4. Rowan Williams, *Anglican Identities* (London: Darton, Longman & Todd, 2004), 1.

5. Williams, *Anglican Identities*, 1.

6. Geoffrey Rowell, Kenneth Stevenson, and Rowan Williams, compilers, *Love's Redeeming Work: The Anglican Quest for Holiness* (Oxford: Oxford University Press, 2001), xx.

7. Rowell, Stevenson, and Williams, *Love's Redeeming Work*, xx.

8. Rowell, Stevenson, and Williams, *Love's Redeeming Work*, xxii.

9. Kenneth J. Collins, *The Theology of John Wesley: Holy Love and the Shape of Grace* (Nashville, TN: Abingdon Press, 2007), 6–16.

10. Simon Barrington-Ward, *The Jesus Prayer and the Great Exchange*, Grove Spirituality Series 124 (Cambridge: Grove Books, 2013).

11. Barrington-Ward, *The Jesus Prayer*, 32.

12. Barrington-Ward, *The Jesus Prayer and the Great Exchange*, 5.

13. For example, the biblical approach of Michael J. Gorman, *Becoming the Gospel: Paul, Participation, and Mission*, The Gospel and Our Culture Series (Grand Rapids, MI: Eerdmans, 2015).

14. Simon Barrington-Ward, *Love Will Out* (Basingstoke, UK: Marshall, Morgan & Scott, 1988), 15.

15. Barrington-Ward, *Love Will Out*, 18.

16. Barrington-Ward, *Love Will Out*, 62.

17. Barrington-Ward, *Love Will Out*, 38.

18. Barrington-Ward, *The Jesus Prayer and the Great Exchange*, 5.

19. Barrington-Ward, *Love Will Out*, 70.

20. Simon Barrington-Ward, "My Pilgrimage in Mission," *International Bulletin of Missionary Research* 23, no. 2 (1999): 61.

21. Barrington-Ward, *Love Will Out*, 107.

22. Barrington-Ward, *Love Will Out*, 107–13.

23. Barrington-Ward, *Love Will Out*, 67.

24. Simon Barrington-Ward, "Dying to Live: The Vocation of Anglicanism," *ANVIL* 12, no. 2 (1995): 106–7.

25. Barrington-Ward, *Love Will Out*, 98.

26. Barrington-Ward, *Love Will Out*, 61.

27. Barrington-Ward, *The Jesus Prayer*, 53.

28. Barrington-Ward, *The Jesus Prayer and the Great Exchange*, 10.

29. Barrington-Ward, *The Jesus Prayer*, 17.

30. Barrington-Ward, "My Pilgrimage in Mission," 64.

31. Barrington-Ward, *The Jesus Prayer*, 16.

32. Barrington-Ward, *Love Will Out*, 92.

33. Barrington-Ward, *Love Will Out*, 92.

34. Barrington-Ward, *Love Will Out*, 30.

35. This theme is more prominent in recent approaches to mission, such as by the Anglican Sue Hope, *Mission-Shaped Spirituality: The Transforming Power of Mission* (London: Church House Publishing, 2006). On intercession see Barrington-Ward, *Love Will Out*, 33.

36. Barrington-Ward, *Love Will Out*, 38.

37. Barrington-Ward, *Love Will Out*, 41.

38. For different approaches to contextualizing the gospel see Stephen B. Bevans, *Models of Contextual Theology*, rev. ed. (New York: Orbis, 2002).

39. Barrington-Ward, *Love Will Out*, 92. More recently, discipleship for mission has been promoted by the Anglican Mike Breen and Steve Cockram, *Building a Discipling Culture: How to Release a Missional Movement by Discipling People Like Jesus Did* (Pawleys Island, SC: 3 Dimension Ministries, 2011).

40. Barrington-Ward, *Love Will Out*, 64.

41. Barrington-Ward, *Love Will Out*, 64.

42. Which the present author appreciated during the 1980s and 1990s.

43. Barrington-Ward, "My Pilgrimage in Mission," 64.

44. Barrington-Ward, *Love Will Out*, 128; Barrington-Ward, "My Pilgrimage in Mission," 64.

45. Barrington-Ward, *Love Will Out*, 63.

46. Barrington-Ward, *Love Will Out*, 29–35.

47. Barrington-Ward, "My Pilgrimage in Mission," 60.

48. Barrington-Ward, *The Jesus Prayer*, 7.

49. Barrington-Ward, *The Jesus Prayer*, 15–22.

50. Barrington-Ward, *The Jesus Prayer*, 50.

51. Barrington-Ward, *The Jesus Prayer and the Great Exchange*, 21.

52. Barrington-Ward, *The Jesus Prayer*, 76.

53. Brother Ramon and Simon Barrington-Ward, *Praying the Jesus Prayer Together* (Oxford: Bible Reading Fellowship, 2001), 133–5.

54. Barrington-Ward, *The Jesus Prayer and the Great Exchange*, 12.

55. See particularly chapters in Ramon and Barrington-Ward, *Praying the Jesus Prayer Together*.

56. Barrington-Ward, *The Jesus Prayer*, 50.

57. Barrington-Ward, "Dying to Live," 109.

58. Barrington-Ward, "Dying to Live," 109.

59. Barrington-Ward, "Dying to Live," 107–8.

60. Joseph Prince, *Grace Revolution: Experience the Power to Live Above Defeat* (New York: FaithWords, 2015).

61. Brown, *Hyper-Grace*.

62. For one treatment of the issue from the time see John F. MacArthur, *Faith Works: The Gospel According to the Apostles* (Milton Keynes, UK: Word Books, 1993).

63. See, for example, David Watson, *Discipleship* (London: Hodder & Stoughton, 1983).

64. Amos Yong, *Spirit of Love: A Trinitarian Theology of Grace* (Waco, TX: Baylor University Press, 2012); Matthew T. Lee, Margaret M. Poloma, and Stephen G. Post, *The Heart of Religion: Spiritual Empowerment, Benevolence, and the Experience of God's Love* (New York: Oxford University Press, 2013).

65. Lee, Poloma, and Post, *The Heart of Religion*, 244–245, 52–53.

66. Yong, *Spirit of Love*, 121–24.

Chapter 11
Law and Grace as Partners:
An Examination of Reformed Theology

1. John Calvin, *Institutes of the Christian Religion*, ed. John T. McNeill, trans. Ford Lewis Battles (Philadelphia: Westminster Press, 1960).

2. John Calvin, "The Necessity of Reforming the Church," in *Calvin: Theological Treatises*, ed. J. K. S. Reid (Philadelphia: Westminster Press, 1954), 190.

3. John. T. McNeill, "Introduction" in Calvin, *Institutes of the Christian Religion*, lviii.

4. Calvin, *Institutes of the Christian Religion*, 5.

5. Calvin, *Institutes of the Christian Religion*, 1013.

6. Augustine, *The City of God*, xxi.xv, in *Basic Writings of Saint Augustine*, vol. 2, ed. Whitney J. Oates (New York: Random House, 1948), 585.

7. Calvin, *Institutes of the Christian Religion*, 292.

8. Calvin, *Institutes of the Christian Religion*, 1236–1240.

9. Calvin, *Institutes of the Christian Religion*, 540.

10. R. Kent Hughes, *Disciplines of Grace* (Wheaton, IL: Crossway Books, 1993), 17.

11. Calvin, *Institutes of the Christian Religion*, 833–49.

12. Evangelical Presbyterian Church, *The Westminster Confession of Faith in Modern English*, 3rd ed. (Livonia, MI: Evangelical Presbyterian Church, 2010), 33.

13. Office of the General Assembly, "W-4.4003 Constitutional Questions for Ordination, Installation, and Commissioning," *Presbyterian Church (U.S.A.) Book of Order Part II, 2015–2017* (Louisville, KY: Office of the General Assembly Presbyterian Church (U.S.A.) 2015), 122.

14. Office of the General Assembly, "W-4.9000 9. Marriage," in *Presbyterian Church (U.S.A.) Book of Order Part II*, 128.

15. Sinclair B. Ferguson, *The Whole Christ: Legalism, Antinomianism, and Gospel Assurance—Why the Marrow Controversy Still Matters* (Wheaton, IL: Crossway, 2016), 13, Kindle.

16. Ferguson, *The Whole Christ*, 14–15.

17. J. Rodman Williams, *The Era of the Spirit* (Plainfield, NJ: Logos International, 1971), 41–43.

Chapter 12
Evidence of Grace in the Old Testament

1. See any recent, good commentary on the Gospel of John. See this *ḥesed-'emeth* pair also in Genesis 24:49; 47:29; Joshua 2:14; Hosea 4:1; and Proverbs 20:28.

2. This section of the chapter relies on Lester J. Kuyper, "Grace and Truth: In the Old Testament and in the Gospel of John," in *The Scripture Unbroken* (Grand Rapids, MI: Eerdmans, 1978), 157–86.

3. Such as Lot toward the heavenly guests at Sodom (Gen. 19:19); the spies toward Rahab (Josh. 2:12, 14); David and Jonathan in their covenant, and David, in honoring that covenant, toward other descendants of Saul (1 Sam. 20:8, 14, 15; 2 Sam. 9:1, 3, 7). One of the most significant of Old Testament words, *ḥesed*, resists being translated into only one English word. Bible translations use a few, such as "mercy," "kindness," "lovingkindness," and, as here, "steadfast love."

4. Kuyper, "Grace and Truth," 161.

5. Kuyper, "Grace and Truth," 162.

6. Kuyper, "Grace and Truth," 163. Applied to John 1, "grace and truth" should also be taken as *hendiadys*: "faithful loyalty."

7. Stephen D. Renn, ed., *Expository Dictionary of Bible Words*, s.v. "Grace, Gracious" (Peabody, MA: Hendrickson, 2005), 447.

8. Kuyper, "Grace and Truth," 164.

9. Kuyper, "Grace and Truth," 164.

10. Kuyper, "Grace and Truth," 164.

11. To be brief, this section simplifies the complexities of the meanings of *ḥesed* in the Old Testament and the ongoing scholarly debate Kuyper could not draw from with his 1978 publication. The basic notion of *ḥesed* offered here seems to express contemporary scholarly consensus, with variations.

12. Space does not allow this chapter to explain why John 1:17 says "grace and truth" rather than "steadfast love and faithfulness." The answer lies in how word meanings change over time and how translations establish traditions other translations follow. I explain this answer more fully in "Obligations of Grace," May 2016, http://digitalshowcase.oru.edu/e21scholars/2016/GraceMER/1/.

13. Kuyper, "Grace and Truth," 177.

14. Kuyper, "Grace and Truth," 176.

15. Shorthand for the old covenant, or Old Testament.

16. As recently as a generation ago, T. Robert Ingram protested the silence of theologians about grace in creation: "Are we...to conclude that grace was not the source of all the spiritual blessings bestowed upon Adam in Paradise before the Fall when he was not a sinner?" And, "When 'God saw everything that he had made, and behold, it was very good' (Gen. 1:31), was it not of grace that it was good? to say nothing of the fact that it existed at all? Was there some merit

in the things God had made that made them good, apart from his grace? Was it not the unmerited love of God which gave existence to all things?" ("The Grace of Creation," *Westminster Theological Journal* 37, no. 2 (1975): 207.)

17. Genesis 1:26–29; 2:18–25.

18. Genesis 1:10, 12, 18, 21, 25, 31; 2:8.

19. Note on Genesis 11:1–9, "The Tower of Babel," *The ESV Study Bible, English Standard Version* (Wheaton, IL: Crossway Bibles, 2008).

20. Jeremiah's New (or Renewed) Covenant (Jer. 31:31–34) deserves the great attention Christians give it, but the AID covenants also influence the events and writings of the New Testament; Jesus Christ fulfills the AID covenants.

21. William Sanford LaSor, David Allan Hubbard, and Frederic William Bush, *Old Testament Survey: The Message, Form, and Background of the Old Testament*, 2nd ed. (Grand Rapids, MI: Eerdmans, 1996), 73.

22. God restates and enlarges this covenant in Genesis 15, 17, and 22. Space prevents further discussion here.

23. Christians understand this covenant to be important from David's time onward, with oracles that demonstrate its value from later prophets, such as Isaiah (chapters 9 and 11), and its fulfillment in Jesus Christ, God's perfect king and descendant of David (Matt. 1:1; Luke 1:32).

24. A few examples (not all include those words) are Exodus 32:7–14; 1 Samuel 12:19–22; Psalm 106; Isaiah 40:1–2; 43:22–25; 48:9–11; and Ezekiel 20:40–44.

25. Lack of space prevents showing how the Sinai Covenant exemplifies ancient suzerain-vassal treaties, which express both the suzerain's kind deeds that justify the vassal's gratitude and loyalty (here, the miraculous Exodus) and stipulate the vassal's response (here, keeping God's covenant). Those stipulations appear in the Old Testament as the Law of Moses. See fuller discussion in "Obligations of Grace" at http://digitalshowcase.oru.edu/e21scholars/2016/GraceMER/1/ and in LaSor, Hubbard, and Bush, *Old Testament Survey*, 73–75.

26. William Sanford LaSor, David Allan Hubbard, and Frederic William Bush, *Old Testament Survey: The Message, Form, and Background of the Old Testament* (Grand Rapids, MI: Eerdmans, 1982), 150.

27. Note on Psalm 119, *ESV Study Bible.*

28. Here abridged from Don Brandeis, *The Gospel in the Old Testament* (Grand Rapids, MI: Baker Books, 1962), 119–20. Used by permission of Baker Publishing Group.

29. LaSor, Hubbard, and Bush, *Old Testament Survey*, first ed., 159–60, where the authors cite several Jewish texts in agreement. Note 19 includes "…[S]alvation by works of the law is nowhere taught in the Old Testament. So the Old Testament was understood by Jesus and the apostles, including Paul—all of whom were Jews."

30. See two other studies that support this position: Ernest F. Kevan, *The Grace of Law: A Study in Puritan Theology* (Grand Rapids, MI: Baker, 1965) and Daniel P. Fuller, *The Unity of the Bible: Unfolding God's Plan for Humanity* (Grand Rapids, MI: Zondervan, 2000). In his "Appendix: The Nature of the Mosaic Law," Fuller exegetes three Pauline texts crucial to John Calvin's view of the Law to support his thesis "that, contrary to Calvin, the law and the gospel are a continuum rather than a contrast" (459).

Chapter 13
Grace and Works—A Johannine Perspective

1. Most scholars believe that more than one author was involved in the composition of the Johannine literature.

2. John 3:19, 20, 21; 4:34; 5:20, 36; 6:28, 29; 7:3, 7, 21; 8:39, 41; 9:3, 4; 10:25, 32, 33, 37, 38; 14:10, 11, 12; 15:24; 17:4.

3. 1 John 3:8, 12, 18; 2 John 11; 3 John 10.

4. Revelation 2:2, 5, 6, 13, 19, 22, 23, 26; 3:1, 2, 8, 15; 9:20; 14:13; 15:3; 16:11; 18:6; 20:12, 13; 22:12.

5. For perhaps the best assessment of this topic from a Johannine perspective cf. Paul A. Rainbow, *Johannine Theology: The Gospel, the Epistles, and the Apocalypse* (Downers Grove, IL: InterVarsity Press, 2014), 327–9.

6. Author's translation.

7. Author's translation.

8. Author's translation.

9. Author's translation.

10. Author's translation.

11. Author's translation.

12. Author's translation.

13. Author's translation.

14. Author's translation.

15. Author's translation.

16. Author's translation.

17. Cf. J. C. Thomas, *1 John, 2 John, 3 John* (Blandford Forum, UK: Deo Publishing, 2011), 41–42.

18. Interestingly enough, this specific formula is also found in 1 Timothy 1:2 and 2 Timothy 1:2.
19. Thomas, *1 John, 2 John, 3 John*, 25–26.
20. Author's translation.
21. Author's translation.
22. Author's translation.
23. Author's translation.
24. Author's translation.
25. Author's translation.
26. Author's translation.
27. Author's translation.
28. Author's translation.
29. Author's translation.
30. Author's translation.
31. Cf. John Christopher Thomas, "The Literary Structure of 1 John," in *The Spirit of the New Testament* (Blandford Forum, UK: Deo Publishing, 2005), 255–66.
32. Author's translation.
33. Here I borrow heavily from John Christopher Thomas, *The Apocalypse: A Literary and Theological Commentary* (Cleveland, TN: CPT Press, 2012), cf. esp. 91 and 688.
34. Author's translation.
35. Here I draw heavily on Thomas, *The Apocalypse*, 111–12.
36. Author's translation.
37. Author's translation.
38. Author's translation.
39. Author's translation.

Chapter 14
Grace and Spirit Baptism

1. Jon Mark Ruthven, *What's Wrong With Protestant Theology: Tradition vs. Biblical Emphasis* (Tulsa, OK: Word & Spirit Press, 2013), 133.
2. Ruthven, *What's Wrong With Protestant Theology*, 133.
3. Peter Hocken, *Azusa, Rome, and Zion: Pentecostal Faith, Catholic Reform, and Jewish Roots* (Eugene, OR: Pickwick Publications, 2016), 66.
4. Hocken, *Azusa, Rome, and Zion*, 66–68.
5. See Judges 6:34; 1 Chronicles 12:18; 2 Chronicles 24:20; Judges 11:29, 13:24, 14:6, 19, 15:14. James D. G. Dunn, *Baptism in the Holy Spirit* (Philadelphia: Westminster Press, 1970), 110.

6. "Conversion-initiation" is a term used throughout Professor James D. G. Dunn's *Baptism in the Holy Spirit* signifying the change that took place upon believing on Christ as Savior and Lord.

7. Ruthven, *What's Wrong With Protestant Theology*, 131.

8. Ruthven, *What's Wrong With Protestant Theology*, 131.

9. James D. G. Dunn, *Jesus and the Spirit: A Study of the Religious and Charismatic Experience of Jesus and the First Christians as Reflected in the New Testament* (Philadelphia: Westminster Press, 1975), 201.

10. Dunn, *Jesus and the Spirit*, 202.

11. Dunn, *Jesus and the Spirit*, 201.

12. Dunn, *Jesus and the Spirit*, 202.

13. Dunn, *Jesus and the Spirit*, 202.

14. Dunn, *Jesus and the Spirit*, 203.

15. Ruthven, *What's Wrong With Protestant Theology*, 163.

16. Dunn, *Jesus and the Spirit*, 203.

17. Ruthven, *What's Wrong With Protestant Theology*, 164.

18. Ruthven, *What's Wrong With Protestant Theology*, 163. See 2 Corinthians 1:11–12, 9:14; Ephesians 1:16–17; 6:18–19; Philippians 1:4, 6–7 (peace=Spirit); Colossians 1:3–4 (faith); 1:9; 4:3–4; 1 Thessalonians 1:2–5; 3:10; 5:17–20; 2 Thessalonians 1:11; 3:1; 1 Timothy 4:5–6; and Philemon 5–6 (cf. Romans 15:29).

19. Dunn, *Jesus and the Spirit*, 205.

20. Dunn, *Jesus and the Spirit*, 205.

21. Dunn, *Jesus and the Spirit*, 206.

22. Dunn, *Jesus and the Spirit*, 208.

23. Dunn, *Jesus and the Spirit*, 208.

24. Ramsay MacMullen, *Christianizing the Roman Empire A.D. 100–400* (New Haven, CT: Yale University Press, 1984), viii.

25. MacMullen, *Christianizing the Roman Empire A.D. 100–400*, viii.

26. Alister E. McGrath, *The Future of Christianity* (Oxford, UK: Blackwell, 2002), 99.

27. McGrath, *The Future of Christianity*, 108.

28. McGrath, *The Future of Christianity*, 108.

29. Harvey Cox, *Fire from Heaven: The Rise of Pentecostal Spirituality and the Reshaping of Religion in the Twenty-First Century* (Reading, MA: Addison-Wesley Publishing, 1995), 107.

30. Peter Hocken, *The Glory and the Shame: Reflections on the Twentieth Century Outpouring of the Holy Spirit* (Surrey, UK: Eagle-Guildford, 1994), 102.

31. Henry I. Lederle, *Theology With Spirit: The Future of the Pentecostal and Charismatic Movements in the Twenty-First Century* (Tulsa, OK: Word & Spirit Press, 2010), 109.

32. Peter Hocken, "Remarks," Charismatic Leaders Fellowship, Regent University, February 2012.

33. Hocken, *Azusa, Rome, and Zion*, 67.

34. Hocken, *Azusa, Rome, and Zion*, 76.

35. Hocken, *Azusa, Rome, and Zion*, 107.

36. Hocken, "Remarks."

37. David Manuel, *Like a Mighty River: A Personal Account of the Charismatic Conference of 1977* (Orleans, MA: Rock Harbor Press, 1977), 205.

Chapter 15
Glossolalia and Groaning:
A Manifestation of God's Grace

1. Barbara Aland et al., *The Greek New Testament*, 4th rev. ed. (Stuttgart, Germany: Deutsche Bibelgesellschaft, 1994).

2. Gordon D. Fee, *God's Empowering Presence: The Holy Spirit in the Letters of Paul* (Peabody, MA: Hendrickson, 1994), 28, 32.

3. Fee, *God's Empowering Presence*, 33, 606.

4. Fee, *God's Empowering Presence*, 606.

5. Richard N. Longenecker, *The Epistle to the Romans: A Commentary on the Greek Text*, The New International Greek Testament Commentary, ed. I. Howard Marshall and Donald A. Hagner (Grand Rapids, MI: William B. Eerdmans, 2016), 594.

6. Walter Bauer et al., *A Greek-English Lexicon of the New Testament and Other Early Christian Literature*, 3rd ed., ed. Frederick William Danker (Chicago: University of Chicago Press, 2000), 945.

7. Bauer et al., *A Greek-English Lexicon of the New Testament and Other Early Christian Literature*, 483.

8. Bauer et al., *A Greek-English Lexicon of the New Testament and Other Early Christian Literature*, 645.

9. Romans 3:4, 6, 31; 6:2, 15; 7:7, 13; 9:14; 11:1, 11; 1 Corinthians 6:15; Galatians 2:17; 3:21; 6:14.

10. Longenecker, *The Epistle to the Romans*, 344.

11. Fee, *God's Empowering Presence*, 582.

12. John Kildahl, *The Psychology of Speaking in Tongues* (New York: Harper & Row, 1972), 83.

13. Bauer et al., *A Greek-English Lexicon of the New Testament and Other Early Christian Literature*, 41.

14. Bauer et al., *A Greek-English Lexicon of the New Testament and Other Early Christian Literature*, 41.
15. John Bertone, "The Experience of Glossolalia and the Spirit's Empathy: Romans 8:26 Revisited," *Pneuma* 25, no. 1 (Spring 2003): 54, https://www.deepdyve.com/lp/brill/the-experience-of-glossolalia -and-the-spirit-s-empathy-romans-8-26-0G2eqbYMYF.
16. Fee, *God's Empowering Presence*, 578.
17. Fee, *God's Empowering Presence*, 577, n.311.
18. Fee, *God's Empowering Presence*, 577, n.311.
19. Dunn, *Jesus and the Spirit*, 86.
20. Bertone, "The Experience of Glossolalia and the Spirit's Empathy," 60–61.
21. A. J. M. Wedderburn, "Romans 8:26—Towards a Theology of Glossolalia?," *Scottish Journal of Theology* 28, no. 4 (1975): 369, https://doi .org/10.1017/S0036930600024406.
22. Keith Warrington, *Pentecostal Theology: A Theology of Encounter* (New York: T & T Clark, 2008), 65–66.
23. Leon Morris, *The Epistle to the Romans*, Pillar New Testament Commentary (Grand Rapids, MI: William B. Eerdmans, 1988), 328.
24. C. H. Dodd, *The Epistle of Paul to the Romans*, The Moffatt New Testament Commentary, vol. 6 (New York: Harper and Brothers, 1932), 135.
25. Dodd, *The Epistle of Paul to the Romans*, 135–136.
26. John Murray, *The Epistle to the Romans: The English Text With Introduction, Exposition, and Notes, in Two Volumes* (Grand Rapids, MI: William B. Eerdmans, 1968), 312.
27. C. K. Barrett, *A Commentary on the Epistle to the Romans*, Black's New Testament Commentaries (New York: Harper & Row, 1957), 168.
28. Ernst Käsemann, *Commentary on Romans* (Grand Rapids, MI: William B. Eerdmans, 1980), 240–1.
29. Käsemann, *Commentary on Romans*, 241.
30. Käsemann, *Commentary on Romans*, 241.
31. Käsemann, *Commentary on Romans*, 241.
32. Käsemann, *Commentary on Romans*, 241–2.
33. C. E. B. Cranfield, *A Critical and Exegetical Commentary on the Epistle to the Romans*, The International Critical Commentary, ed. J. A. Emerton and C. E. B. Cranfield (Edinburgh, UK: T & T Clark, 1975), 422.
34. Cranfield, *A Critical and Exegetical Commentary on the Epistle to the Romans*, 424.
35. Wedderburn, "Romans 8:26," 374.

36. Wedderburn, "Romans 8:26," 377.

37. W. J. Hollenweger, *The Pentecostals: The Charismatic Movement in the Churches* (Minneapolis: Augsburg, 1972), 342.

38. Oscar Cullmann, *Salvation in History* (New York: Harper & Row, 1967), 256.

39. Bertone, "The Experience of Glossolalia and the Spirit's Empathy," 61.

40. Käsemann, *Commentary on Romans*, 240.

41. Portions of the above material originally appeared in the following thesis: Mark Randall Hall, "Glossolalia as Past Phenomena: Occurrences of Tongues-Speech During the First and Second Centuries" (master's thesis, Oral Roberts University, 1989), 12–20.

42. Dunn, *Jesus and the Spirit*, 86. The information in this paragraph originally appeared in the following thesis: Mark Randall Hall, "Glossolalia as Present Phenomena: The Nature and Purpose of Tongues" (master's thesis, Oral Roberts University, 1989), 11.

43. Fee, *God's Empowering Presence*, 587.

44. Douglas Moo, *The Epistle to the Romans*, The New International Commentary on the New Testament (Grand Rapids, MI: William B. Eerdmans, 1996), 510.

45. Bertone, "The Experience of Glossolalia and the Spirit's Empathy," 64.

46. Fee, *God's Empowering Presence*, 591.

Chapter 16
Going Beyond the Debate on Grace:
Learning from a South Asian Tradition

1. I would like to thank Ms. Levino L. Yhoshu for being a fabulous research assistant and for all her help in making the paper I presented in London ready for publishing.

2. John M. G. Barclay, "Pure Grace?," *Studia Theologica—Nordic Journal of Theology* 68, no. 1 (2014): 5.

3. Barclay, "Pure Grace?," 6.

4. Barclay, "Pure Grace?," 7.

5. Barclay, "Pure Grace?," 7.

6. Barclay, "Pure Grace?," 7.

7. Barclay, "Pure Grace?," 7.

8. Barclay, "Pure Grace?," 7.

9. John Wesley, *A Plain Account of Christian Perfection* (Peabody, MA: Hendrickson, 2007), 4.

10. Ellis, *The Hyper-Grace Gospel*, 27.

11. J. Todd Billings, "John Milbank's Theology of the 'Gift' and Calvin's Theology of Grace: A Critical Comparison," *Modern Theology* 21, no. 1 (January 2005): 87.

12. Billings, "John Milbank's Theology of the 'Gift' and Calvin's Theology of Grace," 88; see also John Milbank, "Can a Gift Be Given? Prolegomena to a Future Trinitarian Metaphysic," *Modern Theology* 11, no. 1 (January 1995): 119–61.

13. Billings, "John Milbank's Theology of the 'Gift' and Calvin's Theology of Grace," 88.

14. Barclay, "Pure Grace?," 7.

15. Alasdair MacIntyre, "Epistemological Crises, Dramatic Narrative and the Philosophy of Science," *The Monist* 60, no. 4 (October 1977): 453–72.

16. Alasdair MacIntyre, *Whose Justice? Which Rationality?* (Notre Dame, IN: University of Notre Dame Press, 1988), 396.

17. MacIntyre, *Whose Justice?*, 364.

18. Amos Yong, *Hospitality and the Other: Pentecost, Christian Practices, and the Neighbour* (Maryknoll, NY: Orbis Books, 2008), 36.

19. Yong, *Hospitality and the Other*, 36.

20. Kiyokazu Okita, "Truth as Encounter—A Vaiṣṇava Vedānta Exposition on the Guru's Grace," *ISKCON Studies Journal* 2 (2014): 112.

21. Okita, following Rāmānuja, Madhva, and Caitanya, argues for the same. "Truth as Encounter," 111.

22. Okita, "Truth as Encounter," 117.

23. Jan Gonda, *Change and Continuity in Indian Religion* (Delhi, India: Munshiram Manoharlal, 1997), 282.

24. Okita, "Truth as Encounter," 116–7.

25. Okita, "Truth as Encounter," 116.

26. Joel D. Mlecko, "The Guru in Hindu Tradition," *Numen* 29, no. 1 (July 1982): 33–61.

27. Gonda, *Change and Continuity in Indian Religion*, 279.

28. Okita, "Truth as Encounter," 121.

29. Okita, "Truth as Encounter," 117.

30. Okita, "Truth as Encounter," 127.

31. Okita, "Truth as Encounter," 125.

32. David Norman Smith, "Faith, Reason, and Charisma: Rudolf Sohm, Max Weber, and the Theology of Grace," *Sociological Inquiry* 68, no.1 (January 1998): 44.

33. Smith, "Faith, Reason, and Charisma," 46.

34. Ellis, *The Hyper-Grace Gospel*.

35. Okita, "Truth as Encounter," 125–6.
36. Brian Daley, "The Law, the Whole Christ, and the Spirit of Love: Grace as a Trinitarian Gift in Augustine's Theology," *Augustinian Studies* 41, no. 1 (2010): 143–4.
37. Smith, "Faith, Reason, and Charisma," 43.
38. Daley, "The Law, the Whole Christ, and the Spirit of Love," 143–4.
39. David K. Bernard, *A History of Christian Doctrine: The Reformation to the Holiness Movement: AD 1500–1900*, vol. 2 (Hazelwood, MO: Word Aflame Press, 1956), 275–6.

Chapter 17
Beware of Counterfeit Grace

1. "Ephesians 1:7–8 Commentary," Precept Austin, last updated April 3, 2017, http://www.preceptaustin.org/ephesians_17-8.
2. "Greek Verbs Quick Reference," Precept Austin, last updated September 29, 2017, http://www.preceptaustin.org/new_page_40.htm.
3. William Edwy Vine, *Vine's Expository Dictionary of Biblical Words*, s.v. "NT: 3956," (Nashville, TN: Thomas Nelson, 1985).
4. James Strong, *Biblesoft's New Exhaustive Strong's Numbers and Concordance with Expanded Greek-Hebrew Dictionary*, s.v. "NT: 3956," Biblesoft and International Bible Translators, 1994.
5. *Merriam-Webster*, s.v. "sanctification," accessed October 23, 2014, https://www.merriam-webster.com/dictionary/sanctification.
6. Joseph Prince, *Grace Revolution: Experience the Power to Live Above Defeat* (New York: FaithWords, 2015).
7. The name of the testimony giver has been changed to protect his privacy. His story is used with permission.